Managing Development
in the Third World

Managing Development in the Third World

*Coralie Bryant
and Louise G. White*

Westview Press / Boulder, Colorado

This is a Westview reprint edition, manufactured on our own premises using equipment and methods that allow us to keep even specialized books in stock. It is printed on acid-free paper and bound in softcovers that carry the highest rating of NASTA in consultation with the AAP and the BMI.

Copyright © 1982 by Westview Press, Inc.

Published in 1982 in the United States of America by
Westview Press, Inc.
5500 Central Avenue
Boulder, Colorado 80301
Frederick A. Praeger, President and Publisher

Library of Congress Cataloging in Publication Data
Bryant, Coralie.
  Managing development in the Third World.
  Bibliography: p.
  Includes index.
  1. Economic development projects—Management. 2. Economic assistance—Management. 3. Underdeveloped areas. I. White, Louise G. II. Title.
HD82.B749   658.4'04   81-16494
ISBN: 0-89158-927-9   AACR2
ISBN: 0-89158-928-7 (pbk.)

Printed and bound in the United States of America

10   9   8   7   6   5   4   3   2

Contents

Tables and Figures

Figures

Preface

It is easy to be overwhelmed by the intractable forces at work within and among nations as the decade of the 1980s begins. The interdependence of nations, the divisiveness of their ideologies, and the seeming inevitability of resource depletion all appear likely to diminish efforts for nonviolent and creative change. And for those who maintain that fundamental changes in social and political structures are necessary, as we do, it is difficult to believe that policy design and implementation can effectively accomplish such change. Social change often seems hostage to unmanageable and unpredictable forces and energies. Notwithstanding these factors, we reflect in this book on the possibilities for purposive change and. suggest some directions and specific strategies for accomplishing change within the third world.

Our analysis is based on the premise that development is an increase in both growth and equity, a process empowering rather than demeaning. It is also based on the conviction that public institutions can contribute to development; even if such institutions are often part of "the problem," they can also be part of "the solution." Since we are both sensitive to current excesses and failures in administrative and political institutions and organizations throughout the world, we recognize that this assumption is, in part, an act of faith. A major reason for striving to ensure that public institutions can make a positive difference is the fact that the alternatives are far worse—domination by those with the most resources, violent revolution, or anarchy. There is no evidence that any of these alternatives would accomplish needed changes and considerable evidence that they would make development more difficult and problematic.

In addition, there are numerous instances in the third world and the industrialized West alike where innovative individuals and groups have been creative and effective. Most writers on development in the past decades have overlooked such instances and have focused instead on the difficulties involved and the complexities of the problems. It is thus important to look more closely at those who have initiated change, to analyze their contributions and the reasons for their success.

Although developmental change can come from several sources, we focus on the role that organizations and administrators can play. Often behavior and events that appear idiosyncratic or perverse are actually responses to organizational patterns and incentives. It is therefore crucial to examine organizational structures and designs and to determine which forms are most compatible with the developmental task. Although there appear to be certain constancies in organizational behavior, there is sufficient evidence of planned structural change that we feel justified in considering alternative directions.

This book is written as an introductory text for those who will be working on development programs and projects in this country or abroad. As such it surveys the major issues and topics with which development managers are concerned. Many of these topics readers must examine more intensively as they seek to build their skills in development management. Our objective here is to help those beginning their study of development management to understand what the field encompasses. In some ways our endeavor is as ambitious as the boundaries of the field are ambiguous. It is also adventuresome in that our concept of development administration is different from much that has been labeled as such in the past.

Together we bring to this task a knowledge of the developmental experience in both the third world and the urban centers within the United States. Both of these arenas have expanded our understanding of the several themes in this book — the meaning of development as growth with equity, the importance of organizational patterns, and the possibility for purposeful social and political change. Further, we believe that those involved in each arena have much to learn from those in the other. Both as individuals and as scholars we have been inspired and instructed by those who continue to cope with the realities of underdevelopment, poverty, and inequality. We hope the succeeding chapters will acknowledge this debt and contribute to a conversation among all those who reflect on and participate in the challenges of administering developmental change.

Coralie Bryant
Louise G. White
Washington, D.C.

Acknowledgments

Inevitably ideas that find their way into textbooks have deep roots that are difficult to identify or fully acknowledge. These roots are often entangled with past places, people, and experiences in wonderfully complex and unpredictable ways. Thus there is no way to thank adequately the many to whom we feel indebted. Yet some deserve special mention either for their inspiration, support, or forbearance. And some experiences were pivotal. Teaching at the University of Zambia; working in Botswana, Swaziland, Uganda; visiting in India—all these experiences occasioned meeting people who added to this endeavor. Steve Mulenga, George Simwenga, Tebogo Bothole, Betsy Stephens, Kenneth Grundy, Roger Tangri, Bob Curry, and Raghavendra Hebsur merit special thanks for ideas and insights they shared through these experiences.

The Development Studies Program within the Agency for International Development proved that substantial intellectual freedom and excitement are possible while teaching within a large organization's mid-career training program. The directors of that program, Richard Blue and Michael Calavan, were often a source of ideas and are to be commended for their generation of an exceptionally sound program with a critical, independent faculty. Among these faculty, we are indebted to Chris Field, Stuart Marks, Peter Weil, and John Westley.

Friends in England at the University of London, at Oxford, and at the Institute of Development Studies Program at Sussex were also often very helpful. Special thanks are due to Robert Chambers, Keith Griffin, Issac Marks, Shula Marks, Rita Cruise O'Brien, and Donal Cruise O'Brien.

Our current faculty colleagues and most assuredly our students have tolerated our testing of ideas and experimentation with new concepts. Some of those at George Mason University got involved in data collection and methodology and policy analysis. And the George Mason Word Processing Center proved to be both extraordinarily efficient and careful in the production of the manuscript. Joan Thomassy showed that patience and professionalism can win out; she worked with skill, accuracy, and unfailing good cheer from copy that was rarely clear, and usually messy. Many of the students and faculty in the International Development Program at American University will recognize here materials and ideas that they initially heard in forum and in seminars. Among those who deserve thanks is American University for granting time to complete this manuscript. And other thanks are due to Steve Arnold, Brady Tyson, and Jim Weaver and all the students in the development administration seminar. Russell Stout served above and beyond the call of duty as a colleague by reading and commenting on each chapter. Deborah Steel, the Humphrey fellows, and Beth Shields all helped as graduate students.

We are grateful to the World Bank for the opportunity to participate in the Task Force on Implementation Problems in Human Resource Development during the fall of 1979. To all those involved and especially to Peter Knight, Norman Uphoff, John Montgomery, Milton Esman, and Francis Lethem we owe our gratitude.

Others also shared suggestions and insights, including David Korten, Paul Streeten, Stanley Heginbotham, and William Siffin, as we worked through unwieldy concepts and troublesome issues. We also want to insist on thanking Westview's initially anonymous reviewer, John Powelson. His detailed and carefully drawn comments greatly assisted our revising efforts.

Barbara Sutton's artistic skill was available to us before she left to work with refugees in Thailand. We thank her for all the figures and graphs she drew for us from our scribbled notes.

A word of thanks to our families is also in order; to our children for their patience, our husbands for their endurance, and our parents for their encouragement. All of them in different ways share with us visions of what might be, while coping skillfully with what is.

One would think with such help we might have written with greater wisdom. That we did not always do so is our misfortune to bear. In no way can any of these people share responsibility, except for our gratitude. We did not always heed all advice nor follow it as some would have liked. Thus our errors of omission or commission are ours, while we remain profoundly grateful to many who helped us along the way.

C.B.
L.G.W.

Managing Development
in the Third World

PART ONE

Development Administration: An Introduction

This book is about the administration of development. It is based on the assumption that those involved in the process of planning and implementing development confront organizational problems and dilemmas that warrant special attention. The first two chapters concern two fundamental issues: the meaning of development and the role of administration in bringing about development. These two issues are closely related: alternative definitions of development have different implications for the task of those involved in administration. The next three chapters provide an analysis of organizations, how they function and how people behave within them. Chapter 3 reviews what is presently known about how organizations work. Chapter 4 presents a variety of perspectives on organizations, each implicitly a model for bringing about change. Chapter 5 examines the way that individuals behave within organizations and includes a model of the various factors that influence behavior in order to analyze ways to bring about change. The chapters in Part 1 form the basis for a discussion of the various strategies to implement programs and projects that are considered in Part 2.

1
Redefining Development

Introduction

Development is one of the most compelling concepts of our time. It provokes painful questions about values, techniques, and choices. It raises anew the classical query about the nature of the "good society," as well as the problem of who is to decide on society's content and course. Because these are large and difficult problems, it is easy to lose them in generalizations, using the term *development* as a euphemism for change, modernization, or growth. Development, however, is more complex than any of these words suggests.

Development is a normative concept; it implies choices about goals for achieving what Gandhi called the "realization of the human potential."[1] Growth by itself does not accomplish enough and sometimes has unfortunate consequences. As the microbiologist would remind us, the hallmark of the cancer cell is growth without development. Similarly, development is not always interchangeable with modernization, for there are many aspects of tradition that enhance the human potential and knit cultures together. Michael Todaro indicates several qualities of development when he concludes that it is "a multidimensional process involving major changes in social structures, popular attitudes and national institutions as well as the acceleration of economic growth, the reduction of inequality and the eradication of absolute poverty."[2]

The concept of development is also more broadly applicable than is sometimes assumed. Often it is used in reference to third world nations, and indeed that is the emphasis in this book. However, development can only be fully understood if it is conceived as a process in industrialized countries as well as in the third world. Industrial nations have far to go to "realize the human potential"; they have much to learn about inequality and the alleviation of poverty. Additionally, they are part of the reason why the third world finds development so difficult. Just as development

3

is not synonymous with economic growth, relations with the third world cannot be improved simply by exporting technology and increasing trade. Global inequalities are more intricately rooted. The Brandt Commission on relations between North and South has stated, "We want to make it clear that North and South cannot proceed with 'business as usual' only adding a few bits here and there. What is required is intellectual reorientation, serious steps towards structural change, increased practical cooperation."[3]

In the meantime, developmental choices are being made throughout the world by peasants, farm families, nations, and international organizations. Within the latter, the number of actors has increased dramatically in the last three decades. A United Nations system with 55 members in 1946 had 152 members in 1979. Local and international governments from Allahabad to Zimbabwe make policy choices that directly affect their chances for development. All these official efforts are supplemented by a multitude of workaday decisions that weave different developmental futures for farmers, peasants, squatters, bourgeoisie, and elites as they live and work in rural areas, townships, and exploding cities. The interdependence of that global community bodes both good and ill, carrying the potential for bane or blessing.

One often hears of development but observes the reality of underdevelopment. Poverty and its several aspects deepen; peasants continue to struggle for survival against landlessness; shantytowns spring up daily in urban areas. Buffeted between moneylender and landowner, at the mercy of the weather, and with limited access to seed, water, and draft animals, every action of the peasant must be measured against its risk in a risk-filled environment. Aggregate measures of growth in GNP and life expectancy and of decline in infant mortality tell a tale of uneven improvement, increased suffering for some, debt accumulation, diminished environment, and increased inequalities.

Just as many lay claim to the concept of development, and just as its reality is ambiguous, the term itself has many different meanings. The history of the changes in the conceptualization of development and successive efforts to reshape its definition are instructive in understanding the term's current meanings.

Historical Notes

The study of development can be traced to the concerns of eighteenth-century philosophy, political economy, and the fledgling social sciences. But since World War II, the rate of social and economic change within the countries reaching or struggling for independence catapulted development to the forefront of public debate. The result has been a challenging discussion among and within disciplines about development's origins, nature, and implications. Much of the debate springs from differing perceptions about how and under what circumstances a nation can increase its rate and direction of change. These issues in turn are rooted in deeper concerns over why people behave as they do and what are appropriate and feasible goals toward which change might be directed. There are also different assessments of the extent to which change can, or should, be managed and directed. Underlying these queries are the issues of power and choice—who is to decide the direction and nature of change.

Postcolonial Era: The Dominance of an Economic Perspective

The end of World War II ushered in the beginning of self-government in much of Asia and Africa. India, giant among nations in population and land area, was the first to gain independence. Due to the luminous quality of Gandhi's message and his leadership of the world's largest non-violence movement, India's independence set in motion a more general repudiation of colonial legitimacy. In the wake of dying empires, basic questions took on new urgency: What are the origins of legitimacy for social change? What relationships exist between traditional values and economic progress? How can countries expand opportunities for their populations? What are the causes and sources of economic and political development? How can, or should, new nations most effectively govern themselves?

During the 1950s and on through the 1960s, economists tended to dominate the development debates and essentially determined their intellectual scope. Understandably, planners in this period were also heavily influenced by economists in the development field. For some planners, development was synonymous with growth and in turn with industrialization and productivity. Most economists of the 1950s assumed industrialization was essential for growth and hence concentrated on what needed to happen in order for industrialization to proceed. There were two approaches to increasing industrialization. The first, and the one most frequently pursued, was to stimulate the fledgling industrial sector. It was essentially a dualist approach in which the traditional economy was seen as a competing alternative, and imports were designed with industrial productivity in mind. The second approach, less frequently adopted, was to mobilize the traditional sector of the economy to the task of industrialization. The reasoning was that the poorest peoples living in rural areas were a potential and badly needed labor force.

Economic policy should therefore focus on harnessing the traditional and underdeveloped sectors for the process of growth and industrialization, rather than on importing Western technology.

The power of the economists rippled through the related disciplines. Unique among the social sciences, economics had a metric — money — and hence could readily measure and quantify in areas where other social sciences could not. Academics in other fields — anthropology, political science, sociology, public administration — tried to interject additional factors into the economists' equation of industrialization with development. For example, it was felt by some that certain forms of government would encourage development while others would not. But since proponents of such a theory could not provide evidence as compelling as that available to economists, members of other disciplines tended to accept the economists' prescriptions and to focus on the consequences of the industrialization process for their areas. Anthropologists talked of the need to change traditional attitudes and to induce a work ethic; political scientists talked of the need for political control; administrators talked of the need for merit civil service systems; and sociologists talked of the need for elites to provide the necessary savings, role models, and leadership.

Following the academic lead, planners and politicians adopted the same economic arguments and combined them with their own ideologies and commitments to modernity. This acceptance of an economic perspective on the development task had two crucial implications. First, it was strikingly clear that modernity would not always fit easily or painlessly into the traditional cultures of developing nations. To take but one example, the ongoing relationships and kinship patterns in a village could be totally disrupted by the demands of industrial organizations and recruitment. The culture, attitudes, and preferences of the people therefore came to be viewed as obstacles to development. Drawing such a conclusion, planners and policymakers of this period assumed that people, especially the rural poor, needed to be led into modernity. The incompleteness of the peasants' information and the inadequacies of rural and traditional institutions meant that change had to come from external forces and events. It followed that persuasiveness and authority must be brought to bear on choices. The political implications of that assumption were used to justify political control, coercion, and often military rule.

A second key assumption often made was that during the initial stages of growth, development required heavy investment in productive activities. As a result, planners concluded that questions of equity and distribution had to be postponed for decades, if not for a generation. This conclusion reinforced the argument that development required strong control mechanisms. Only an authoritative regime could cope with a transition period in which only a few would benefit from development.[4]

Shortcomings of the Early Development Decades

Some political scientists and commentators raised objections to these views. But with time, the strongest criticism arose within the third world countries themselves, especially from opposition groups within Latin American countries who saw military rule as carrying too high a human cost. They were primarily troubled about the impact of political coercion on the social fabric of the country.

In the meantime economists were examining evidence about the actual course of growth and were finding uneven results. Some argued that real growth in aggregate terms (GNP — gross national product — or GDP — gross domestic product) declined during the 1970s in terms of income for the poorest of the third world nations.[5] In many instances this growth was not even keeping up with population growth. Figure 1.1 provides a comparison of trends in per capita GNP including projections through 1990.

Table 1.1 presents this same information in another way, showing both the relative growth rate of GNP and the annual rate of population

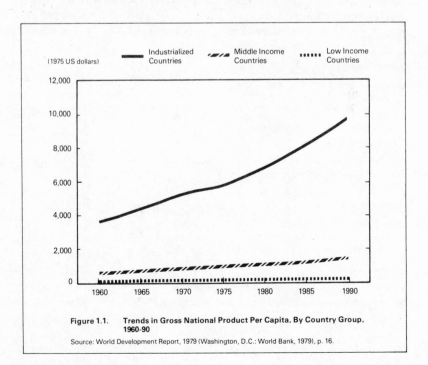

Figure 1.1. **Trends in Gross National Product Per Capita, By Country Group, 1960-90**

Source: World Development Report, 1979 (Washington, D.C.: World Bank, 1979), p. 16.

growth. The GNP figures indicate that the income gap between rich and poor nations is *widening* at a rate of more than 2 percent per year. And the differential in population increase means that the actual gap between per capita incomes in the developed and underdeveloped worlds is widening at an annual rate of 3.8 percent.[6]

An increase in inequality is also becoming evident, both within countries and between them. One study found that the poor were actually worse off in some countries than they had been at the beginning of the push for growth.[7] The amount of inequality often increased even in those instances where the welfare of the poor had improved.[8] One measure of inequality is the percentage of national income received by the top 5 percent of the population. In effect the question is how much of the total national income goes to the wealthiest people within the country. For example, although Brazil has had significant growth in GNP since 1965 (about 5.6 percent a year), the share of national income going to the top 5 percent of the population rose from 29 to 38 percent. Table 1.2 provides data on this distribution for some other countries.

Revisions In Economic Views

Economists responded to these deepening inequalities by critiquing the earlier models of development and the underlying assumption that the newly generated wealth would "trickle down" to those less fortunate. The new hypothesis proposed was that inequality would follow the course of

TABLE 1.1

Relative Growth Rate of GNP and Population

	Annual growth rate 1965-1974	Annual rate of population growth
42 poorest nations[a]	1.1	2.9
55 developing nations[a]	3.3	2.5
35 developed nations	4.6	.8

a. UN classification of "least developed" and "developing"

Sources: Michael Todaro, Economic Development in Third World (London: Longman, 1977), p. 26. World Bank Atlas, 1979: Population, Per Capita Product, and Growth Rates (Washington, D.C.: World Bank Group, 1979).

an inverted *U*; as growth proceeded, it would first increase and then decrease. The increase would occur initially as some groups were able to exploit new opportunities more fully than others. The result, according to Irma Adelman and Cynthia Morris, was that "development is accompanied by an absolute as well as a relative decline in the average income of the very poor."[9] Over time presumably other groups would enter the wage economy, and at this point inequality would gradually decline.

The evidence about the relationship between growth and equity remains mixed, however. As indicated above, studies done in the 1960s and 1970s were skeptical of the earlier assumption that the benefits of growth would "trickle down" to the poor. But by 1980 several economists were citing evidence that in a few countries at least capitalist growth was generating wider benefits, and thus they were finding partial confirmation of the 1950 models. For example, economists William Loehr and John Powelson questioned the accuracy of the inverted *U* hypothesis; they have found no conclusive evidence that growth "generates inequality in and of itself." They pointed out that studies to the contrary are not based on time-series data and seldom take into account the amount of inequality in the society prior to growth. They also confirmed several studies that find political and structural issues key influences on inequality, including the opportunities of the poor to take advantage of economic development, the extent to which fiscal policies are progressive, and the distributional impact of various substantive policies such as education and agriculture. Development economist James

TABLE 1.2

Percent of National Income Going to Top 5 Percent of Population

Country	1960	1970
Bangladesh	19.0	17.0
Malawi	na	27.0
Tanzania	na	34.0
Bolivia	na	36.0
India	27.0	25.0
Pakistan	20.0	18.0
Sri Lanka	27.0	19.0
Ecuador	42.0	42.0
Canada	14.0	14.0
Denmark	16.9	22.0
United States	16.0	13.3

Source: World Tables, 1976 published for World Bank by Johns Hopkins University Press.

Weaver has also pointed out that very recent data in such countries as
Brazil and Taiwan indicate that growth has meant an increase in
equity.[10]

Another development in economic thought came with the gain in influence of "political economy" during the late 1960s and early 1970s. Its
key point is that economic issues can only be understood in the context of
political reality. Political economists start from the assumption that
political questions of resource ownership, power, and distribution have a
great influence on the process of development, and they arrive at two
major conclusions. First, growth and development are two distinct,
albeit related, processes. Growth by itself is not the same as development. Growth they equate with actual production and greater ouput;
development, on the other hand, can be defined as capacity for production. The significance of this distinction is that capacity depends on the
structures in a society; to increase capacity these structures have to be
changed. "This change is done by introducing new outputs, establishing
new sources of inputs or new uses for them, and finding new demands
for outputs."[11] The position that development is distinct from growth
has taken on added conviction with time. Structural change is seen as
essential in order to expand capacity.

The second conclusion of the political economists is that production
and distribution are closely related. Earlier economists focused on productivity and either left the problem of distribution to the political scientists or implied that inequality is necessary to stimulate the requisite rates
of investment. What became clearer upon closer examination was that
the kind of production chosen and the way in which it had been organized directly affected who benefited from increases in productivity.
Since different modes of production lead to different distributions, these
effects cannot be ignored.[12]

Economists from the mid-1970s on began to collect evidence that
redistribution was possible without sacrificing growth; since equity was
feasible (and they agreed it was desirable), they could now define
development to include concern for distribution. One of the seminal
works presenting this argument came from no less-established a citadel
for mainstream development economics than the World Bank and was
entitled *Redistribution with Growth*.[13] One of the interesting points
about this collection of studies is that it grew out of a joint study by the
Bank's Development Research Center and the Institute of Development
Studies at the University of Sussex, England, and represented the influence of political economists upon the Bank.[14]

Its contributors argue that there are economic reasons for increasing
equality. For example, investment rates may be improved with a more
egalitarian distribution policy. At the same time, growth is inherently in-

egalitarian, and, as a result, economic models are insufficient by themselves to deal with inequality. It is therefore necessary for policies to include social as well as economic objectives. Positive actions are needed to limit concentration of wealth through such measures as education, land reform, and redistributive taxes. A first step can be to categorize different groups in the society by income and then see how each group is affected by development policies. Given this information, and the preferred social objectives, packages of appropriate policies can be designed.[15]

The role of economics was further refined by those economists who identified themselves with the field of "development economics" as a distinct study within the broader discipline.

> Development economics to a greater extent than traditional economics or even political economy is concerned with the economic and political processes necessary for affecting rapid structural and institutional transformations of entire societies in a manner that will most efficiently bring the fruits of economic progress to the broadest segments of their populations.[16]

Development economics therefore underscores the importance of distributional issues and the necessity for structural change in society in order to accomplish any redistribution.

Dependency Theorists

Another group of economists who participated in the continuous debates over the meaning and nature of economic development were the dependency theorists. Their name comes from the main thesis of their argument: third world countries are made dependent, often under the guise of development, upon the developed countries. One of the processes that fosters this dependency is the transformation of the middle class within third world countries to the comprador (compromised) class, looking outside to the West for political leadership rather than inward to their own countries. For the dependency theorists, many countries are *underdeveloped* rather than developing, and they attribute this underdevelopment to external factors, such as the adverse terms of trade most third world countries experience. They argue that the functioning of international trade and finance frequently places developing countries at the mercy of factors beyond their control.[17]

As part of this international perspective, dependency theorists reiterate the emphasis of others on the importance of social and political structures in society. They hold that international forces work to create "structures of poverty" — institutions that respond to the priorities of the industrial world and in so doing reinforce the poverty and dependence of the third world. This economic analysis has important political implications. First, the benefits of growth do not spread throughout the economy as the classical economists theorized. Even more importantly, there are conflicting interests in a society; those with power use growth to promote their own interests. Terms of trade, choices about what to produce, and patterns of investment all strengthen the interests of certain groups in the society at the expense of others. A nation is not just a single national entity; it is composed of many and often conflicting interests. The work of Colin Leys, particularly his analysis of Kenya, offers an example of the dependency argument. He notes that "the question of 'whether there will be meat in the kitchen is never decided in the kitchen'" and continues,

> Among their major deficiencies both "political development" and "economic development" theories have had in common a marked disinclination to distinguish clearly between the different interests at stake in the countries of the third world, let alone to make the antagonisms between them into the central focus of enquiry. One must start out from an analysis of the way in which different "patterns of development" embody the dominance of different combinations of class interests.[18]

Dependency theorists insist upon going behind events and leaders to determine the use and abuse of power, whose interests are being served, and what alternatives exist. This approach began among economists from, or concerned with, Latin America, and it quickly spread. Some argue that its applicability to the Latin American case was not as readily transferable to other parts of the world. Others, however, disagree, pointing out that the dependency argument in essence makes a new and generally valid interpretation of events.[19] Basil Davidson argues eloquently for more comprehension of the revolutionary nature of the change Africans must make for themselves and against the dependency that comes with foreign assistance.[20] David Gould illustrates how the dependency argument affords a different understanding of the potentially oppressive role administration can, and sometimes does, play. He notes the inefficiency and arbitrariness prevailing in the Zairian bureaucracy and points to the ways in which they reduce the poor to an increasingly marginal existence. Most discouraging, he points out that such behavior on the part of administrators is not an aberration, but rather a rational response to the system within which they are living. The elites, he adds, in contrast to the poor, remain indifferent to this administrative behavior because they are able to share in the profiteering or, at least, to avoid its abuses.[21]

Some dependency theorists draw heavily on Marxist theory; others do not. One of the issues that remains unresolved among the different groups of "dependistas" is the role of scarcity in their analysis. Some Marxists insist that there is little or no "real" scarcity, that the scarcity that exists is induced and maintained by social organizations and institutions in order to keep people under control. Scarcity, according to this argument, is engineered in order to maximize the profits of the capitalists. The disagreements over this argument are intense among those of the Left, and not all of those who use Marxist analysis accept the argument. Harold Brookfield, for example, who adopts other aspects of Marxist analysis, takes strong exception to the Marxist view of scarcity. He argues that resource scarcities exist in nature and that the way in which the world community comes to terms with these shortages is important. He also argues that the underdevelopment of the third world is related to the generation of poverty in the first world. In *Interdependent Development* he makes a case for a global restructuring—a case supported by many scholars in the World Order Models Project, as well as many United Nations forums.[22] In stressing the extent to which the industrialized nations experience many of the problems confronting the third world, Brookfield raises an interesting issue. As resource scarcity becomes more pronounced, it will be increasingly apparent that the characteristics of dependency can be applied to many of the more developed countries. Not all of the dependency theorists appreciate these commonalities.

Humanist Views

Other analyses focus on the human and ethical dimensions of development. One of the most eloquent is entitled *The Cruel Choice,* by ethicist Denis Goulet. In this important book, Goulet emphasizes the impact of underdevelopment on the human condition.

> Underdevelopment is shocking; the squalor, disease, unnecessary deaths, and hopelessness of it all! . . . The most empathetic observer can speak objectively about underdevelopment only after undergoing, personally or vicariously, the shock of underdevelopment. This unique culture shock comes to one as he is initiated to the emotions which prevail in the "culture of poverty." . . . [The] prevalent emotion of underdevelopment is a sense of personal and societal impotence in the face of disease and death, of confusion and ignorance as one gropes to understand change, of servility toward men whose decisions govern the course of events, of hopelessness before hunger and natural catastrophe. Chronic poverty is a cruel kind of hell and one cannot understand how cruel that hell is merely by gazing upon poverty as an object.[23]

Viewed from this perspective development is defined as liberation from poverty and from a stunted view of self. Development means enhancing self-esteem and a sense of efficacy or ability to make choices about the future. The humanists also insist that the appropriate question is, Development for what? Merely increasing consumption or expanding material benefits is insufficient and in the end dehumanizing.

The economist Michael Todaro builds on this analysis and writes that development implies three different core values:

Life sustenance: the ability to provide basic necessities. All people have certain basic needs without which life would be impossible. These "life-sustaining" needs indisputably include food, shelter, health, and protection.

Self-esteem: the ability to be a person. A second universal component of the good life is self-esteem — a sense of worth and self-respect, of not being used as a tool by others for their own ends.

Freedom from servitude: the ability to choose. A third and universal value that should constitute the meaning of development is the concept of "freedom." Freedom here is not to be understood in the political or ideological sense, but in the more fundamental sense of freedom or emancipation from alienating material conditions of life and, from the social servitudes of men to nature, ignorance, other men, misery, institutions, and dogmatic beliefs.[24]

The Meaning of Development

The view of development that informs the following chapters is drawn from these contributions and critiques, and like them it is based on certain specific values. Fundamentally, we argue that development involves both "being" and "doing." Deprivation, degradation, poverty all indicate underdevelopment wherever they are found, and it is crucial to *do* certain things in order to reduce such poverty. One could even argue that in severely deprived circumstances doing is primary. Thus much of our concern is with designing and administering projects and programs to bring about visible and significant change in people's circumstances.

We also believe that poverty dehumanizes and diminshes the human spirit and human capabilities; change therefore needs to take account of the uniqueness of individuals. We propose that development means increasing the capacity of people to influence their future. It thus involves being, as well as doing. It means that projects and programs not only need to accomplish physical and concrete changes, but need to do so in such a way that people have a greater capacity to choose and respond to these changes. It means that planned change has to be concerned with the potential of individuals and with the inviolability of their persons.[25]

This view of development differs from both modernization and growth as they are commonly defined. In spite of the rich theory that has grown up around the concept of modernization, it is virtually impossible to disengage it from an identification with westernization and industrialization. Modernization is frequently defined in terms of developing specializations and a variety of structures and institutions, but in common parlance it means adopting the symbols, styles, and technologies of first world countries. Yet a country can be modern in style and technique and not any closer to an ability to influence its future or pursue its potential. And even though growth may improve conditions, it is not sufficient in itself.[26] The infant who only adds to gross body weight is hardly considered by parents, doctors, or teachers as "developing." Nor do leaders within developing countries consider aggregate increases in GNP alone as the only indicator of development.

Development as an increase in the capacity to influence the future has certain implications. First, it means paying attention to *capacity,* to what needs to be done to expand the ability and energy to make change. Second, it involves *equity;* uneven attention to different groups will divide peoples and undermine their capacity. Third, it means *empowerment,* in the sense that only if people have some power will they receive the benefits of development. And finally it means taking seriously the interdependence in the world and the need to ensure that the future is *sustainable.* Unless we recognize and deal with problems of scarcity and finite resources, any capacity we achieve will be very short run.

Capacity

First, development involves expanding capacity to determine one's future. As used here, capacity includes such economic factors as productive facilities. It is very difficult for a person or state to increase his or its control over the future if major factors of production are crippled, or if basic needs are not met. Thus development encompasses a concern with production and growth, but it has a much broader meaning. It includes the capacity of the nation and community to develop political and social institutions responsible for production and allocation. And drawing from humanist thought, capacity includes a concern for people's self-esteem, their ability to invest themselves in caring about and shaping their own future. Development therefore has both a micro and a macro aspect: it involves changes in the individual and the community as well as the nation.

Equity

Second, development includes distributional issues. No matter how "developed" an economy is, if only a small segment of the population benefits from it, development has not occurred. Although economists have supported the argument for equity, it does not ultimately depend upon an economic rationale. In the long run economic development is stimulated by increasing the human resources in a country and by equalizing the ability to consume. Even without this argument, however, equity is a part of development. It is also a normative concept implying that ensuring more equality in access and benefits is a value in itself.

Empowerment

Third, development includes acquiring leverage for the poor. Since economic growth will not automatically be broadly distributed, the question of its benefits is a political issue. Politics in fact can be defined as the resolution of conflicts over the allocation of benefits from growth. The only way to have a built-in mechanism for correcting grossly unfair allocative decisions is for people to have influence. They can then use that influence to raise their issues onto the agenda. Loehr and Powelson suggest that "leverage is gained from the ability to shift alliances, plus a knowledge of how to do so advantageously." Thus it is a form of strategic behavior, and the more information and freedom people have, the more leverage they will have over policy.[27]

Events have shown that benefits tend to go to those in power. The fact that those who are poor are also the powerless has a great deal to do with the amount of inequity that continues to exist.[28] Although many studies document this point, an interesting analysis comparing the course of development in several countries in Latin America concludes:

> Conservative authoritarian regimes often fail to anticipate or recognize popular demands for policy expansion. Instead as in Nicaragua, their development programs respond to a small elite or to the demands of international agencies. . . . Costa Rica illustrates the other extreme. Its president faces overwhelming demands for the expansion of welfare programs from an active and vocal legislature and from his own bureaucracy. He is concerned with satisfying demands not repressing them. . . . In contrast to most of his neighbors, the Costa Rican president has begun to distribute the benefits of development to a majority of his countrymen.[29]

Powerlessness therefore reduces the demands and pressures on political leaders, and without such demands leaders are unlikely to focus on distributional issues.

Powerlessness is problematical for a second reason. We have said that development means increasing people's capacity to make choices about their future. Without a sense of personal efficacy, without any experience in expressing their needs, without an awareness of where to go with their demands, individuals can hardly develop such a capacity. In the following passage an experienced authority on development administration raises the central issue. He argues that if we see dependency as crippling, we are forced to deal with the problem of powerlessness:

> A basic question in development management . . . is whether desired social outcomes can be achieved through central technocratic allocation of resources to provide services intended to benefit the poor, or whether the real problem of poverty is rooted in basic social structures which relegate the poor to conditions of dependency. If the former, then the central problem may be one of increasing the effectiveness of service delivery. If the latter, then the central problem may be to reduce dependency by measures which increase the potential of the poor to take independent and instrumental political action on their own behalf.[30]

Sustainability

Lastly, development includes a long-range concern for the future; the term that captures this issue is *sustainability*. Because of such factors as fragile soils, finite energy, limited mineral sources, and pollution problems, production decisions need to take the future into account. The question is whether present production decisions allow us to sustain ourselves over time, a question that has become important as people have become more conscious of ecological and environmental issues. Natural resources that were once taken for granted or even abused in the past are now looked upon with new appreciation and real concern. Many of them are nonrenewable; their finiteness propels us to consider the prospects for a sustainable future. Others might be damaged by modern man's manipulation of chemicals and energy sources to come up with new substances.

Developing countries understandably find this new argument heavy with irony. Just as many of them are on the threshold of modern advances in industrialization, they are told to beware of the environmental hazards that will come in its wake. Having come late to the process of industrialization, they are to bear costs that forerunners simply neglected.

Interdependence

The issue of sustainability in turn raises the elusive and complex issue of interdependence. As the dependency theorists note, the third world is economically dependent upon the industrialized nations. But it is also true that the industrialized nations are dependent on the third world for much of their growth. An increasingly large share of exports from the United States, for example, is sold within the third world.[31] In fact, U.S. trade expansion depends upon developing countries purchasing increasing amounts of U.S. goods and services. This mutual dependence can only be characterized as interdependence.[32]

As trade among nations increases, so does their interdependence; this phenomenon is inherently conflictual. But before considering the sources of potential conflict in the relationship, the system aspect warrants attention. Interdependence is a major characteristic of a system. And systems analysis gives us some insight into the nature of interdependence. Interdependence has two central properties: (1) the behavior of each part has an effect on the behavior of the whole, and (2) no one part has an independent effect. For example, the behavior of the lungs, and the effect that they have on the human system, depends in part on the behavior of the heart. Neither one can work well without the other. In this instance, they are completely interdependent.

There are degrees of interdependence in systems, however. Whereas the human body is a very interdependent system, many aspects of the world economic system are obviously not that interdependent. Yet with increased international trade, communication, and technology one of the characteristics of our times is the increasing *rate* of interdependence, as captured in Marshall McLuhan's term the *global village*.[33]

Interdependence offers great potential, as well as intense conflict. Interdependence in human relationships allows people to be and become more than they might be or become alone. In this respect, it has an enabling function. The system is more than the sum of its parts. Yet there are also strains in the relationship. The loss of control over determining direction causes strain. International monetary flows mean that no one economy can completely control its own money supply as it did prior to the increased interdependence. Such a situation is politically difficult to explain to a public accustomed to great independence of action. The steady loss in the degrees of freedom decision makers prized in earlier times causes anxiety and hence conflict. Decision makers experience real frustration when that which was once controllable becomes not only uncontrollable, but even less predictable. We only vaguely understand the contours of this issue at the international level. Yet consider its functioning at the human level. Specialists in family law tell us that interdependence causes real anger even among people committed to one another's welfare. Consider the process of family budgeting. If many family members all write checks on one account, planning becomes simultaneously more difficult and more essential. In a world of finite resources, 150 nations are writing checks on the world account. And planning has become both more essential and more difficult.

Administrative Incapacity

Development conceived as broadly as it has been here raises special problems within each of the social sciences. Within the field of management and administration, these issues have received far too little attention. And yet within communities, countries, and the international forum, administrators play a variety of influential and important roles. As a result, it is central that we consider the management processes and methods that are available to cope with the problems ahead. Management is not just a question of efficient service delivery or of effective control over the existing allocative systems. It is a change-oriented field concerned with the institutional dynamics of social justice. The problem is that administration in most third world nations is more marked by incapacity than by imaginative, responsive institutions. This book is about ways to increase administrative capacity. In chapter 2 we will deal specifically with the role of administration in underdevelopment and the causes of the problems it encounters. In the remainder of the book, we will examine methods, approaches, and techniques for more responsible and responsive administration.

Conclusions

In this chapter we have reviewed the competing paradigms of development, as well as some of the results of the first development decades. Some of the early expectations for development proved unduly optimistic. Not only did much of the poverty remain unrelieved, but inequalities increased and some of the poor were absolutely as well as relatively worse off. Jolting as this fact has been for decision makers, economists, and planners, it has been far more devastating for the people whose story it tells. As the empirical evidence has accumulated, new approaches have been developed and old approaches revised in an attempt to explain, interpret, and advise on what is to be done.

From each of the competing perspectives on development, a broadened conception of development emerges. This conception of development encompasses not only growth, but capacity, equity, and empowerment as well. Development defined as a process for evolving a capacity to influence one's future, however, is fraught with difficulties. Not the least of these difficulties is that of scarcity in an interdependent world. Development administrators are already deeply engaged in these issues and processes within developing states. It is to assist them in their task of building more responsive approaches and institutions that this textbook is written.

Notes

1. Mohandas K. Gandhi, *An Autobiography, The Story of My Experiments with Truth,* 8th ed. (Boston: Beacon Press, 1968). (The first edition of Gandhi's autobiography was published in two volumes in 1927 and 1929.)

2. Michael Todaro, *Economic Development in the Third World* (London: Longmans, 1977), p. 62.

3. Report of the Independent Commission on International Development Issues (Chairman: Willy Brandt), *North-South: A Programme for Survival* (Cambridge, Mass.: MIT Press, 1980), p. 26.

4. For an excellent summary and critique of the contribution of U.S. political scientists, see Donal Cruise O'Brien, "Modernization, Order, and the Erosion of the Democratic Ideal: American Political Science 1960-1970," *Journal of Development Studies* 8 (July 1972).

5. Barrington Moore's major study, *The Social Origins of Dictatorship and Democracy* (Boston: Beacon Press, 1966), details how this assertion reappears in different epochs for different cultures. As a precursor to the politics of the basic needs approach that was to follow in development assistance, see Robert Ayres, "Development Policy and the Possibility of a 'Livable' Future for Latin America," *American Political Science Review* 59 (June 1975):507-525.

6. Todaro, *Economic Development in the Third World,* p. 26.

7. Hollis Chenery et al, *Redistribution with Growth* (London: Oxford University Press, 1974), p. xiii. For an excellent empirical update of this literature see *Growth and Poverty in Developing Countries,* World Bank Staff Working Paper no. 309, prepared by M. S. Ahluwalia, N. Carter, H. B. Chenery, and Development Policy Staff, rev. (Washington, D.C.: World Bank, 1979). One of their conclusions is that "on balance, the results suggest that focussing on improvements in distribution may be as effective in reducing world poverty as the accelerated growth option" (p. 44).

8. Charles Frank and Richard Webb, *Income Distribution in the Less Developed Countries* (Washington, D.C.: Brookings, 1977).

9. Irma Adelman and Cynthia Taft Morris, *Economic Growth and Social Equity in Developing Countries* (Stanford: Stanford University Press, 1973), p. 189. For a summary of capitalist, political economy, and growth-with-equity development models, see James H. Weaver and Kenneth P. Jameson, *Economic Development: Competing Parables,* Development Studies Program, Occasional Paper no. 3 (Washington, D.C.: Agency for International Development, 1978).

10. William Loehr and John P. Powelson, *The Economics of Development and Distribution* (New York: Harcourt Brace Jovanovich, 1981), pp. 130-141. James Weaver, personal conversation, 1981.

11. Norman Uphoff and Warren Ilchman, *The Political Economy of Development* (Berkeley: University of California Press, 1972), p. 88.

12. Ibid., p. 78.

13. Chenery, *Redistribution with Growth.*

14. Some of the earliest work in political economy was done by scholars who were teaching or doing research at the Institute of Development Studies. Two of those involved in the joint study by the World Bank and the Institute of Development Studies that led to this book are the well-known political economists Dudley Seers and Richard Jolly. Their landmark study of Cuban development, *Cuba, The Economic and Social Revolution* (Chapel Hill: University of North Carolina Press, 1964), set a standard for work in this field.

15. In a way, this approach added to the strength of the argument T. W. Schultz makes on the importance of investment in human resources in his famous study *Transforming Traditional Agriculture* (New Haven, Conn., and London: Yale University Press, 1964).

16. Todaro, *Economic Development in the Third World*, p. 6.

17. One of the earliest and most important works in this field is Paul Baran's *Political Economy of Growth* (New York: Monthly Review Press, 1957). Keith Griffin also looks at South America in *Underdevelopment in Spanish America* (London: George Allen and Unwin, 1969). Added to these is the valuable contribution of the Brazilian Andre Gunder Frank, *The Development of Underdevelopment* (New York: Monthly Review Press, 1971).

18. Colin Leys, *The Underdevelopment of Kenya* (London: Heinemann Educational Books, 1975), p. ix. Leys not only extends the dependency analysis to Africa, but discusses its political and administrative mechanisms more directly than have previous economists.

19. Peter C. W. Gutkind and Immanuel Wallerstein, eds., *The Political Economy of Contemporary Africa* (Beverly Hills, Calif.: Sage Publications, 1976).

20. Basil Davidson, *Can Africa Survive?* (Boston and Toronto: Little, Brown, 1974).

21. David Gould, "From Development Administration to Underdevelopment Administration: A Study of Zairian Administration in the Light of Current Crisis," *Les Cahiers du Cedaf* 6 (1978):21.

22. Harold Brookfield, *Interdependent Development* (Pittsburgh: University of Pittsburgh Press, 1975), p. 205. See also Gerald Mische and Patricia Mische, *Toward a Human World Order* (New York: Paulist Press, 1977). The Institute for World Order under the World Order Models Project sponsors a considerable amount of research and writing on this same theme.

23. Denis Goulet, *The Cruel Choice: A New Concept in the Theory of Development* (New York: Atheneum, 1971), p. 24.

24. Todaro, *Economic Development in the Third World*, p. 63.

25. Abdul Said and Brady Tyson, "Education and Development: The Emerging Dialogue," *Harvard Educational Review* 1981 (forthcoming).

26. Edgar Dunn distinguishes between growth as a change in scale, or an in-

crease in size, and development as an increase in the complexity of behavior. This view also take variation and individuality into account. *Economic and Social Development* (Baltimore: Johns Hopkins, 1971), p. 9.

27. Loehr and Powelson, *Economics of Development,* pp. 16-19.

28. One of the most thorough expositions about this relationship is R. H. Tawney's *Equality* (London: George Allen and Unwin, 1931; 4th ed., rev., 1952; 7th ed., 1970)

29. Gary Wynia, *Politics and Planners: Economic Policy in Central America* (Madison: University of Wisconsin Press, 1972), p. 197.

30. David Korten, *Population and Social Development Management* (Caracas: Instituto de Estudios Superiores de Administracion — IESA, 1979), p. 17.

31. See Joseph Peckman, *Setting National Priorities: Agenda for the 1980s* (Washington, D.C.: Brookings Institution, 1980). Within this volume, see especially Ralph C. Bryant and Lawrence B. Krause, "World Economic Interdependence," pp. 71-98, and John W. Sewell and John A. Mathieson, "North-South Relations," pp. 497-530.

32. Brookfield, *Interdependent Development;* Ralph C. Bryant, *Money and Monetary Policy in Interdependent Nations* (Washington, D.C.: Brookings Institution, 1980); Report of the Brandt Commission, *North — South: A Programme for Survival.*

33. R. L. Ackoff, *Redesigning the Future* (New York: John Wiley, 1974).

2

Administration and Underdevelopment

Introduction

Buried in the thousands of pages of five-year plans throughout the third world are programs that purport to bring development to rural regions — to expand the economy and to increase the income of the people who live there. But once the political battle to gain power, formulate the plan, and raise the funds is won, the next phase is less clear. What is to happen to move the plan into practice? Where are the skilled project designers who can mount projects in key areas? How are communities to be mobilized? In short, how is development to be implemented? These are the questions of development administration; they are often the key to whether or not the elusive phenomenon development occurs. Conversely, the fact that development often does not happen, or is very uneven, is partially rooted in management and organizational problems. Although administrative capacity is in short supply everywhere, its serious scarcity in the third world is particularly crippling.

In the following chapters, the range of skills, techniques, and approaches the development administrator needs to have at his command is spelled out in some detail. But before proceeding to these issues, we need to place administration in a broader context and explore the relationship between underdevelopment and administrative incapacity and also between administrative and political power. Taken together they present a troubling paradox: administrative incapacity deepens underdevelopment, but strengthening administration can also retard the course of political development. A strong administration can inhibit the generation of political power — both the power of leaders and of the public.[1] At the same time, political leaders are ambivalent about their own role. They are often frustrated and maddened by administrative weakness; they need a capable bureaucracy to implement policies, and yet addressing the problem is less glamorous and more long range than their short-term political horizons. Political leaders are also easily threatened by skilled administrators and thus wary of expanding administrative resources.[2] It is for this complex of reasons that we emphasize a participatory developmental approach to management that takes into account the larger political system within which administration functions. It is important to understand the relationships in order to address the possibility of change and the directions that such changes should take.

Underdevelopment and Incapacity

In Chapter 1 underdevelopment was defined as a process of steadily increasing inequity and the marginalization of people and resources. Because this process is rooted in political powerlessness, many observers have questioned whether those in administration can alter its course. The reason for their doubt is straightforward—more often than not, administrators appear to be part of the problem rather than part of any solution. For example, administrators usually have a vested interest in the status quo and hence have little investment in social change. By this reasoning, they are unlikely to attempt any redistribution of power or resources or even to be concerned with basic needs.

Stated in this manner, the argument suggests that administrative problems are deeply rooted in the behavior of administrators and thus can be attributed to administrators themselves. But it is also true that these problems are partly—indeed largely—the result of administrative incapacity, of structural and organizational flaws, rather than simply of what administrators do. It is the argument of this book that just as development has its obverse in underdevelopment, development administration has its obverse in administrative incapacity. Administrative incapacity is an inability to respond to needs conveyed by citizens. It is characterized by swollen bureaucracies encumbered with formalistic procedures that delay rather than expedite service delivery and program implementation. Administrative capacity, on the other hand, is rather like good housekeeping; when it is really good, it is also unobtrusive, enhances the environment, and facilitates getting on with the job. At this point, however, two interesting and related issues arise. The first is what we will call the paradox of administration, which in turn raises the second issue—the relationship between administrative and political power.

The Paradox of Development Administration

Most simply put, the paradox of development administration is that effective administration is essential to accomplish development, and yet its very effectiveness can also stifle and inhibit political development. The problem is that political development is about the issue of power. It requires the effective administration of scarce resources, but it also requires expanding access to decision making about those resources. The latter is necessary to enhance the capacity of people to determine their own future. Thus as administrators develop their ability to manage resources, they are likely to halt the expansion of political institutions — institutions that are essential to further distribute power. The point is made very nicely by Stanley Heginbotham in his study of the Indian bureaucracy.

> The adoption of modern elements of structure and process in any bureaucracy creates the potential for increases in institutional capacity that result from greater differentiation, better communication, or more effective control. At the same time, such innovations are likely to generate new conflicts and incongruities that reduce institutional capacity. The challenge of administrative development is to modernize in such a way that the first dynamic achieves greater force than the second.[3]

It is evident that as administrators increase their technical skills, they tend to dominate policy decisions and foreclose public discussion of alternative strategies. Hence the paradox exists — administrative incapacity prevents development from occurring, yet increased capacity can also impede development by stifling the generation of political power.

Administrative and Political Power

The classic way to deal with this paradox is to insure that political institutions are sufficiently strong that they can generate the participation and power necessary to hold the bureaucracy accountable. It is an approach used by democratic regimes as well as by those of the far Left and Right (witness the upheavals in China associated with the Cultural Revolution).[4] And yet it is particularly difficult for political leaders in the third world to carry out that function. Part of the problem goes back to the historical experience of colonialism.[5] A colonial state was the administrative state par excellence. Colonies were administered rather than governed; resources were managed with the goals of the metropolitan power in mind. Yet colonial administration was also a complete merger of political and administrative functions. So complete was this merger that confusion reigned over the distinguishing characteristics of either role. District commissioners were administrators; they were also political officers.[6] As independence approached, there was a flurry of activity to divorce these married functions. But it was too little and too late. The colonized had learned from experience rather than from a text, and they too wanted to politicize the administrative function. The difference was that they had a new set of goals. Some, such as Julius Nyerere, tried duplicating the administrative apparatus with a political party apparatus. Some tried to use a one-party system to achieve control. But nowhere was there a complete or satisfactory solution to merging administrative and political power.

If we are to define the respective roles for political and administrative power, we must begin by noting that administrative power is a subset of political power, combining as it does, both authority and influence.[7] Military power in turn is a kind of administrative power that adds coercion to the authority of position and usually forecloses participatory power.[8] Throughout history the problem has always been to find ways to hold accountable, or even to influence, administrators whose authority springs from the positions they hold. In some political systems, administrative power was merged with religious or cultural authority as, for example, in the Mandarin Chinese rule or within some traditional chiefdoms and kingdoms as in precolonial Africa.[9] In more recent time, regimes of the Left (China in the Cultural Revolution) and of the Right (Nigeria in the civil elections of 1979) have concerned themselves with balancing administrative power with political power to achieve greater popular control over decision making.[10]

The issue of the balance between administrative and political power resurfaced in the development administration literature. Fred Riggs and a group known as the Comparative Administration Group (CAG) argued that the attention to administrative development, which marked the early postindependence period, was actually impeding political development. For example, one of the hallmarks of administrative reform is to institute merit systems and to get rid of "spoils systems," where positions are given in return for support. The problem, according to these writers, is that spoils are very useful in building political parties and that preemptory introductions of merit systems inhibit the development of parties. Not only are administrative reform and political development often contradictory, but if a choice has to be made between them, political development is the more critical task.[11]

The relationship of reform and social change to administration is an old and complex problem. In the 1930s, long before Riggs, Harold Laski in England was convinced that even if the Labour party came into power, it would not be able to carry out nationalization. He feared that the civil service would be reluctant to implement far-reaching social change because that would diminish the power of the social class from which that civil service was drawn.[12] He proved to be wrong, and the reason he was is very instructive. He underestimated the complexity of organizations and their effect on perceptions and motivations. In short, he underestimated the potential for innovation by administrators and their opportunities to build and join coalitions built on either personal objectives or social ideals. There is far more permeability in a system than some of the static revolutionary models assume. Revolutionary models assume a rotten, unjust, and unreformable society that, through the catalyst of the revolution, becomes rational, harmonious, and self-improving. It is more accurate to see that administrative power can be changed in a variety of ways and that many of the same problems will recur after revolution has occurred.

Changing Approaches to Development Administration

In several respects development administration is different from its parent field of public administration. This is partly because the very definition of development includes specific policy goals — equity and structural change. Increasing both equity and access is particularly difficult and challenging. In addition, the environment within which such a combination must work is marked by critical scarcity, high uncertainty, and great risk. It is important to emphasize these factors; otherwise it is easy to expect too much of administrators and to assume they have more control over project resources than they do. The development administrator needs special skills, approaches, and knowledge if the problems he confronts are not to overwhelm him. Rural development programs, literacy programs, effective extension services, health clinics, schools, land reform, and effective taxation systems all require creative, flexible, and innovative administration.

The history of the development administration field is essentially a history of various efforts to address the needs of third world bureaucracies and to find ways to increase their capacity.[13] And just as there have been changes in the way in which development is perceived, there have also been changes in the kind of help that has been offered and in the way in which administrators describe what they need.

In the 1950s and 1960s, many states were just gaining their independence. It was therefore probably natural that much of the literature on administration at the time centered on issues of nationhood and on problems confronting the system as a whole. Essentially there were three different groups interested in development administration: (1) those who were most interested in the transmission of specific administrative techniques and skills,[14] (2) those interested in political-administrative relationships,[15] and (3) those within the third world who were struggling to achieve their own administrative styles.[16] The first group, those focusing on specific tools, worked mostly through multilateral organizations, especially the United Nations.[17] The second group, those concerned with political relationships as well as some of those from the first group, were part of a privately funded movement in the United States known as the Comparative Administration Group.[18] They tried to combine a series of case studies with an overall framework detailing how different parts of a political system relate to other parts. The third group, the indigenous leaders, tended to be very critical of the others and raised compelling questions about problems they were actually facing. This criticism, the decrease in financial support, and changing events in the third world all meant a decline in the field of development administration.[19]

Three major shortcomings of the older approaches these groups took are immediately apparent. First, their concerns were fairly limited. They were caught up in nation-state-level problems. The CAG group in particular showed little concern for immediate and pressing management issues with which administrators were dealing daily. Second, they drew from a relatively narrow range of organization theory and research. Many of them used models that were loosely defined as a "scientific management" approach, where management was considered a culture-free technology. An even greater shortcoming was that they neglected many of the developments that were taking place within organization theory, reflecting on and qualifying the earlier models. Third, and perhaps most unfortunate, those in the field were not learning from the third world. Although the West has only recently become enamored with the concept Small is Beautiful, based on the writings of the English economist Edward Schumacher, Gandhi had raised many of these issues years before. Similarly many of the ideas now so influential within the behavioral sciences have been current in India and Sri Lanka (Ceylon) for years through the work of Hindu and Buddhist scholars.[20] In short, the development administration field was not a learning field—it learned little from these local sources, and it fed little back to its parent discipline.[21]

The criticism can be taken one step further. According to Bernard Schaffer, many of the efforts to accomplish administrative reform during this period only served to reinforce the elitism and power of the bureaucrats. In other words, this period of development administration reflects the paradox of administration described earlier.

Schaffer traces the process back to the postindependence period, which was marked by efforts to strengthen the central management capacity of the state, most often at the expense of local units and existing organized interests. During the 1950s and 1960s the major problem of development administration was identified as manpower development. First, most of the training agenda was set by foreign institutions, which linked the new administrators to international rather than to internal networks. Thus learning within a nation and among nationals was not encouraged. Second, the training itself was defined in terms of *central control* and thus served to justify the existing bureaucracy rather than to challenge it to tackle problems of change. The problem was that management techniques were emphasized without being related to the task of development, and so they served only to enhance the power and control of central elites. According to Schaffer, "The processes of preparation and training in the public services of the new states have created beliefs and institutions producing quite different results than would be indicated by the demands of that agenda: a passion for certification, for example; a use of international networks; bureaucratic institutional ideologies; and a structure of centralized patronage and levies."[22]

Symptoms of Incapacity

Administrative incapacity is a common ailment in all systems, including those that claim to be "developed." But in the third world it is the severity of the illness that is striking, not the realization that the virus has been seen before. There are a variety of symptoms of administrative incapacity:

1. Too few of the skilled can be spared to work in rural areas even though it is known that that is where the greatest need exists.
2. Those few administrators who are capable are constantly shuffled about between tasks and ministries.
3. Most ministries are highly centralized and lack any serious structures to reach distant regions, even if they have the commitment to do so.
4. Local-level institutions are very weak and are steadily undermined by centralized ministries and staff shortages.
5. The wide social distances between administrators and the public grow with time and reflect differential access to education and resources.
6. Those lacking regular access to decision makers resort to bribes; corruption becomes a part of the process and undermines the respect and legitimacy that the administration needs.
7. National governments, feeling their fragile legitimacy, make few demands on the public. This phenomenon has been termed the

soft state. There are few obligations to work in the interest of the community, or to avoid actions prejudicial to that community (like corruption). Taxation, for example, is poorly administered and incomplete in coverage.[23]

These symptoms would be less deeply worrisome if the public sector were relatively small, or if the private sector were flourishing and dynamic. In many developing countries, the public sector is already larger than the private sector. Table 2.1 ranks fifty-five countries by the percentage of the total budget that is spent on the civil service. (No data

TABLE 2.1

Country Expenditures on Civil Service as Percentage of Total Budget

Country	Expenditure on Civil Service as Percentage of Total Budget
Bahamas	48.12
Bolivia	46.52
Greece	42.37
Costa Rica	41.45
Ethopia	38.43
Zaire	36.13
Dominican Republic	32.50
Uruguay	31.29
Guatamala	30.45
Botswana	29.33
Nicaragua	27.55
Peru	27.14
Spain	26.62
Philippines	20.19
Venezuela	25.88
Tanzania	25.73
Chile	25.46
Mexico	23.57
Thailand	21.81
Sri Lanka	21.20
Nigeria	19.37
Zambia	19.22
France	16.33
United Kingdom	15.71
United States	14.34
India	12.98
West Germany	9.99
Sweden	9.03

Source: George T. Kurian, The Book of World Rankings (New York:

Facts on File, 1979).

are available for communist countries.) Almost all of those with the highest proportions of their work force in the civil service are developing countries, whereas industrialized countries typically have a much lower percentage. Two interesting exceptions are India and Indonesia, both of which rank among the lowest in terms of money spent on civil service salaries.

The reasons for this disparity are easy to understand. Primarily, the problem is in the timing of development; the later it begins, the more the government feels the need to engage in large-scale purposive change. For example, the major manpower study for Namibia states, "Past experience in Africa, Asia, Latin America and Europe has demonstrated that the later in time serious efforts to achieve development have begun, the greater has been the role of the state in providing infrastructure, services, finance, and state sector productive enterprises."[24] In addition, savings and investments are low and hence do not stimulate investments that pull people into the private sector.

Countries have tried to deal with the rapid growth of the public sector, but the results are uneven. For example, in Tanzania in 1961 a government commission recommended reductions in the number of civil service posts. By the end of the decade, however, the civil service had more than doubled, at an annual growth rate of 111 percent. Similarly between 1975 and 1979, the civil service in Ghana grew at the rate of 17 percent per annum.[25]

The salary scales in the civil services are part of the problem for they are often much higher than any other salaries within the country and hence exert a serious pull away from other employment. In part these scales stem from the colonial experience when they were based on the salaries of expatriates. Bernard Schaffer adds that most efforts at administrative reform have led to even greater contrasts between the civil service and other employment and between high and low levels within the service. "The actual outcome in each case (of civil service reform) is almost exclusively and apparently inescapably a more or less radical improvement in salaries and conditions for the public service, and frequently of a highly gross and inegalitarian kind, even within the public service itself."[26]

External Causes of Incapacity

Just as there are competing explanations for the difficulties of development, there is a similar variety of explanations proposed for the incapacity of administration. Basically these competing explanations can be divided into those that focus on external causes of incapacity and those that focus on internal causes. The first group finds its roots in Marxist thought, particularly as it has been developed by dependency theorists. The second group has several roots, but can primarily be traced to the thought of Max Weber. We will examine both sets of arguments and then consider how they are interrelated.

The dependency explanation focuses on the external factors that constrain the development of an effective and autonomous administrative system.[27] Some of its intellectual roots go back to Marx's analysis of the preeminence of economic relations in influencing all other institutions in a society. Administrative behavior is then said to be determined by the influence of external economic structures, and thus it is often referred to as "structuralist" analysis.

Structuralists emphasize the way in which the international economic system influences and constrains the path of development. International terms of trade, the functioning of international financial and monetary markets, and flows of military and security assistance are most commonly cited for their impact on underdevelopment and administrative incapacity. According to this view, third world nations skew their development choices to take advantage of the market demands of industrialized countries. This skewing affects the ways in which the bureaucracies organize themselves and function. Administrators anticipate the reactions of external powers that control financial resources rather than focus on internal resource mobilization. As a result organizational structures tend to develop around these international channels and opportunities, rather than around the needs or priorities in the less-developed sectors of their own economies. Similarly training and recruitment tend to conform to these external agendas, rather than to internally developed priorities. And salaries reflect the standards of international networks rather than national priorities.[28]

The structuralists (or dependency theorists) go on to say that these external economic forces function through economic and political elites within third world nations. Frequently these elites are referred to as compradors, or those who are compromised by their ties to external economic interests. Dependency theorists also argue that the civil service reflects the interests of a middle class, which is dependent upon the West for its behavioral cues and life-styles as well as for political support. Foreign capital, both public and private, is important to the political regime, and the behavior of administrators accommodates and reflects the compromised position of the system.

The relationship between these elites and the administrators can take several forms. Some refer to a "bureaucratic *corps d'élite* controlling and dramatically expanding the 'modern sector' in partnership with western capital."[29] The bureaucrats become the vehicle for modernization and often the major beneficiaries of it. Another view suggests that the weakness of governing institutions encourages elites to turn to foreign alliances leaving the bureaucracy highly vulnerable to external influence. For example, in Senegal this vulnerability led to the erosion of strong socialist commitments to development.[30] Others point to instances where the bureaucrats have in fact become the economic elites and "pillage the country for their own enrichment."[31] These elites are then able to use external resources to maintain their influence and co-opt bureaucrats by providing them additional resources for turning development to their advantage.

An Alternative Explanation: Internal Causes

The second model focuses instead upon the internal characteristics of a state. About the time in his life when Max Weber was trying to mollify his mother's concern over his refusal to take his first communion, David Livingston was making his historic first trip to the kingdom of Buganda. From their vastly different beginnings, they set events in motion that were eventually to influence one another as well as the course of African history. The colonialist regimes that grew out of Livingston's exploits drew heavily upon Weber's concern with the system of authority in each nation.

Weber held that the key to understanding social and political events was to determine how people related to authority. On what basis do they accept some people or institutions as having legitimate authority over them? Such relations exemplify what is here termed an *internal* explanation. In his studies Weber found that authority often was based either on tradition or on the charisma of a leader. In the first instance, people accept others to lead them because they represent traditional values and time-honored authority. In the second instance, they offer their loyalty to a leader because of his personal dynamism or his individual characteristics. To Weber, both of these models had obvious limitations; therefore he tried to find a different basis for rule and authority. The model he wrote most about is what he called the "rational-legal state."[32] People accept such authority because it is based on clear and impersonal rules. They are thereby freed from the status quo of tradition and the idiosyncracies of personal or charismatic leadership. Within the bureaucracy, a hierarchy is established to carry out these rules; tasks are delegated to specialists, who are then accountable to those above them.

In later chapters we consider the effects of hierarchy on the development tasks. The point we wish to make here is that the characteristics of the internal political and administrative system have been important causes of administrative incapacity. This influence is seen most clearly in the role played by the colonial administrative system.[33] (A similar influence was felt in Latin America where the Spanish administrative system was also laced with formal bureaucratic controls.[34]) By developing the myth that bureaucrats are neutral experts who should be protected from political influence, the colonial system left the technocrat secure in his position and power. By focusing on central administrative coordination, the system prevented the growth of political institutions at the local level and stifled effective organization of the public.

For our discussion of the causes of administrative incapacity, Weber's emphasis is an important one. He reminds us that internal practices, habits, and procedures all influence the ability of the bureaucracy to perform. He directs attention to the way people are selected for their positions, to the roles they are assigned, and to the lines of authority and communication that are established.

Many observers of the third world during the postindependence period agree that characteristics of the political systems themselves are crucial to understanding administrative incapacity. Colonialism emphasized the role of administration in bringing about change in these nations and in creating independent states. The political institutions frequently retained their traditional authoritarian characteristics. They were less developed in the sense that there were few ways to hold them accountable to the public, and the public had limited means for access and choice.[35]

The traditional argument is that we need to establish a balance by strengthening political institutions. Several recent studies, however, challenge this conclusion, identifying the problem as the weakness of bureaucratic performance rather than the weakness of political institutions alone. Schumacher's study of Senegal points to "resource constraints and organizational weakness in both the bureaucracy and the governing party."[36] He argues that in Senegal, the patronage ties of the leadership were the major obstacle to transforming the bureaucracy into a means to accomplish development. What is needed, he says, is a stronger administration that can remain independent of client groups and can increase the loyalty of the top civil service.[37] Sigelman in another study of the role of bureaucracy in development concludes that development does not occur *unless* the bureaucracy is highly organized. As a result he argues that administrative capacity does correlate with development.[38]

An Interdependent Model to Explain Incapacity

Both explanations—external and internal—are essential parts of the story. It may be argued that the two are not competing explanations, but rather interrelated. Some of the external factors *interact* with some of the internal factors, and the cumulative effect of their interaction undermines administrative capacity. It is not only that both kinds of constraints contribute to administrative malfunction, but that they feed one another. It is, in short, a systemic relationship. The internal and external factors are interdependent and work together to weaken the country's chances for development. Figure 2.1 is a diagram of how this interdependence functions.

Consider, for example, the impact of an International Monetary Fund (IMF) standby agreement on a third world country. The working of the international financial market (an external factor) brings country X to the point of requesting IMF help. This help comes in the form of

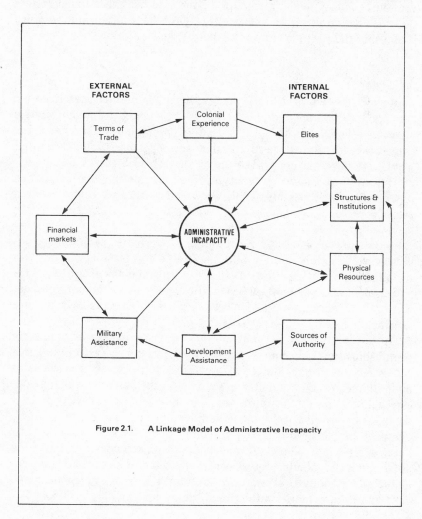

Figure 2.1.　A Linkage Model of Administrative Incapacity

rigorous and profoundly interventionist policy guidelines on monetary policy, price controls, and deregulation. The weak planning and management capacity in the country provides few resources with which to counter the powerful arguments of the IMF staff. The internal political repercussions of the agreement weaken the party's capacity to mediate and aggregate the conflicting interests. The political structures are further weakened and, being debilitated, are less able to generate analysis of alternative responses to the growing fiscal and financial crisis. Lack of administrative capacity means that the flow of international assistance may not be strategically targeted, adding to the downward spiral of the economy. The systemic interaction of the external and internal factors increases administrative incapacity, and that incapacity in turn diminishes the potential for redistributive policies in the future.

Conclusion

In this study we wish to incorporate what has been learned from the dependency literature and to consider its implications for administrative change. As one authority has said, "The administrative and the dependency literature have remained inconveniently separate."[39] In other words, we have not considered the extent to which the failings of administration are caused by external forces. In part they have remained separate because the analytical task of tracing the relationships between external explanations and internal explanations for incapacity has not been done.

Second, we argue that the external and internal explanations of administrative malfunction are both applicable and interdependent. This formulation is important because it reminds us that any effort to change one element in the system will be insufficient. Changes and improvement will have to occur in several places and even simultaneously to have satisfactory results.

Third, development administration can play an important role in accomplishing developmental change.[40] It is most apt to perform this role well when alternative sources of power exist to provide the muscle to hold administration accountable. Because of the impact of internal and external factors, administrators are not complete masters over their decisions. Yet it is also true that administrators and, more to the point, organizations, institutions, and development projects can contribute to development. The point is to understand both the constraints and the possibilities that administrators confront. In the rest of the book we examine the various organizational options that exist to enhance the developmental potential within the third world.

Notes

1. For a discussion of the marginalization of the poor by lower-level administrators, see Janice Perlman, *The Myth of Marginality* (Berkeley: University of California Press, 1976). Also see David Gould, "From Development Administration to Underdevelopment Administration: A Study of Zairian Administration in the Light of Current Crisis," *Les Cahiers du Cedaf* 6 (1978):1-34.

2. Irving Louis Horowitz, *The World of Development* (New York: Oxford University Press, 1972), discusses this tension at length. There is also an empirical examination of these tensions in survey research by Raymond F. Hopkins, *Political Roles in a New State; Tanzania's First Decade* (New Haven: Yale University Press, 1971), pp. 108-140. See also a case study by Merilee S. Grindle, "Power, Expertise and the Technico: Suggestions from a Mexican Case Study," *Journal of Politics* 39 (1977):399-426.

3. Stanley Heginbotham, *Cultures in Conflict: The Four Faces of Indian Bureaucracy* (New York: Columbia University Press, 1975), p. 223.

4. Joan Robinson, *The Cultural Revolution in China* (London: Penguin, 1969).

5. Bernard Schaffer provides a good review of literature on the colonial experience, "Administrative Legacies and Links in the Post-Colonial State: Preparation, Training, and Administrative Reform," *Development and Change* 9 (1978):175-200.

6. Close examination of district commissioners' archives in Uganda revealed this finding. For an exposition of the implications of the colonial administrative legacy, see Coralie Bryant, *Some Problems of Public Administration in Uganda* (Ph.D. diss., University of London, 1963; also available at Makerere College, Uganda).

7. A good, direct exposition of these concepts is found in Robert Dahl, *Modern Political Analysis,* 3rd ed. (Englewood Cliffs, N.J.: Prentice-Hall, 1976).

8. Amos Perlmutter, *The Military and Politics in Modern Times* (New Haven: Yale University Press, 1977), p. 34; Brian Loveman, "Military Regimes, National Development Strategies and Local Politics in Latin America, 1964-1977," (Paper presented at the Joint Annual Meetings of the Latin American Studies Association and the African Studies Association, Houston, Texas, November 1977). Morris Janowitz also made this argument in *The Military in the Political Development of New Nations* (Chicago: University of Chicago Press, 1964).

9. See, for example, Lloyd Fallers, *Bantu Bureaucracy* (Chicago: University of Chicago Press, 1965).

10. Robinson, *The Cultural Revolution in China;* Jean Herskovits, "Democracy in Nigeria," *Foreign Affairs,* Winter 1979/80.

11. Fred Riggs, "Bureaucrats and Political Development: A Paradoxical View," *Bureaucracy and Political Development,* ed. by Joseph LaPalombara (Princeton: Princeton University Press, 1963), pp. 120-167. See, also, Fred Riggs, *Administration in Developing Countries* (Boston: Houghton Mifflin, 1964).

12. Harold J. Laski, *Parliamentary Government in England,* 6th ed. (London: George Allen and Unwin, 1960).

13. For a good selection of major articles on this approach as it existed in the United States, see John D. Montgomery and William J. Siffin, eds., *Approaches to Development: Politics, Administration and Change* (New York: McGraw-Hill, 1966). Another collection that pulls together writing from most of the leading American writers is Fred W. Riggs, ed., *Frontiers of Development Administration* (Durham, N.C.: Duke University Press, 1970). It is interesting to note that in England, interest in administrative processes as they related to development was approached differently. Much of the work was carried in journals such as the *Journal of Local Administration Overseas* or the *Journal of Commonwealth Political Studies.* Works such as Margery Perham's *The Colonial Reckoning,* Reith Lectures (London: Fontana Books, 1963); Lucy Mair's *Safeguards for Democracy* (London: Oxford University Press, 1961); William Robson's *Nationalized Industry and Public Ownership* (London: George Allen and Unwin, 1960); and Kenneth Robinson's *Dilemmas of Trusteeship* (London: Oxford University Press, 1965) were the mainstays of those interested in development administration.

14. Dennis Rondinelli and Marcus D. Ingle make this distinction in "Administrative Decentralization and Local Participation in Development Management," (Paper delivered at annual meeting of the American Society for Public Administration, San Francisco, April 1980).

15. For example, LaPalombara, *Bureaucracy and Political Development.*

16. *The Journal of Local Administration Overseas* carried many of the articles written by African scholars and administrators, whereas within India there was a rich lode of material by Indian scholars. Kusun Nair's *Blossoms in the Dust: The Human Factor in India's Development* (New York: Praeger, 1961) deserves to be remembered as it was the beginning of the wave of Indian criticism of development that was to follow. Chief Obafemi Awolowo, *Awo: The Autobiography of Chief Obafemi Awolowo* (Cambridge: Cambridge University Press, 1960); Jomo Kenyatta, *Facing Mount Kenya* (New York: Vintage Books, 1960); Patrice Lumumba, *Congo, My Country* (New York: Praeger, 1962); Oginga Odinga, *Not Yet Uhuru: An Autobiography* (London: Heinemann, 1967) retold Africans' response to modernization. There were many more works. One of the fortunate aspects of this earlier period was that many statesmen took the time to write their autobiographies, which often richly detailed the administrative experience of their countries. One of the most readily available books with selections from the most famous of the African writings is that of Wilfred Cartey and Martin Kilson, eds., *The African Reader: Independent Africa* (New York: Vintage Books, 1970).

17. The United Nations documents in public administration are so numerous that they have filled many shelves in libraries. For an overview of their perspectives, see United Nations, Technical Assistance Bureau, *A Handbook of Public Administration: Current Concepts and Practice with Special Reference to Developing Countries,* 1961.

18. For a good summary of the Comparative Administration Group, see Dwight Waldo, ed., "Comparative and Development Administration: Retrospect

and Prospect," *Public Administration Review* 36 November-December 1976:615-654. In this same issue, see especially Brian Loveman, "The Comparative Administration Group, Development Administration," pp. 648-655. Another summary discussion of this group is in Ferrel Heady, *Public Administration: A Comparative Perspective* (New York: Marcel Dekker, 1979).

19. For a good summary of the Rockefeller Foundation's view of early public administration training, see L. D. Stifel, J. S. Coleman, and J. E. Black, eds., *Education and Training for Public Sector Management in Developing Countries* (New York: Rockefeller Foundation, 1977). The Comparative Administration Group was originally funded by the Ford Foundation. It is interesting to note that the Ford Foundation has continued to be interested in improving developmental management, but prefers to work directly with those institutions within developing countries that are most committed to developmental management. For a discussion of some of the work of these institutions, see David Korten, ed., *Population and Social Development Management* (Caracas: Instituto de Superiores de Administracion, 1979).

20. It is interesting to read the two exchanges between Herbert Simon and Chris Argyris that appeared in *Public Administration Review* 33 (May-June and July-August 1973). See Chris Argyris, "Some Limits of Rational Man Organizational Theory," pp. 253-267; Herbert Simon, "Applying Information Technology to Organization Design," pp. 268-277, and "Organization Man: Rational or Self Actualizing?" pp. 346-353; Chris Argyris, "Organization Man: Rational and Self Actualizing," pp. 354-357. In many respects this debate is rather like the arguments about heart and mind as separate ways of knowing. It is also, in many respects, an echo of the quarrel between the earliest colonial administrators and the older Sanskrit and Buddhist scholars in the East, especially India and Ceylon. Simon says Argyris's focus on self-actualization and self-fulfillment (a very Zen Buddhist concept as Maslow admits) will not achieve much production, build bridges, or produce the physical infrastructure upon which our civilization rests. Argyris responds much in the manner of the wise religious scholar throughout traditional religions that perhaps being is superior to doing. This issue lies at the core of much of the developmental debate.

21. Many of the members of the CAG group have done some very creative work since then. William Siffin publishes a newsletter on development, which is regularly sent to those in the field, the *PASITAM Newsletter* (Bloomington: Indiana University). In addition he has produced collections of articles on development and management problems. See *Analytic Skills Programs* (Bloomington: Indiana University, 1976-1979). See also John Montgomery, *Technology and Civic Life* (Cambridge, Mass.: MIT Press, 1974). His major assumption is that development requires changes in the quality of civic life. Milton Esman's *Landlessness and Near Landlessness in Developing Countries,* Rural Development Committee, Center for International Studies (Ithaca, N.Y.: Cornell University, 1978) is a very significant study because it reminds the development community of the importance of a seriously neglected group—the landless poor.

22. Schaffer, "Administrative Legacies," p. 187.

23. John Montgomery and Milton Esman write about some of these symptoms

in their background papers for the *World Development Report, 1980* (Washington, D.C.: World Bank, 1980).

24. Reginald Green, *Manpower Estimates and Development Implications for Namibia* (New York: United Nations Institute for Namibia, 1978).

25. Irving Kaplan, ed., *Tanzania,* Foreign Area Studies (Washington, D.C.: American University, 1978), p. 115.

26. Schaffer, "Administrative Legacies," p. 191.

27. For an example of this approach see, Colin Leys, *The Politics of Underdevelopment in Kenya* (London: Heinemann, 1975).

28. Kaplan, *Tanzania,* pp. 115–116.

29. Leys, *Politics of Underdevelopment in Kenya.*

30. Edward Schumacher, *Politics, Bureaucracy and Rural Development in Senegal* (Berkeley: University of California, 1975), pp. 220–227.

31. David Gould, "From Development Administration."

32. One of the best sources on Weber's thought is found in Reinhard Bendix, *Max Weber* (New York: Anchor Books, 1962). For a collection of his writings see H. H. Gerth and C. W. Mills, eds., *From Max Weber* (New York: Oxford University Press, 1946, 1972).

33. Samuel Huntington and Barrington Moore, eds., *Authoritarian Politics in Modern Society* (New York: Basic Books, 1970). The studies compiled in this text concern the impact of the civil service and its predecessor, the colonial service, as a major factor leading to one-party rule. For an excellent summary of the impact of colonial administration on subsequent administration, see Goren Hyden, Robert Jackson, and John Okumu, *Development Administration: The Kenyan Experience* (Nairobi: Oxford University Press, 1970).

34. Gary W. Wynia, *Politics and Planners* (Madison: University of Wisconsin Press, 1972).

35. Samuel Huntington, *Political Order In Changing Societies* (New Haven, Conn.: Yale University, 1968).

36. Schumacher, *Politics, Bureaucracy,* p. 27.

37. Ibid., pp. 230–231.

38. Lee Sigelman, "Modernization and the Political System: A Critique and Preliminary Empirical Analysis," *Sage Professional Papers in Comparative Politics* 2 (1971).

39. Schaffer, "Administrative Legacies," p. 194.

40. J. Fred Springer, "Observation and Theory in Development Administration," *Administration and Society* 9 (1977):13–44; Nelson Kasfir, "Theories of Administrative Behavior in Africa," *African Studies Review* 1 (January 1972):155–165; and Howard McCurdy, *Public Administration: A Synthesis* (Menlo Park, Calif.: Cummings Publishing, 1977), Chapter 9.

3
The Dynamics
of Organizations

Introduction

A recent study of a third world nation concludes that the present bureaucracy operates in much the same manner as the colonial regime that preceded it. The claim is particularly striking since the country in question is Tanzania, a nation avowedly socialist, committed to participation and bottom-up planning. According to the study, the similarity is both in structure and administrative style. The present bureaucracy "responds to the same imperatives — getting production up, getting visible results — that its precursors did. But none of this is to point fingers at offenders. It is simply a fact that people placed in a similar structure with a similar task to perform are likely to behave in similar ways. The behavior of Tanzanian bureaucrats is unremarkably predictable."[1] This chapter examines the nature of organizations, the dynamics of which seem to form a pattern whether we are discussing Dar es Salaam, Delhi, or Washington, D.C. and whether we are considering 1960 or 1980. When organizations do function differently in these arenas, it is because their environments differ and the people in them are responding to different pressures and opportunities. The organizational dynamics are nevertheless the same.[2]

As discussed in Chapter 2, third world nations are characterized by administrative incapacity resulting from the interdependence of internal and external factors that constantly influence their decisions and actions. In order to design ways to counter that incapacity, it is first necessary to examine how organizations function and how they handle these internal and external problems. It is important to clarify these organizational dynamics and the influence that they have on the development task in order to explore realistic changes.

Understanding how organizations function has implications beyond the formal bureaucracy. Much of the work of the development administrator is through organizations — either existing ones or new units created to allow project beneficiaries (small farmers, urban squatters, or landless rural laborers) to become involved in addressing their problems. Organizations come in a variety of forms. The Kenyan Ministry of Agriculture is an organization; Exxon is an organization; the Canadian International Development Agency is an organization. And so are smaller entities, such as Tanzanian village councils, panchayats, Guatemalan farmers' credit associations, or the Botswana Federation of Women. In short, organizations are clusters of people, each with its own needs and interests, interacting to accomplish certain tasks and operating within resources and constraints in the environment. We need to know more about each element within that definition in order to understand the problems that confront organizations involved in development.

Analyzing Organizations

Organization Goals

Almost every organization has a task or goal. It may produce goods (large industries or small cooperatives); it may provide services (departments of health or education); it may market goods (retailers); or it may be a vehicle for a community to mobilize its own resources (cooperatives). Some goals are clear and specific, whereas others stem from vague mandates or are multidimensional and abstract. An agency, for example, may be given the task of building an irrigation project, a fairly straightforward task. Another may be charged with improving health care, a much more open-ended and ambiguous goal. These differences generate very different organizational arrangements and communication systems within an organization. The best processes for building the irrigation system, for example, will not necessarily be appropriate for a nutrition program. Whether the kind of structures and processes used is appropriate to the organization's goals is a major organizational issue. A major implication is that incapacity often stems from the incompatibility of processes and goals, and that administrative processes in third world nations are not always those best suited to the development task. (We return to this question in Chapter 4.)

An organization's goals are not always obvious, even to those within. There may be only minimal agreement on what they are or are supposed to be. Or there may be controversy over how to interpret them, or how they are to be achieved. Similarly, goals change over time. Organizations often take on new dimensions as they continue in existence, and their goals and tasks grow by steady accretion without much purposeful design.

Even when an organization is new or is trying to establish a new program, it is seldom easy to clarify goals or to arrive at them rationally or consistently. First, goal setting may require a great deal of information about a wide variety of alternatives. For example, setting goals for rural development requires information about the region, the latent technology, the habits and preferences of farmers, and the capacities of extension workers. Few individuals or organizations have all the relevant information available. Second, goals reflect the values and commitments of individuals. Thus people will differ on what the goals should be and will have emotional investments in some goals rather than others. One administrator will be committed to educating farmers, another to building roads. Finally, political considerations often favor one goal rather than another. Political feasibility influences many projects and programs.

Because of these difficulties, goals are often compromises, according to organization theorist Herbert Simon. Goals are frequently used to make adjustments to a situation rather than to solve it once and for all. For example, it is difficult for an agricultural organization to define what policies will most effectively accomplish agricultural development. Therefore, it will tend to set what Simon calls a "satisfactory" goal, one that appears feasible and will at least improve the situation.[3]

Formal Organizational Structures

Although very small groups of people can work together to accomplish a task on the basis of personal interactions, as an organization grows in size it tends to develop a formal structure. Different people are assigned different tasks and soon develop specializations. The more complex the goal of the organization, the more specialization tends to occur. In the process, information generated by doing different tasks becomes more selective. Once such specialization occurs organizations need to find ways to coordinate the activities. Almost inevitably, coordination involves some degree of hierarchy.[4]

Max Weber was one of the first to stress that coordination is commonly done through hierarchical decision making and that hierarchical patterns are natural in large organizations. Weber was deeply concerned about the growth of bureaucracy and the stifling effects bureaucratic behavior might have for the modern state. Yet he was also among the first to point out that large-scale organizations need to be structured so that each actor and department can play its role effectively.[5]

The conditions in many third world countries have also encouraged hierarchies to flourish. Colonial administrations, whether English, French, or Dutch, were hierarchical, and the earliest entrants from within colonies into these colonial services were socialized into hierarchical patterns. The classic example is the elite Indian civil service.[6] In some instances hierarchy was compatible with more authoritarian aspects of the local culture. The British colonial model, for example, was able to co-opt traditional norms of authority in India and enforce them more strictly than before.[7]

Hierarchy is a means for delegating orders down the line and separating functions into progressively narrower assignments. Each level is accountable to the next one above it. Hierarchy is also a communication system; each level simplifies the information it receives and relates it to other information. This process means that information is gathered in bits and pieces and aggregated as it travels upward in the hierarchy. Much information, however, is lost as that aggregation process continues. Even if one is generous about the summarizing skills of all actors in the organization, information will inevitably be lost as it travels through successive layers.[8] For example, field agents, who are responsible for instructing farmers in new methods, usually accumulate much useful information about the perceptions and problems of local farmers. The formal reports that they give to their supervisors, however, tend to be routine and formal, frequently omitting useful information on the receptivity and needs of farmers.[9] Even if information is transmitted, it is often misused as it is passed up the line. For example, supervisors may use reports from field agents as a way to evaluate and control them, rather than as a source of information. When this occurs, less useful information will be included in the reports and they will become increasingly formal and routine.[10]

As Weber and others have argued, hierarchy can be a useful way to structure an organization. At the same time the information loss in a hierarchical system can lead to inefficiency and inflexibility. There are, however, different degrees of hierarchy. Some are "steep," which means that all decisions are made at a top level and handed down. Others are "flat," which means that some decisions are made by consulting with others at the same level. Whether and under what circumstances the goals or tasks of the organization are better accomplished by broader participation and bottom-up planning are important questions to address in analyzing any organization. Given the tendency of agencies to develop into hierarchies, efforts to establish a flatter hierarchy with consultation will have to be purposive and carefully orchestrated.[11]

Hierarchies in public and private organizations differ in many respects. One distinction lies in the kinds of information they receive and the messages that consumers and beneficiaries send. Since private organizations sell goods or services in the marketplace, consumers communicate what they want through their purchases. However, those who consume the services of a public organization cannot send messages in the same way. Therefore, public administrators have to find other ways to decide what they should do. And usually they rely on internal experts rather than the public to evaluate their work.[12] Often the experts who do these evaluations are professionals with specialized training that has its own standards and norms. The problem is it is easy for experts to lose touch with the way in which their products are perceived by others. Professional standards may prescribe that a certain nutrition program be instituted even though it is unsuited to the cooking and eating habits of the residents. And if the training of the professionals has been relatively narrow, they may not welcome others' opinions. The dilemma is that hierarchies originally develop in response to a need for specialized information; but once members develop special expertise, they tend to block out other relevant or even crucial information.

Thus far, organizations have been described as groups of people who come together to accomplish certain goals or tasks. Organizations, therefore, are *instruments* to do things. If they do not perform well, we can try to convince those at the top that reforms are necessary and then design ways to make them more effective or efficient. This approach may be unsuccessful, however, because it ignores the "difference between instrumental and institutional bureaucracies. In fact many governmental agencies, particularly in new states, were institutional bureaucracies. They had built up their autonomy, become used to working virtually independently of political overseers and cherished their ability to decide their own arrangements."[13] Philip Selznick uses the concept of an institutional bureaucracy to describe agencies that acquire a value of their own separate from what they actually accomplish.[14] Organizational survival becomes more important than goals. Robert Merton calls this "goal displacement," where goals are displaced by an organization's effort to survive.[15] This tendency is one evidence of what many analysts refer to as bureaucratic pathology. Its primary impact is to insulate organizations from other institutions, from the public, or from traditional goals. Traditional reforms are not effective with such agencies.

Another sign of pathology is the tendency of bureaucracies to become rigid and routinized. Hierarchical organizations exert considerable pressure on members to be disciplined. As a result organizations turn to rules and come to define loyalty in terms of adhering to rules. "Against such a background of rigidity, the executives of the organization will find it increasingly difficult to make even minor adjustments in the rules. Positions of authority will come to be occupied by persons who lack the ability to consider adjustments to the organizational routine," giving us what Victor Thompson refers to as "the growing imbalance between ability and authority."[16]

A third pathology occurs when all decisions are effectively made at the top, thereby undermining the authority of officials at various levels. Dr. Luis Prieto, former minister of education in Venezuela, describes the extreme form of centralization that has developed in his country.

> When a request is denied by an immediate supervisor, it is sent to the President and approved without even consulting the immediate supervisor. This practice damages the principle of authority and responsibility. It then follows that all interested parties send their request to the highest authority and the immediate supervisors do not make decisions fearful that they will be overturned. . . . The real reason why there is so much running around and paper work generated in public offices is due to the extreme centralization of functions and responsibilities. The result is a strangulation of administrative activities.[17]

Organizational Role

In addition to decision-making patterns, the formal structure of an organization includes patterns of individual behavior. An individual's job description carries certain expectations no matter who holds the position. These expectations are commonly referred to as roles. For example, a person's role may mean that he/she is expected to exercise initiative or alternatively to follow orders closely. This role may or may not coincide with personal interests and style. One person may prefer to take charge of others, but his/her role requires a more collaborative style. Field agents may prefer to work in structured settings, while their roles require considerable initiative and self-motivation in relating to the farmers.

The concept of role has been used to identify characteristics of an organization. James March and Herbert Simon, for example, argue that roles make environments more predictable for people, but that when roles are not clear they can produce uncertainty and conflict. Sometimes people may feel clear about their roles, but feel that they are placed in a position where they have to fill two different and often conflicting roles.[18]

How do people learn about their roles? Often administrators are selected because they have traits that match the role. Recruiting the right people for a job is an important part of an administrator's job. Organizations also socialize members into their roles; they subtly reward some actions and not others. Agents who make visits to farmers can be rewarded; those who never leave the village can be penalized. Organizations can structure incentives as well as undertake a range of in-service training approaches to induce more favorable performance. (See Chapter 5 for further discussion of role.)

Informal System

In addition to their formal structures and prescribed roles, organizations have informal patterns. They are also social collectivities, and as such they stimulate friendships, rivalries, personality conflicts, and deep loyalties. The pattern that is reflected in the chart of an organization's formal structure and in an organization's budget, then, represents only the theoretical flow of authority. It tells little about how an organization functions in reality. Informal structures are neither so apparent nor so discoverable; they crisscross throughout the organization in elaborate and complex ways. Employees may come from various ethnic groups and develop special ties or informal networks among others in their group, which in turn influence the way in which work is carried out.

Often informal systems emerge because the formal structure is inadequate, too cumbersome, or does not encompass all the important relationships and factors in a situation. If workers feel ignored in decision making, they may develop their own networks to pass on information. These informal networks may be functional and useful in an organization; they may facilitate goal accomplishment. For example, conversations may lead to new insights into a problem; social networks may increase the flow of useful information. Alternatively, according to Anthony Downs, their major effect may be to "divert a great deal of its members' activities from achieving the formal purposes of the bureau to manipulating conditions of power, income, and prestige within the bureau."[19]

The Environment of Organizations

The Role of the Environment

Organizations are not isolated bodies; rather they exist alongside many other institutions, groups, and traditions in a society. An organization is in fact part of a larger system that includes all societal characteristics that influence it. This system is the environment of an organization. Organizational analysis has increasingly come to stress the effect of the environment on the ways in which organizations function and on the kinds of policies that develop.[20] For example, in order to understand how an organization delivers nutrition education, it is useful to examine the organization's goals, its formal and informal structures, and the roles of its members. But it is also important to consider the resources it receives from other groups such as the local government, the public, or the Department of Health.

The environment is important to an organization for two different reasons. First, it can provide resources. Other agencies may allocate financial support, client groups may offer political support, new technology may make its products cheaper. Second, the environment may offer limits or constraints. Groups may oppose actions or compete for resources, local beneficiaries may ignore services, political pressures may undermine effort. An organization therefore needs both to accumulate as many resources as possible and to protect itself against the actions and threats of others.

From this perspective all organizational actions are ways to handle environmental opportunities or threats. Coordination in this view is not simply a way to integrate specialization; it is primarily a way to cope with external demands. Field agents, for example, are placed in very difficult situations because of the pressures on them.[21] Whether they teach nutrition to villagers or work with farmers to plant new seeds, they are caught up in the feelings and demands of beneficiaries.

Classifying Environmental Influences

Determining what parts of the external world are parts of an organization's environment is a major management job. Donald Warwick suggests that any list should include influences from both the remote and more immediate environment. The remote environment "consists of those physical, historical, socio-cultural, ecological and technological conditions with distant effects on planning."[22] To illustrate their impact he describes an education reform project in Peru. The government tried to install a bilingual education program to teach both Spanish and the local dialect in the early grades. The assumption was that the dialect would give the children an easier entrée to school and enhance pride in their own heritage.

This noble scheme, which seems to have been developed by the planners *for* the Indians, rather than with them, failed miserably for socio-cultural reasons. For their part, the parents were indifferent to hostile. "Since social and economic power was associated with the language of the elite, they actually approved of teaching the children in Spanish from the first day of school. . . . Only after they reached a secure middle-class status did socially mobile Quecha speakers show interest in advertising their knowledge of the language."[23]

The immediate environment includes three factors. First is the *power setting,* which means any groups or organizations that have some degree of power over an agency. Second is the *issue context,* which is concerned with how vital the organization is to the society. Are others very interested in its work, or does it have a low priority? And third, there is the *operating environment,* or the immediate circumstances that influence the operation of the organization.

A second way of classifying environmental forces is provided by Daniel Katz and Robert Kahn.[24] They want to show how aspects of the environment are related to organizational tasks. First, they define five sectors of the environment (see Figure 3.1). Second, they examine four different dimensions of influence that these sectors have on an organization: Do they increase its stability? Are they congruent with other influences? Do they occur randomly or are they organized? Finally, do they create scarcity?

Each of these dimensions can be applied to conditions in the third world. Looking first at the "stability-turbulence" dimension, it is probably accurate to say that all of the sectors reflect turbulent conditions. Cultural values are changing, political regimes are fragile, labor is making increased demands, and the value of physical resources is constantly changing in the international arena. At higher rates of turbulence the direction of change becomes increasingly difficult to predict, and survival problems squeeze development issues from the public agenda.

Nations and communities vary, however, as to whether the environment generates uniformity or diversity, the second dimension of influence. Some countries have a diverse economic structure; other economies are tied to the export of a single commodity. Some have a much more pluralistic society; others have a single dominant culture or ethnic identity. This second factor has profound implications for organizations. Evidence suggests that the extent to which different ethnic groups can enter the bureaucracy is a major determinant of conflict in a country.[25] Some organizations have purposefully tried to recruit members from different ethnic groups; others have tried to insulate themselves and recruit from a single ethnic community.[26] One could generalize and predict that the more diverse the environment, the easier it is for an organization to develop its own client groups and resources and insulate itself from external checks.

The third dimension refers directly to the extent of organization within

FIGURE 3.1

The Environment of Organizations

Environmental Sectors or Types of Functional relationships	Stability-Turbulence	Uniformity-Diversity	Clustered-Random	Scarcity-Munificence
1. Societal values: Cultural Legitimation				
2. Political: legal norms and statutes				
3. Economic: markets and labor				
4. Informational and technological				
5. Physical: geography and natural resources				

Source: Daniel Katz and Robert L. Kahn, Social Psychology of Organizations (2nd ed.), p. 125.

Copyright (c) 1978 by John Wiley and Sons. Reprinted by permission.

the polity. Almost by definition, developing countries have fewer organizations, weaker institutions, fewer mass communications, and less extensive media resources. In some countries, the environment is virtually consumed by anarchy, whereas in others the environment is rigidly controlled by highly authoritarian regimes.

The last dimension is "scarcity-munificence." Developing countries vary widely in the wealth of their natural resources. The physical geography also has a direct effect on the way in which organizations function. Geography influences communication networks and the possibilities of logistical support for projects. Nepal's beauty becomes her bane in transportation. Indonesian islands are especially difficult to service in support of projects.

The Special Impact of Poverty

Scarcity, or poverty, in third world countries is so pervasive that it has a special influence on organizational dynamics. The nature of the vicious circle of undernourishment, high birthrates (but high infant mortality), illness, subsistence work, illiteracy, and early death all contribute to administrative incapacity. Few well-trained people, sparse support for those few, fragile institutions through which they work, little managerial infrastructure, weak information sources, little feedback, and high political turbulence influence the strategies of local administrators. Some try to exit; others look for patrons to ease their burdens. Exiting is sometimes referred to as the "brain drain," which is an exit made by those who become discouraged or threatened by close proximity to the circle of poverty. Often officials are unwilling to subject themselves and their families to conditions of poverty or to life in rural areas. The conditions of poverty are so overwhelming that officials easily become discouraged and turn to filling routine tasks. In various ways, they insulate themselves from dealing with poverty or escape from those agencies that do.

A second response to widespread poverty is to establish patron-client relationships. Poor peasants attach themselves to slightly wealthier peasants who can plead their cases to those more strategically located. Thus in return for services or goods, the wealthier peasants will represent clients about school fees, licenses, or credit. A patron-client relationship is an exchange that develops under many circumstances and takes on many implications. Although often thought of as political behavior because of its relationship to access, this phenomenon is as much administrative as it is political. The organizational hierarchy may help those who negotiate such an arrangement. The lower-level administrator will undertake services for another (moving applications faster or processing his claims more expeditiously) in order to gain access to some services in return.

Corruption

A much discussed aspect of organizational environments in third world nations is the widespread evidence of corruption. Gunnar Myrdal makes the problem of corruption the centerpiece in his argument that third world nations are "soft states," with fragile governing institutions that have little hold on the country. "Corruption is part and parcel of the general condition in the underdeveloped countries of their being soft states. It is a major inhibition and raises serious obstacles against all efforts to increase social discipline. Not only are politicians and administrators affected by the prevalence of corruption, but also businessmen, and, in fact, the whole population."[27] By this reasoning, Myrdal argues that corruption undermines political stability because it causes people to lose respect for government.

Although most would agree that corruption has a very debilitating effect, there is less agreement on the reasons why it is so prevalent. Traditionally corruption has been traced to such social factors as the lack of a commitment to the nation-state or the breakdown in traditional values. In a contrasting argument, James Scott contends that corruption is most usefully viewed as a means of political influence, rather than as an expression of moral degradation. The problem is that the nature of political institutions in third world countries encourages certain kinds of influence rather than others. Whereas nations with more developed political institutions encourage the exercise of such influence *before* laws are made, in third world countries, where political opportunities are limited, this exertion is more apt to occur at the enforcement or *implementation* stage. Scott says, for example, "Where organizational skills are scarce and where, as a result, interest group associations are either weak or nonexistent, the corruption of law enforcement may be a more economizing way to exert influence over policy outcomes."[28]

As he explains this idea, peasants who avoid a regulation by bribing the enforcing official are influencing policy outcomes just as much as they would had they formed a peasants' association and agitated against the regulation in the first place. But forming the association is harder and more costly in terms of time and energy; hence the bribe is more economical and "rational." Likewise businessmen who buy protection from civil servants in order to avoid a licensing fee are similarly affecting policy at its implementation stage, rather than organizing to change the regulation at the legislative stage. To the extent that bribery requires less effort and fewer resources it is a more rational form of political influence.

This approach to political corruption has two major implications. First, it emphasizes that political corruption is an intrinsic part of the problem of development and social change rather than a cultural aberration. During periods of rapid change the boundary between social norms and legal rules may shift and become blurred. This approach therefore provides an explanation for the rampant corruption that occurred in sixteenth-century England and in the United States during the nineteenth century, as well as in the contemporary third world.

Second, this approach to corruption emphasizes how debilitating it can be to the task of administration. Such corruption sets up the expectation that groups and interests must always intervene at the implementation stage and in so doing greatly complicate the work of administrators. At the very least, corruption will undermine the legitimacy that the development administrator needs in order to smooth the way for development programs. One major way to reduce it is to pull groups into decision making earlier so that laws and regulations command greater legitimacy during their implementation stage. By contrast, coercive measures to insure cooperation during implementation may have negative repercussions, generate resentment toward administrative decisions, and ultimately increase corruption.

These strong and systemic pressures can easily overwhelm administrators working at the field level. They are apt to be particularly vulnerable, to feel neglected by their supervisors, to be underpaid, and to believe that everyone else is caught up in corrupt practices. The result is that their resistance to bribery and to other forms of corruption steadily diminishes. One criterion for successful administration is therefore to find ways to enhance the self-respect of lower-level officials, to develop processes and structures to support them, and to increase their responsiveness to their clients' needs.

Organizational Maintenance

Earlier in the chapter there was a discussion of the tendency within bureaucracies to institutionalize and to seek autonomy. This same behavior occurs in response to pressures from the environment. Organizations need to find ways to maintain and protect themselves from efforts to dilute their influence or to alter policies. Although organizations work toward attaining such goals as increasing agricultural output, much of what they do can only be explained as efforts to retain their autonomy and independence. And their leadership tends to be most protective when lines of responsibility are not clear, when mandates are vague, and when the organization is more vulnerable to incursions from others. For example, when several agencies are brought together to run an integrated development project, each organization's leadership will try to protect the organization and control its employees.[29] Organizations' leaders will also go to great lengths to protect their existing budgets and staff and to prevent their work from being assigned to others. This natural tendency can be a problem in a development project if one of the goals is to develop capacity in a local government by sharing responsibilities.

One way in which organizations often try to protect themselves is to show or claim success. They may even go so far as to change what they do from a difficult task to a more manageable one. Job training programs, for example, may ignore the neediest or least educated in order to achieve success in their training. Studies of organizations serving the blind in the United States find that these organizations focus on the younger and potentially employable blind rather than the elderly and those who most need their help.[30] Similarly, in the Comilla project in Bangladesh, field agents gave loans to the more well-to-do farmers, rather than the poor ones, because they felt that the former would be better risks. They felt they could not afford to risk loaning money to those who needed it most because the agents themselves need to show their superiors how successful they were.[31]

Organizations may also seek protection by insulating themselves from other groups. One study of educational planning in Mexico stressed the tensions that surround any effort to consult with other groups. "If the planners reveal the content of the plan ahead of time, they may immediately be under pressure to alter it, to accommodate the needs of that group. It therefore seems preferable to present all interested parties with a *fait accompli,* because it will be that much more difficult to alter a coherent whole with an inherent logic of its own."[32] Consultation and interaction may in fact be very threatening.

Thirdly, environmental uncertainty and scarce resources may encourage organizations to become rigid. In an unpredictable, threatening, and complex environment, the temptation is to establish routines and rules in order to cope and establish some predictability. A classic way to deal with limited administrative capacity and external threats has always been to "dig in" and avoid taking any risks or sharing power with other groups.

Organizational Innovation

Organizational leadership also responds to environmental complexity by adapting and being innovative. Under what conditions do leaders react creatively? Some studies find that the most important factors are those internal to the organization. For example, Paul Lawrence and Jay Lorsch stress the importance of the norms and values leaders establish. "Usually the best support for innovation among the . . . upper level members of a bureaucratic system is a set of re-inforcing or peer group norms centered on adaptive and creative behavior."[33] If leaders expect and exemplify creativity they are more likely to see it in others. Other research indicates that the ways in which organizations are structured are important to innovation. For example, innovation may well be suppressed in organizations with a steep hierarchy and internal control.[34]

According to Wesley Bjur and Gerald Caiden institutionalism cannot be handled by traditional reforms, nor will internal change occur naturally; organizational change is a political as well as a management task.[35] This observation means that external pressure is necessary, rather than relying solely on internal processes and intentions to effect change.

To the extent that organizations do innovate and grow, they tend to develop momentum for further growth, what Anthony Downs calls an "accelerator effect."[36] Support and resources tend to increase and more groups look to the organization for services. There are also forces within the organization—in leadership and membership—that encourage growth. "Growing organizations tend to have less internal conflict and higher morale because there are opportunities for individuals and groups to increase their rewards, power or prestige without decreasing the share of other organizational participants. This factor creates an especially strong incentive for leaders to strive for bureau expansion, because the morale and effort of employees can be more easily maintained under these circumstances."[37] These tendencies have a particular relevance in developing countries where bureaucracies are frequently described as "swollen" and, as noted in Chapter 2, have grown far faster than other sectors of the country.

Conclusions

Because the problem of administrative incapacity can often be found rooted in organizations, this chapter has described some of the dynamics of organizations, how they work and how people behave within them. An organization can be diagnosed using such criteria as formal structure, the shape of its hierarchy, information flows, informal systems, and the roles of individuals. Similarly the concept of the environment is a useful tool to examine external influences on an organization and how it adapts to external resources and constraints.

These concepts suggest universal tendencies that can exist within an organization in any setting. They describe problems and possibilities that are intrinsic to behavior within organizations. Not all of these tendencies are desirable or facilitate the task of development. Hierarchical authority, rigidity, and corruption contribute to the incapacity of bureaucracies to accomplish development. Understanding how organizations work provides insights into possible changes and ways in which they can be more effective. The rest of this text examines which aspects can most profitably be changed and strengthened.

Notes

1. Louise Fortmann, *Peasants, Officials and Participation in Rural Tanzania* (Ithaca, N.Y.: Cornell University Press, 1980), p. 40. The same similarity between

a colonialist predecessor and a present regime has been traced in Venezuela by Mark Hanson, "Organization Bureaucracy in Latin America and the Legacy of Spanish Colonialism," *Journal of Inter-American Studies and World Affairs* 16 (1974):199–219.

2. For the argument that development organizations function similarly to those in other cultures, see David Leonard, *Reaching the Peasant Farmer: Organization Theory and Practice in Kenya* (Chicago: University of Chicago Press, 1977), p. 231. By contrast, Fred Riggs writes that organizational behavior in the third world is best understood as a unique response to the conditions of underdevelopment. *Administration in Developing Countries: The Theory of Prismatic Society* (Boston: Houghton Mifflin, 1965).

3. Herbert Simon, *Administrative Behavior* (New York: Macmillan, 1947); James March and Herbert Simon, *Organizations* (New York: John Wiley and Sons, 1958).

4. For a classical and positive analysis of the role of hierarchy, see Paul Appleby, *Morality and Administration in Democratic Government* (Baton Rouge: Louisiana State University, 1952). For a more recent defense, see Charles Perrow, *Complex Organizations* (Glenview, Ill.: Scott, Foresman, 1972).

5. Max Weber, *The Theory of Social and Economic Organization,* ed. Talcott Parsons (New York: Free Press, 1917).

6. W. J. Morris-Jones, *The Government and Politics of India* (London: Hutchison University Library, 1964).

7. Stanley Heginbotham, *Cultures in Conflict* (New York: Columbia University Press, 1975), pp. 29–40.

8. Two of the many studies that relate hierarchy to communication are Anthony Downs's *Inside Bureaucracy* (Boston: Little, Brown, 1967), p. 117; and Gordon Tullock's *The Politics of Bureaucracy* (Washington, D.C.: Public Affairs Press, 1965), pp. 137–141.

9. For studies of field agents, see Robert Chambers, *Managing Rural Development* (New York: Holmes & Meier, 1974); Heginbotham, *Cultures;* and Leonard, *Reaching the Peasant Farmer.* Also see Chapter 9 of this book.

10. Heginbotham, *Cultures,* pp. 164–165.

11. Organizational development interventions and "management by objectives" are two of several interventions designed to do this. See Chapter 4.

12. Downs, *Inside Bureaucracy,* pp. 29–31.

13. Wesley Bjur and Gerald Caiden, "Administrative Reform and Institutional Bureaucracies," in *Dynamics of Development,* ed. Sudesh Sharma, vol. 1 (Delhi: Concept Publishing, 1978), p. 369.

14. Philip Selznik, *Leadership in Administration* (Evanston, Ill.: Row, Peterson, 1957), p. 5.

15. Robert Merton, "Bureaucratic Structure and Personality," in *Reader in Bureaucracy* (New York: Free Press, 1952). Philip Selznik, Robert Merton, and Alvin Gouldner all write extensively on the manner in which rules developed to maintain an organization can have indirect dysfunctional results. Alvin Gouldner, *Patterns of Industrial Bureaucracy* (New York: Free Press, 1954); Philip Selznik, *TVA and the Grass Roots* (Berkeley: University of California,

1949). For a study of bureaucratic pathology derived from economic methods, see William Niskanen, *Bureaucracy and Representative Government* (Chicago: Aldine, Atherton, 1971). Howard McCurdy, referring to Western organizations, comments that "unfortunately the study of bureaucratic pathology seems to be dying out just as bureaucratic dysfunctions are becoming most pronounced." *Public Administration: A Synthesis* (Menlo Park, Calif.: Cummings Publishing, 1977), p. 104.

16. McCurdy, *Public Administration*, p. 88.

17. Luis Prieto, cited in Hanson, "Organization Bureaucracy," p. 201.

18. For example, see March and Simon, *Organizations*, p. 4. Also see discussion in Harold Gortner, *Administration in the Public Sector* (New York: John Wiley and Sons, 1977), p. 197.

19. Downs, *Inside Bureaucracy*, p. 63. The classic study of informal activity is found in Gouldner, *Patterns of Industrial Bureaucracy*.

20. Daniel Katz and Robert Kahn, *The Social Psychology of Organizations*, 2nd ed. (New York: John Wiley and Sons, 1978); B. Guy Peters, *The Politics of Bureaucracy* (New York: Longman, 1978), also presents a good discussion of the impact of the environment on bureaucracy from a comparative perspective.

21. Katz and Kahn, *Social Psychology*, Chapter 2.

22. Donald Warwick, Integrating Planning and Implementation: A Transactional Approach," mimeographed (Cambridge, Mass.: Harvard University, June 1978), p. 14.

23. Ibid., pp. 15–16.

24. Katz and Kahn, *Social Psychology*, Chapter 5.

25. Donald Horowitz, "Multiracial Politics in the New States: Towards a Theory of Conflict," in *Issues in Comparative Politics*, ed. Robert Jackson and Michael Stein (New York: St. Martin's Press, 1971), pp. 164–180.

26. David Leonard did a survey of agricultural field agents in Kenya. He found that while group dynamics occurred along ethnic lines, work-place identities to some extent crossed ethnic lines. *Reaching the Peasant Farmer*, Chapter 3.

27. Myrdal mentions the problems of the soft state in *Asian Drama* (3 vols. [New York: Random House, 1968]); however, he gives it his fullest attention in *The Challenge of World Poverty* (New York: Vintage, 1970), p. 237.

28. James Scott, "An Essay on the Political Functions of Corruption," *Asian Studies* 5 (1967):505.

29. George H. Honadle, "Anticipating Roadblocks in Organizational Terrain: How Development Project Organization Design Makes a Difference," mimeographed (Washington, D.C.: Development Alternatives, October 1977).

30. Donald A. Schon, "The Blindness System," *Public Interest*, no. 18 (Winter 1970), pp. 25–38.

31. Harry W. Blair, "Rural Development, Class Structure and Bureaucracy in Bangladesh," *World Development* 6 (1978):65–82.

32. Warwick, "Integrating Planning," p. 31.

33. Paul Lawrence and Jay Lorsch, *Organization and Environment: Managing Differentiation and Integration* (Homewood, Ill.: Richard Irwin, 1969), p. 206.

34. Victor Thompson, *Bureaucracy and Innovation* (Tuscaloosa, Ala.: University of Alabama Press, 1969), pp. 1–10.

35. Bjur and Caiden, "Administrative Reform," pp. 365–378.

36. Downs, *Inside Bureaucracy,* pp. 10–18.

37. Gortner, *Administration,* p. 24.

4

Perspectives on Organizations

Introduction

Underdevelopment persists, and at least part of the reason lies in the kinds of organizational behavior and patterns described in the last chapter. The question therefore arises whether these are inevitable. Can we design an organization that can handle turbulence in the environment? Is there an effective way to organize and facilitate the work of field agents? The answers to these and similar questions depend on how one thinks about an organization and describes its functions. It may appear that the answer is obvious, that everyone would agree on what an organization should do and what should be changed. In fact it is not, and there are a number of different perspectives on organizations and on the source of their problems. One focuses on organizational inefficiency, another on relationships between supervisors and workers. In this chapter we describe several models of organizations; each represents an effort to identify what is most essential to an organization, hence where the problem lies and what kinds of changes are most useful. We then examine the implications that can be drawn from each of these models for development work.

The models are grouped into two broad clusters. The first group of explanations focuses on the organization as a system for making decisions and accomplishing goals. It examines the organization *internally* as a discrete body with its own dynamics, purposes, and methods to work more effectively. It helps us look at the internal dynamics of a ministry and understand why it functions as it does and with what results for those who work within it. The second group of explanations emphasizes the extent to which organizations interact with their environment.[1] They are limited by outside factors and can learn and incorporate strength from their environment. In the case of a ministry, for example, this approach explains how and why it learns or fails to learn from its interactions with other organizations and from the larger more remote social, political, and cultural environment.

Organizations as Autonomous Actors

The dominant trend in Western theory has been to view organizations as autonomous bodies and to examine how they can accomplish their goals most efficiently and rationally. This perspective is concerned with what goes on *within* the boundaries of the organization and has been greatly influenced by economic models, with their emphasis on goals, choices, and incentives.[2]

Scientific Management

Scientific management follows closely in the tradition of Max Weber, with his stress on rational organization and hierarchy. Organizations are defined by their ability to manage, control, and to find "the one best way." An early proponent, Frederick Taylor, spent many hours actually observing workers, how they moved and paced themselves. He was impressed that if work was carefully organized and specified in fine detail, efficiency could be greatly increased, and he spent his time designing jobs and routines to increase productivity. Taylor even went so far as to measure how muscles operate in order to indicate how much rest time is needed.[3] Although the excesses of scientific management are renowned, the basic thrust of the model has been very influential. A stress on designing routines and rewards to encourage productivity continues to influence management studies as well as development administration. For example, the recent UN *Handbook of Public Administration* prescribes ways to organize hierarchies and improve the regular routines in an agency, illustrating the observation that "this emphasis on control pervades management education and training."[4]

Decision Theory

A second model is also based on the assumption that the primary problem for an organization is to accomplish its goals more efficiently. The model's two major architects, Herbert Simon and James March, were also impressed by the limited capacity of an organization to deal effectively with a very complex environment. The problem is that the human mind is limited in its ability to absorb all this information or to process it into an eventual solution. Rational decisions are therefore very difficult, if not impossible. The major task of an organization, they conclude, is to find ways to handle this complexity. Since decisions and implementation both require vast amounts of information, the way in which an organization handles information is in fact "*the* central activity in which the organization is engaged."[5] Administrators thus operate under what Simon calls "bounded rationality" and end up "satisficing" or making satisfactory decisions rather than optimal ones.[6]

Simon has continued to be impressed by the importance of learning to handle information wisely and creatively and has tried to design organizations with these limitations in mind. One way to deal with the "richness of the informational environment" is to further specialize tasks so that each person can focus more fully on his task or role. More recently he has advocated the use of routines and tools such as management information systems to handle all the relevant information. Dealing with information becomes a moral responsibility. "Today, we can trace minute and indirect effects of our behavior; the relation of smoking to cancer, the relation of the brittleness of eagles' eggs to the presence of DDT in the environment. With this ability to trace effects, we feel responsible for them in a way we previously did not. The intellectual awakening is also a moral awakening."[7]

Simon's model is an affirmation that organizations exist to carry out certain tasks and challenges them to improve their internal capacity to arrive at appropriate decisions. One example that captures some of the flavor of this approach is the effort of the Indonesian Family Planning Project to establish routines to handle problems of information overload and communication gaps. Project designers knew that in order to be successful in delivering contraceptives, they would have to have supplies available where and when they were wanted. The traditional way to handle the problem was to have suppliers send goods out as soon as they were requested by local areas. Such an arrangement, however, can create frustrating delays. In this instance they decided to ship supplies routinely to each local area on the basis of reported usage in the past, rather than wait for specific requests. An evaluation of the project listed this prompt and routinized delivery process as a major factor in its widely noted success.[8]

Peter Drucker, a noted management lecturer, has also been concerned with designing more effective internal procedures. Executive leadership needs to recall the goals of the organization, as well as the particular strengths the organization has to offer. Priorities can then be set around the best way to accomplish these goals.[9] Peter Blau, a sociologist, emphasizes the value of clear goals in getting members to be more effective. If people are evaluated by their accomplishments and not by certain routines, they are much more apt to be creative and effective.[10] This effort to design organizations around their goals has recently been used to develop what is called a management-by-objectives (MBO) approach, with goals, operating plans, and performance reports carefully laid out. (In Chapter 9 we describe some efforts to apply this model to the supervision of field agents.)

Human Relations Model

A third model offers a more expanded view of what is important and relevant in an organization. Members are not only invested in achieving the purposes of the organization, they are also motivated by their needs, values, and feelings. And unless an organization is able to deal with these, it will not be effective no matter how rational its procedures.

This model got its initial thrust in 1927 from a series of studies conducted in the United States to examine how people behave in organizations. One purpose of the studies was to observe whether workers behaved differently as their working conditions were changed. It seemed reasonable to suppose that if the conditions were improved, the workers would perform better. Surprisingly, however, the studies found that no matter what changes were made, either positive or negative, the workers produced more. Apparently, the conditions themselves were not as important as the attention the workers received from the researchers; as long as they were surveyed, questioned, and observed, they worked harder.[11] The implication for theories of organizations is that the human side of organizations — the ways in which workers feel and interact — has a real effect on their productivity.

Given the importance of this informal system, Chris Argyris concludes that organizations need to make changes in their procedures in order to elicit contributions from their members. Simon suggests improving information processes, but that is not enough. Because Simon ignores the role of emotions within organizations, he also ignores the extent to which they can distort information. Instead it is necessary to stimulate organizations to develop in ways that are compatible with people's emotional needs and energies.[12] (These ways we discuss in Chapter 5.)

Sociotechnical Model

This approach to understanding how organizations function stresses the importance of the social-psychological aspect of an organization. Its main tenet is that the social aspects of the work place must "fit" with the task of the organization — its economic role — and with existing technology, in order that the organization fulfill its function efficiently.[13] Studies of coal mining in England have revealed that as technology changes, traditional work patterns are often inappropriate, and yet they tend to be carried over to the new tasks. Ideally, a work group is given a period in which to design more appropriate social organization and role definitions for its members. Often management needs to encourage such changes to occur. According to this model, changes need to take account of the social-psychological dimension of the work place and to generate social arrangements appropriate to the economic task and the technology of an organization. In one study of coal mining in England, the authors found that after new coal-mining technology was introduced, the miners developed social organizations that were both appropriate and fit the changed technology. This change came about in spite of the fact that the particular forms they developed had been thought to be infeasible. The point, therefore, is that no single mode of organization is optimal; rather the important task is to find one that fits the particular task and technology available.

Conflict Model

A fourth model, one that has been less influential in the West, emphasizes the conflicting interests that exist within an organization. Systems theories and rational models, for example, stress the extent to which every member has a stake in the success of the organization and tend to overlook any conflicting interests that may be present. The conflict model Ralf Dahrendorf describes, however, is based on the assumption that those in authority have different interests than those who work for them. Employers and employees form two distinct groups, each with their own interests. The conflict between them does not stem from personal animosity, but simply from the fact that some hold power, while others do not.[14]

David Leonard uses this model to examine the Ministry of Agriculture in Kenya and finds that it is helpful in explaining why the ministry has performed very poorly in agricultural extension programs. He found distinct cleavages between those with authority (supervisors) and those without (field agents). This junior staff felt isolated from those in authority and had no investment in their work. The problem was that they were not aware that they shared these mutual interests and so did not band together to demand changes that would enable them to be more effective.[15] The first models described above essentially represent efforts to mobilize different groups in an organization around a single purpose. According to conflict theory, however, conflicting interests are a legitimate reality, and as a result organizations need to find ways of sharing power among their members.

Sociological Models

All of the above models focus on the organization as a distinct entity and on the ways in which it functions internally. Another cluster of models emphasizes the extent to which an organization is part of a much larger environment. Sociological and political pressures within this environment have a profound influence on organizational procedures, decisions, and behavior.

Open-Systems Models

An open-systems model is well exemplified by a farming cooperative. In addition to farmer members and a professional staff, a farming cooperative has a varied environment—firms that sell it machinery, market groups, clients, government regulatory agencies. The only way to understand how the co-op functions is to take into account all of its external relationships and pressures. As Russell Ackoff describes, the co-op is a system in and of itself, composed of many interdependent parts, and a part of a larger system as well. Its effectiveness depends on three related activities: accomplishing its goals, enabling each of its parts to work, and relating to the purposes of the larger system.[16] In other words, the co-op needs to function as a co-op, to facilitate the work of each farming and marketing unit, and to understand its relationship to the overall development of the region.

An "open-system" model includes both the organization and its relations with external groups. A most influential version has been developed by Daniel Katz and Robert Kahn, who draw on both sociology and psychology to describe these relations. In their model, an organization has to function in two ways simultaneously. First, it has to find ways to maintain itself, to elicit the support, energy, and cooperation of its members. Second, it has to try to protect itself from pressures in the environment.[17] Third, it needs to solicit resources and support from others and build linkages with other groups.[18] Thus the co-op needs to protect itself from private firms that might try to assume its functions or lure farmers away. Simultaneously, it needs the support of private marketing groups, suppliers, and clients in order to survive. All these groups and pressures continue to intervene, making it difficult for the organization to operate efficiently. Since participation is usually a way to influence how benefits are distributed, it is easy to see why project managers might choose to limit the extent of public involvement; organizations naturally want to retain control over these issues. The project directors of the Chilalo Agricultural Development Unit (CADU) in Ethiopia, for example, were aware that they were operating in a relatively hostile political environment, and so they limited the kinds of information with which they would deal.[19]

James Thompson has tried to integrate Simon's concern with purposeful goal achievement with the more inclusive open-systems model, through what he calls an "open system subject to criteria of rationality." He distinguishes between three functions of an organization. The first is technical — an organization *does* something, marketing milk for example. The second is institutional — an organization operates as part of the larger political arena in the community. The technical part of an organization can be organized rationally, whereas the institutional part is least rational and most sensitive to pressures from other groups and interests. The task of management, the third function, is to mediate between the first two functions, to decide how much milk to produce, who the clients will be, what distribution system to use.[20] The point is that not all parts of an organization are, or need be, as vulnerable as other parts.

Contingency Models

Insofar as open-systems theory posits that what organizations do is partially contingent or dependent on their environments, it is referred to as "contingency theory."[21] The major point is that there is no single best way to structure organizations; rather their structures emerge in response to external pressures. And further, unless we appreciate the constraints set by the environment and the extent to which bureaucracies reflect and absorb pressures from others, we will tend to place too much responsibility on administrative units. We will tend to hold them accountable for being more in control of their processes and outputs than they are able to be.[22] This same point was made in a review of projects in East Africa. "The socio-cultural environment of the project area determines how rapidly innovations will be accepted, how much cooperation is given to project personnel, how project objectives will be perceived by the intended beneficiaries." The report's conclusion was that most of the time, problems do not stem from management's failure, but from environmental pressures.[23]

Others argue that organizations are in fact able to exert some control over their environment, "that an organization only responds to as much uncertainty as its managers choose to perceive; therefore decisions about the organization's information gathering and processing capability determine the kind of environment in which it functions."[24] A review of several development projects suggests that each did respond selectively to different forces in their environments. The Vicos project in Peru, for example, dealt with the values in the community and tried to change them. The CADU project in Ethiopia ignored the values in its community and dealt almost wholly with economic conditions instead. The outcomes were not always successful; the problem was that although project personnel were able to exert some control over their environments, only those who were also able to build political alliances accomplished their goals.[25]

Bureaucracies and Private Interests

Another perspective that emphasizes the relation between an organization and its environment comes from elite theory. According to this theory, elite interests in a society use their resources to form alliances with members of the bureaucracy who in turn protect elite interests. The above models, by contrast, fail to ask if organizations use their power on behalf of some groups rather than others. They also fail to examine whether organizations use coercion when they deal with groups in the society. As discussed in Chapters 2 and 3, this concern is critical, especially where political institutions are weak and patron-client relations and corruption are prevalent.

Impact Analysis

A final model in which the environment is a significant factor can be called "impact analysis." According to this model, the most important aspect of an organization is not what makes it function effectively, but what impact its policies have. Whereas traditional organization theory is focused on what factors make an organization function effectively, this view raises a different question. According to one proponent, "We should seriously consider turning the more common perspective on its head. Instead of starting with elites, or the bureaucratic process, or institutional intricacies of various levels of government, we should begin by understanding the individuals affected by policies and work our way up from there through collectivities and to government."[26] The impact of policies is more crucial than the process of selecting them.

Among other virtues, gathering information on impacts means that we have a way to evaluate organizations. Other models consider ways to make organizations more effective in accomplishing their goals. The problem is that they only ask whether or not the goals are achieved. They do not ask if the goals are worth achieving. Or as one critic puts it, "The ethical dimension of the goals is none of its business."[27] Impact analysis allows us to ask whether a project is serving the interests of elites or the poor and thus to evaluate the goals and purposes of the organization. Its major implication is that data collection and evaluation are very important parts of the administrative process.

Organizations and Their Environments

Administration Under Uncertainty

If one single point can be drawn from these various models, it is that organizations need to find ways to cope more effectively with their environments in order to accomplish their purposes. As described in Chapter 3, the major characteristic of the environment in developing nations is the extreme and pervasive uncertainty. Uncertainty can be a problem for organizations for several reasons; however, a major difficulty is that it can lead to administrative errors. It is worth our attention to examine the different kinds of errors possible and different methods of dealing with them.

According to the economist Albert Hirschman, the environment of development projects presents two unknowns. The first he calls "uncertainties," or unforeseen problems that can occur during implementation. These problems include uncertainties in both supply and demand. Supply uncertainties include technological breakdowns, such as the failure of a transportation linkage or the unavailability of crucial supplies. Or it may be unclear whether manpower with sufficient training exists to implement a given task. Demand uncertainties include whether there is sufficient demand for a project, whether or what conflict might arise as a result of its implementation, or who will get the benefits of a project.[28] Hirschman describes uncertainties that occur when it is not clear how other groups will respond to a project. A project may lead to conflict with other agencies if these agencies feel they should be in charge of it, or political officials may oppose it because they feel they should get credit for it.

The second unknown Hirschman calls "latitudes," or opportunities for creative adjustment to problems. Designers and administrators always have a certain latitude that gives them room to adjust creatively to constraints, to find new possibilities, to explore unforeseen resources. Among his many examples, Hirschman cites the response that administrators of a pulp and paper mill in Pakistan made when an unanticipated crisis occurred. The paper was made out of bamboo, but soon after the start of the project, 85 percent of the crop died. Temporarily the project directors imported new pulp; at the same time they began collecting bamboo throughout other villages in East Pakistan and started a research program to identify other usable raw material.[29] Due to their creative response to the problem, they ended by having a much more flexible supply of resources. Ironically, had this problem been anticipated, the project would never have been started.

These unknowns are relevant to organization decision making because they can generate two kinds of error. Decision making under uncertainty has in fact received considerable attention from organization theorists. Assume that we are deciding on the nature of a certain project and whether or not to include a certain component or activity. For example, in a project aimed at increasing agricultural productivity, the issue at hand is whether to promote a particular type of new seed that has been developed. We can decide either yes or no, a decision we have to make in the face of many unknowns. There are four possible choices. Table 4.1 illustrates that you would be right in two of the four cases, but that you also have the possibility of making two different kinds of errors. Error means that a decision has to be made on the basis of insufficient information. In this case, someone has to make a best guess about the right course of action; if he guesses wrong it is called an error.[30]

Type I error occurs when a project is rejected because the best guess is that it will not work. It is an error because if all the facts were known, we would proceed with it. Type II error is the reverse of this; it occurs when we decide to proceed with a project because we estimate or guess that it will be a success. In this case, however, more information would tell us that it would not work out. By proceeding with it we have made a Type II error.

Most of those concerned with organizational decision making worry most about the ease with which we make Type II errors, or act when we should not. This error occurs very readily. In order to cope with uncertainty, managers try to exert more and more control. This control in turn tends to limit the amount of information and feedback that they receive. Because they want to protect themselves they tend to assume they have all the information they need. The result is that they end by deciding to act on the basis of insufficient information.[31] Russell Stout and Martin Landau are concerned that national plans fall into this trap. Because managers usually presume more information than they actually possess, they are very liable to make Type II errors, or to engage in precipitous moves. (See Chapter 11.)

Hirschman suggests that there is also an opposite danger; or in Russell Ackoff's terms, there can be "errors of omission" as well as "errors of commission."[32] As we mention above, Hirschman finds evidence of many possibilities for creative adaptation that only become apparent once a project is under way. He worries that administrators are overcome by the many uncertainties that exist and overlook the potential for creative use of opportunities. They are apt to be risk averters and overestimate the problems, and underestimate the benefits. They therefore fall into Type I error by not embarking on a project that could in fact work.

Organizational Designs to Learn from Error

Better management alone cannot adequately handle errors of either type; rather organizations must be designed to take such errors into account. The point is not that administrators should become preoccupied

TABLE 4.I

Type I and Type II Errors

	SUCCESS Introducing the seed would be successful	FAILURE Introducing the seed would be a failure
ACTING You introduce the seed	Correct choice	Type II error acting when you should not
NOT ACTING You do not intro- duce the seed	Type I error not acting when you should	Correct Choice

with avoiding errors, but that they should establish methods of learning from errors. And although the two types of error described above are different in nature, organizational designs to deal with them are remarkably similar. In part this is because they are both problems of *inadequate information.* The issues then are how to incorporate more information into the ongoing processes of decision making and implementation and how to maintain an organizational flexibility to respond to this information. In part information and flexibility are *political* problems. Information is after all a form of influence; acquiring it depends on the amount of support that exists in the community and the extent to which agreements can be forged with potential opponents. Another political unknown is the possibility for eliciting commitments and contributions from beneficiaries. Some prescriptions for organizational design follow.

Management and Experimentation. Because of the many unknowns and the possibility of acting on insufficient information, Landau and Stout describe management as an experimental process. Decisions and policies are actually hypotheses, and the task of the administrator is to manage and not to control. "It bears much repetition that solutions to problems cannot be commanded. They must be discovered: found on the basis of imagination, analysis, experiment, and criticism. There is no other way, the pressure of real time notwithstanding." Any errors that occur become valuable pieces of information and permit correction.

Stout has expanded on this argument and written a book reflecting on the difference between controlling and managing. "The real art of management turns on that which requires the highest degree of creativity and sensitivity; it is not planning or control. It is to keep an organization functioning reasonably well in its continuous battle with uncertainty, as well as the unintended consequences of organizational politics."[33]

A Learning Organization. According to David Korten, designing projects to benefit the poor is a difficult but not impossible task. One problem is that members of the public often possess information crucial to the project. The only way to incorporate their knowledge and support is to establish what he calls a "mutual learning process" and "a continuing process of creative adaptation." In the course of dealing with all the change and uncertainty that occur during development, the possibility of error creates a second problem. To cope with error organizations usually develop ways to deny its existence. Information about failure is not reported, or polished briefings are used to distort reality. An alternative response is to externalize error, which means projecting any failures on others. In time this stance leads to impotence and demoralization as organization members doubt that they can make any difference.

By contrast he writes,

> The "Learning Organization" embraces error. Aware of the limitations of their knowledge, members of this type of organization look on error as a vital source of data for making adjustments to achieve a better fit with beneficiary needs. An organization in which such learning is valued is characterized by the candor and practical sophistication with which its members discuss their own errors, what they have learned from them, and the corrective actions they are attempting. Intellectual integrity is combined with a sense of vitality and purpose.[34]

The key element in Korten's model is the development of an organization that can build on experiences and results. "In fact," he writes, "the effectiveness of a given program design is at least as dependent on the presence of an organization with a well developed capacity to make it work, as it is on the specifics of the design itself." For this reason he criticizes the practice of promoting separate projects that have a beginning and an end and where learning is not institutionalized.[35]

Korten offers examples of two projects that encouraged the development of learning organizations:

> The National Dairy Development Board (NDDB) is perhaps a prototype of this bottom-up program and organization building process. The outlines of the model were worked out largely by a group of small village dairy producers to meet their own needs. The young Kurien brought technical and

marketing skills, and out of their collective knowledge and commitment a strong supporting infrastructure was fashioned — eventually resulting in an official program of national scope.

The Community Based Family Planning Services (CBFPS) provides a parallel experience involving less complex technologies and support requirements. Another young man of strong personality and village experience, Mechai, engaged in collaborating with villagers to try out an idea for making contraceptives more available. Out of early experimentation a program model and a well defined supporting organization emerged, growing and adapting with the expansion of the program.[36]

A Transactional Model. A slightly different model emphasizes the presence of multiple and often conflicting interests. Both organizations and their environments are clusters of varied interests. As a result, management consists of negotiation, bargaining, and pragmatic agreements among interests within the organization in order to encourage feedback and learning.[37] At the same time, administrators are making constant transactions with the various groups in the surrounding environment. Their interaction allows them to take account of any available resources and supports and also of their eventual impact on others.[38]

Organizational Flexibility. As new information becomes available during the course of a project, it is important for an organization to be able to respond to it and learn from it. One way to accomplish this goal is to delegate sufficient decision making to local units, enabling them to explore and take advantage of the possibilities. According to Hirschman, "When considerable authority is delegated to the local manager of an irrigation project, he is likely to identify with the success of the project as a whole and to become involved in the 'next' phases, that is, those following the construction of the irrigation structures; on the contrary, if the irrigation activities of a wide area are handled centrally, the purely engineering outlook is likely to prevail."[39]

Support for Local Administrators. Organizationally, it is important to appreciate the impact of uncertainty and risk on local project administrators and therefore to provide support and feedback at the local level. According to open systems theory, agency personnel who are constantly interacting with external groups or individuals are pulled between the pressures from these groups and the claims of their agencies. Organizations therefore need to be sensitive to these multiple pressures and demands and to give local staff the support they need.

Implementation Reconsidered. Several of these models suggest that the process of implementation needs rethinking. Often implementation is evaluated in terms of how closely a policy matches the original goals and intent.[40] And often it is very helpful to stress the purposive nature of organizations and the goal-oriented nature of implementation. For example, when elite groups attempt to divert a project's benefits, it is useful to recall that the project was originally designed to redistribute goods. But achieving original goals is not always the best measure of implementation. Implementation is also an ongoing process of goal redefinition and development, dependent upon learning, flexibility, and experimentation. Thus local groups often need some discretion to monitor and adjust projects and to change course as new problems and information arise.

Dealing in Different Environments

There can be conflict between the efforts of an organization to accomplish goals and its efforts to learn and adapt. As we discussed, a learning model is useful when organizations have to deal with many unknowns. The environment is not equally unknown or uncertain, however. Similarly organizations are not equally vulnerable to all aspects of the environment. It may be that under some conditions it is very appropriate to design projects and organizations around certain goals and under others less appropriate. Next we describe two different models that are designed to distinguish among aspects of the environment and consider their implications for development organizations.

One survey of development projects concludes that organization theory is incorrect to identify everything external to an organization under the rubric of "the environment" and beyond the control of the agency. Managers are then given very little guidance as to how to relate to external groups and thus focus on the internal life of their organization. The authors present an alternative and more selective model of the environment. It includes only "those *entities whose actions affect* organizational performance, directly or indirectly." They then make three distinctions: First, there is the variety of groups and activities that are under the control of the organization, including the organization itself. Second, there is that part of the environment over which the organization has an influence. Third, there is that part that affects the agency, but is beyond its influence (see Figure 4.1).[41]

One of the utilities of the model is that it clarifies distinctions among specific projects. For example, if a project is set up to build a road or other physical infrastructure, the managing organization will probably be able to exercise considerable control over various resources and supplies. If, however, it is a rural development project, designed to change the well-being in an area, the "influenceable" and especially the "appreciated" environments will be much more significant. In these cases, "control" techniques are less relevant, and organizations need to find ways to influence, understand, and work with those outside of it.

Several of the theories we described in the first part of this chapter

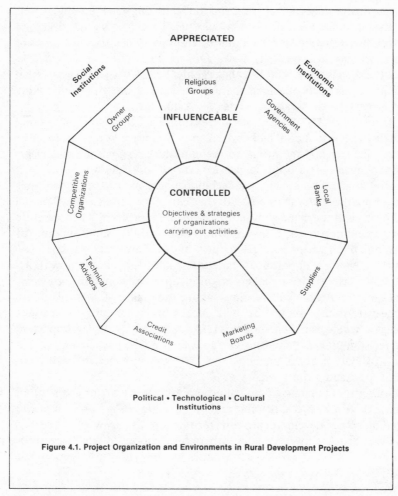

APPRECIATED

Social Institutions

Economic Institutions

Religious Groups

INFLUENCEABLE

Owner Groups

Government Agencies

Competitive Organizations

CONTROLLED

Objectives & strategies
of organizations
carrying out activities

Local Banks

Technical Advisors

Suppliers

Credit Associations

Marketing Boards

Political • Technological • Cultural
Institutions

Figure 4.1. Project Organization and Environments in Rural Development Projects

Source: William Smith, Francis Lethem, Ben Thoolen, *The Design of Organizations for Rural Development Projects*, p. 12. Copyright 1980 held by the World Bank. Reprinted by permission.

outline ways to make organizations more efficient, to rationalize procedures, to focus on goals, to establish more effective coordination. This model affirms the value of these rationalizing techniques; however, it suggests that they will be most successful within that part of an organization's world that can be controlled. Organizations also need to interact with groups and interests whom they can only influence; when they do so, rational techniques have to be modified.

The model above distinguishes among aspects of the environment according to how much influence and control organizations can exert and how purposive they can be. A second model distinguishes among aspects of the environment from a different perspective. Its basis is not degree of control, but degree of certainty. James Thompson identifies two kinds of organizational decisions: the first concerns goals and the second concerns the means to accomplish these goals. This gives us four different situations, for each of which there is an appropriate decision-making model and type of organization.[42] (See Table 4.2.)

There is certainty about goals, for example, when the task is to build an irrigation system; in fact most capital-intensive projects are clear about their goals. If the means to accomplish these goals are also clear, then managers use a decision process Thompson calls "computation." Decision makers can use analytic techniques such as cost-benefit analysis to compute the best way to proceed; they can rely on standardization and repetition and borrow some of the techniques from the scientific management approach. Computation is also useful in small subunits of an organization where political support and resources are stable.

If the means are not clear, if there is less knowledge about how to accomplish a task, decision makers are more apt to rely on their *judgment*. For example, if there was certainty about the goal of family planning, but less certainty about the best means to accomplish it, project managers would use their judgment. In such cases, it is very important that decision makers be purposive about their goals, but remain open to new information about methods and processes in order to learn from both Type I and Type II errors.

At other times managers are not clear about their tasks or goals, often because there are several possible and appropriate goals. For example, in designing a rural development project, some groups may want to use it to distribute benefits more equally; others may choose to emphasize pro-

TABLE 4.2

Decision Contexts and Organizational Models

Means to Accomplish goals	Goals of the Organization	
	Certain	Uncertain
Certain	I COMPUTATION	II NEGOTIATION
Uncertain	III JUDGMENT	IV INSPIRATION

ductivity and growth. Even if there is no agreement on what to do, it may still be clear how to do each one of the alternatives. Then it is appropriate to engage in *negotiation and bargaining* among the different interests. Finally, if it is uncertain how to achieve any of these several goals, then the appropriate response is what Thompson calls "inspiration." Somewhat more realistically, Stout suggests that in such circumstances some form of decentralization may be the only way to avoid chaos or authoritarianism.[43]

Thompson's typology suggests that we should examine the decision context in order to determine the most appropriate organizational model. When the goals and means are clear, then a more purposive and routinized approach is possible. When either or both of these are absent, other more open-ended organizational designs are more useful. Or as Stout puts it, in the former case, *control* is appropriate; in the latter, *management* is needed. The management task is to know precisely when each is relevant, rather than being lured into a too easy acceptance of control and of planning. Production tasks often warrant control and need to be insulated from external pressures. And part of the task of management is to provide this protection. As Stout states, however, "Problems of development are the key management task. They are ill structured; they require an innovation, a novel application of existing knowledge, or a renegotiated organizational position." Thus in any of the last three of Thompson's types, management, not control, is crucial.[44]

It does not follow from either of these models that organizations will adopt the most appropriate processes. In our discussion of bureaucratic pathologies in Chapter 3, we suggest how readily organizations assume much more certainty than in fact exists. Leaders threatened by experimental and learning processes assume they know more than they do in order to maintain some control. It is therefore revealing to pay close attention to those projects and leaders who actually do develop more open and flexible processes and who are sensitive to environmental pressures. One of the purposes of this book is to take note of such successes and to indicate some of the reasons for them.[45]

Conclusions

The task of administering development is difficult and complex. Administrative problems may be due to faulty management, but more often the basic problem is one of organizational design. What kinds of structures and processes are best able to facilitate development? The rest of the book represents an effort to address this question. In this chapter we considered various models of organizations — each of them stressing a different cluster of factors from information systems to human feelings to environmental influences. Administrators may find that one particular model is especially relevant to their context and concerns. Generally the more information they have and the more certainty they have, the more control is appropriate. But such control can only work within a broader approach to administration. This broader meaning is variously defined as management, or as establishing a learning organization. It is particularly relevant in development administration where the environment has a profound influence—where political, social, and economic forces all shape and influence the administrative process, perhaps even more than elsewhere. If these external forces are ignored several problems arise. First, the political dimensions of administration are ignored. Second, managers are held accountable for success even when they cannot control or influence all the relevant forces. Third, it is easier to make errors of judgment, either by acting precipitously, or by ignoring the potential for creative adjustment to the environment. Finally, it is much more difficult to include the public in program design and implementation if all the emphasis is on internal procedures rather than on relations with the environment.

The implications of these findings is that implementation is best conceived as a learning process. The learning has to occur in two different arenas. An organization first has to learn to form and shape its environment—to establish relations with other groups and utilize outside resources. Second, it has to learn how to incorporate and achieve its mandates, tasks, and goals. Such an organization has the best chance of learning from the two kinds of error—the error of making wrong decisions and the error of not doing enough.

Notes

1. This same distinction is made by William Smith, Francis Lethem, and Ben Thoolen in *The Design of Organizations for Rural Development Projects—A Progress Report*, World Bank Staff Working Paper no. 375 (Washington, D.C., 1980), p. i. Two useful summaries of organization theory are Harold Gortner's *Administration in the Public Sector* (New York: John Wiley & Sons, 1977), Chapters 5-6, and Howard McCurdy, *Public Administration: A Synthesis* (Menlo Park, Calif.: Cummings Publishing, 1977), Chapters 1-3.

2. Clarence Stone traces these two approaches to economic and sociological paradigms respectively in "Implementation of Social Programs," *Journal of Social Issues* 36 (1980): 13-34.

3. Frederick Taylor, *Scientific Management* (New York: Harper and Brothers, 1947). For another early classic statement, see Luther Gulick and Lyndall Urwick, eds., *Papers on the Science of Administration* (New York: Institute of

Public Administration, 1937). The empirical basis of Taylor's work has since been challenged by Charles Wrege and Amedeo Perroni, "Taylor's Pig-Tale: A Historical Analysis of Frederick W. Taylor's Pig-Iron Experiments," *Academy of Management Journal* 17 (March 1974): 6–27.

4. Russell Stout, Jr., *Management or Control? The Organizational Challenge* (Bloomington: Indiana University Press, 1980), p. 53. United Nations, Technical Assistance Bureau, *A Handbook of Public Administration: Current Concepts and Practice with Special Reference to Developing Countries*, 1961.

5. Herbert Simon, "Applying Information Technology to Organization Design," *Public Administration Review* 33 (1973): 269.

6. James March and Herbert Simon, *Organizations* (New York: John Wiley & Sons, 1958), pp. 137–172.

7. Simon, "Applying Information Technology," p. 277.

8. James Heiby, Gayl Ness, and Barbara Pillsbury, "AID's Role in Indonesia Family Planning," mimeographed (Washington, D.C.: AID, Bureau for Asia, July 1979), p. 76.

9. Peter Drucker, *Managing for Results* (New York: Harper and Row, 1964).

10. Peter Blau, *Bureaucracy in Modern Society* (New York: Random House, 1956).

11. The experiment is reported in F. J. Roethlisberger and William Dickson, *Management and the Worker* (Cambridge, Mass.: Harvard University Press, 1937). A classic statement of human relations theory is Elton Mayo's *The Human Problem of an Industrial Civilization* (New York: Viking Press, 1933). Recent research indicates that the original Hawthorne studies in fact did not demonstrate the importance of human relations factors. Richard T. Franke and James D. Kaul reanalyzed the data used in the original studies and found that "managerial discipline" explained most of the change in output. *American Sociological Review* 43 (October 1978): 623–643.

12. Chris Argyris, *Management and Organizational Development* (New York: McGraw-Hill, 1971); "Some Limits of Rational Man Organization Theory," *Public Administration Review* 33 (1973): 258. This last article is part of the debate with Herbert Simon (see note 20 in Chapter 2).

13. E. L. Trist, G. W. Higgen, H. Murray, A. B. Pollock, *Organizational Choice* (London: Tavistock Publications, 1963). See also F. E. Emery and E. L. Trist, *Socio-Technical Systems* (London and New York: Pergamon Press, 1960).

14. Ralf Dahrendorf, *Class and Class Conflict in Industrial Society* (Stanford: Stanford University Press, 1959). Another book that has a broader definition of conflict in an organization is Lewis Coser's *The Functions of Social Conflict* (New York: Free Press, 1956).

15. David Leonard, *Reaching the Peasant Farmer* (Chicago: University of Chicago Press, 1977), pp. 43–80.

16. Russell Ackoff, *Redesigning the Future* (New York: John Wiley & Sons, 1974), pp. 16–18.

17. Daniel Katz and Robert Kahn, *The Social Psychology of Organizations*, 2d ed. (New York: John Wiley and Sons, 1978), Chapter 3.

18. Ibid., Chapter 8.

19. Derick Brinkerhoff, "Participation and Rural Development Project Effec-

tiveness" (Ph.D diss., Harvard University, 1980), p. 244.

20. James Thompson, *Organizations in Action* (New York: McGraw-Hill, 1967), pp. 10–13.

21. In addition to Thompson, *Organizations in Action*, major works on contingency theory include Thomas Burns and G. M. Stalker, *The Management of Innovation* (London: Tavistock Publications, 1961), and Paul Lorsch, *Organization and Environment* (Homewood, Ill.: Richard D. Irwin, 1967).

22. Stone, "Implementation," and Dennis Rondinelli and Marcus Ingle, "Administrative Decentralization and Local Participation in Development Management" (Paper delivered at annual conference of the American Society for Public Administration, April 1980).

23. Cited in Smith, Lethem, and Thoolen, *Design of Organizations*, p. 8.

24. Brinkerhoff in "Participation and Rural Development," p. 13., cites the work of Charles Christenson, "Contingency Theory of Organizations: A Methodological Analysis" (Ph.D. diss., Harvard University Graduate School of Business Administration, 1973).

25. Brinkerhoff, "Participation and Rural Development," pp. 241–253; also see Katz and Kahn, *Social Psychology*, p. 135.

26. David Schumann, *Bureaucracies, Organizations, and Administration* (New York: Macmillan, 1976), p. 175.

27. Alberto Ramos, "Misplacement of Concepts and Administrative Theory," *Public Administration Review* 38 (November-December 1978): 554.

28. Albert Hirschman, *Development Projects Observed* (Washington, D.C.: Brookings, 1967), pp. 37–38.

29. Ibid., p. 10.

30. For a discussion of Type I and Type II errors, see any statistics text.

31. Martin Landau and Russell Stout, "To Manage is Not to Control: Or the Folly of Type II Errors," *Public Administration Review* 39 (March-April 1979): 148–156. See, also, Stout, *Management or Control?*

32. Ackoff, *Redesigning the Future*, p. 24.

33. Landau and Stout, "To Manage Is Not to Control," and Stout, *Management or Control?* pp. 53–54.

34. David Korten, "Community Organization and Rural Development: A Learning Process Approach," *Public Administration Review* 40 (September-October 1980). Two other sources for models of learning organizations are Donald Michael, *On Learning to Plan—Planning to Learn* (San Francisco: Jossey-Bass, 1973), and Jay Galbraith, *Organization Design* (Reading, Mass.: Addison-Wesley, 1977).

35. Ibid., pp. 53–54.

36. Ibid.

37. Landau and Stout, "To Manage Is Not to Control."

38. Donald Warwick, "Integrating Planning and Implementation: A Transactional Approach," Harvard Institute for International Development, Development Discussion Paper no. 63 (Cambridge, Mass., June 1979).

39. Hirschman, *Development Projects*, p. 72.

40. Merilee Grindle, "Introduction," *Politics and Policy Implementation in the Third World* (Princeton: Princeton University Press, 1980).

41. Smith, Lethem, and Thoolen, *Design of Organizations*, p. 10.
42. Thompson, *Organizations in Action*, pp. 134–45.
43. Stout, *Management or Control*, pp. 114–117.
44. Ibid., pp. 151–53.
45. Kal Silvert, *Man's Power* (New York: Viking, 1970), and David Korten, "Community Organization." Both writers stress the importance of looking for successful cases.

5
Administrative Behavior

Introduction

An observer of the bureaucracy in Nepal notes the striking change in its behavior over time.

> In 1952 when I was first employed by the Royal Nepal Government, what was most noticeable to the foreign observer was the buoyant, risk-taking response of the younger civil servants whose careers were budding. Policy matters were being debated openly. . . . There was enthusiasm and there was confusion. Yet only a decade later much of that initial verve had tapered off. In 1963, my Final Report described the system as concerned primarily with the promotion of protective and security services; as a system modest in scale but also divisive and separatist.[1]

What had made the difference? A major theme of our text is that a large part of the answer lies in the ways in which such organizations are designed. And the design is based partially on what is known about the ways in which these organizations function, as described in the last chapter. The design should also be based on what we know about human behavior and motivation. In considering the Nepal example, we need to know under what conditions bureaucrats are apt to be "risk-taking" and "enthusiasts." When are they more apt to function as a team, and when are they more apt to be "divisive and separatist?" In this chapter these questions will be examined from the perspective of the manager. What does a manager need to understand about his own behavior as well as his employees' in order to increase the effectiveness of an organization? What is useful to know in order to design organizations for implementing change?

There are two major approaches to explaining behavior, corresponding to the two approaches to organizational analysis described in Chapter

4 (see Figure 5.1). The first, a rational model, focuses on the individual member and his goals. Thus it is very similar to organizational models that emphasize the internal patterns in organizations. The second approach to behavior is frequently called a sociological, or a social-psychological, model; it examines the various influences that affect both an individual's attitudes and behavior and the way in which behavior also influences attitudes. It is analytically very similar to open systems approaches that stress the relations of an organization to outside groups and influences. A third approach is called a developmental, or human relations, model. It uniquely represents the kinds of goals that people pursue and emphasizes the ways to design organizations so they can elicit more desirable motives from people.

A Rational Model

When organizations function poorly, it is tempting to ask what has gone wrong. This model suggests, however, that it is more useful to ask a somewhat different question. People have reasons for behaving the way they do; therefore, the appropriate question is, What makes people act in

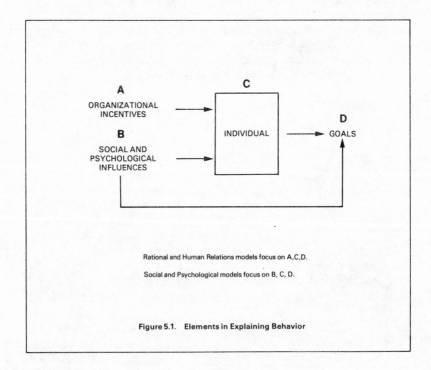

Rational and Human Relations models focus on A,C,D.

Social and Psychological models focus on B, C, D.

Figure 5.1.   Elements in Explaining Behavior

this manner? Or, what made this behavior right from the view of the local manager or the field agent?[2] Peoples' actions are purposeful; if someone is unresponsive, it is because there are no reasons to be otherwise. The strategy for the supervisor is then to tackle those reasons to give the person an incentive to change.

The major tenet of this model is that people pursue their own goals and interests. Those who work for a business firm usually pursue profits, but members of public organizations have no such clear goals to adopt and are therefore freer to pursue their own. Moreover the model is based on the assumption that they pursue these goals rationally. They balance the gains they hope to achieve against the costs they have to spend and only work for these gains if they exceed the costs. Although goals vary in nature, most analysts assume that basically they serve the interests of the individual. "We assume that every official acts at least partly in his own self interest, and some officials are motivated solely by their own self interest. . . . Thus whenever we speak of rational behavior, we mean rational behavior directed at least partly towards ends that serve the self interest of the actors concerned."[3] And this self-interest can encompass any one of several specific goals — power, income, security, convenience, personal loyalty, pride in workmanship, commitment to a program — that individuals establish for themselves.[4]

Anthony Downs gives us one example of what rational, self-interested behavior means in practice. He suggests that the different motives described above can be combined to give us five types of officials:

Climbers (power, income, prestige)
Conservers (convenience, security)
Zealots (commitment to a specific program)
Advocates (commitment to broader policy goals)
Statesmen (loyalty to society as a whole)

Each of these emphasizes a different style and behavior, but all can be described as pursuing his own interest. Herbert Simon agrees that people have different motives — namely achievement, affiliation, and power; and underlying all of these is a "high *need* for power among the participants (managers and managed alike)."[5]

This model has significant implications for the nature of organizations and the role of managers. Because people are both rational and self-interested, they will not automatically serve the goals of the organization. Therefore, organizations need to develop structures and incentives that channel members' interests and capacities, making them consistent with those of the organization. Left to themselves, people will do whatever enhances their interests; however by careful design, organizations can use this same energy to serve the goals of the organization. Immediately after stating that people need power, Simon continues, "A classical issue in the design of organizations and societies is to determine how these dysfunctional consequences can be avoided or mitigated, at the same time permittting the accomplishment of the organization's tasks."[6]

This strategy is functional for organizations and also for members. People need structures, goals, and specific tasks. They need "an understandable, reasonably stable environment for their acting, for their thinking, for their creating, for their dreaming,"[7] Such structures can allow people to work together and settle their differences in a useful way; they can "provide a setting for ordered controversy and accommodation."[8]

The ways in which organizations structure individual behavior center around their use of rewards and incentives. Most simply the task is to find ways to reward behavior that are functional for the organization. Rewards can assume a variety of forms. Amitai Etzioni describes three kinds of sanctions that organizations use to achieve compliance: physical, symbolic, and material. Etzioni's point is that incentives vary with the purpose of the organization. When the purpose is to produce actual goods and services, it is appropriate for a public bureaucracy to use material incentives such as financial rewards and security to motivate members to work for its goals.[9]

The varieties of incentives and their implications are nicely illustrated by Stanley Heginbotham's study of field agents in India. He was interested in how supervisors encouraged agents to comply with their work assignments and found three different types of incentives. The first is *material*. A tax collector, for example, might be told that he could keep anything he gets over a certain amount. The second is *feedback control.* Feedback control is a system whereby staff members are rewarded — given bonuses or simply commended — for submitting their regular required reports. A third way of gaining compliance from workers is by the use of what Heginbotham calls *preprogrammed control.* Instead of using external incentives, managers try to get the worker to adopt the agency's goals as his own, or to internalize them in his own value system. This way is a very subtle, and yet powerful, means of providing incentives and controlling behavior. Training programs, newsletters, reunions of trainers are all possible ways to socialize workers and imbue them with agency goals.

Heginbotham goes on to describe how each of these forms of control has been used at different times in Indian history. The colonial administration was built on feedback and required a constant stream of reports. These reports were then used to control peoples' behavior by serving as a means to evaluate what they were doing. The community development approach that was very influential during the 1950s and 1960s illustrates an effort to preprogram or to socialize workers into the values of the system. It emphasized the ideology of local involvement, and workers gradually absorbed its norms and outlook into their own values. In recent agricultural policy, the method of gaining compliance has changed. Workers are no longer inculcated with the value of community development; instead they are encouraged by formal feedback to submit a constant stream of memos and records. The results have not been positive. According to Heginbotham, these formalities have created a vicious circle. As field agents encounter problems, they are given more supervision. This supervision generates more resistance and in turn more feedback control.[10]

The use of incentives and structures to encourage people to serve the interests of the organization can therefore easily become dysfunctional. Some structure, however, can be helpful to members. As Simon says in the following passage, authority in moderation can be very useful.

> Our task is to design institutions that perform their essential social functions—produce a society's food, for example, or educate its young—at the same time that they satisfy important human needs of those who manage and man them. Among those needs is the need to live in a social environment that gives structure and calculability to life; to have access to norms and rules that guide action until creative discovery suggests interesting and useful ways to modify them. Man is not an imperious creature, unable to tolerate any and all authority exercised over him. He often welcomes authority, when it is exercised with moderation, and when it helps him and his fellows to achieve goals they think important.[11]

Social-Psychological Model

A second approach to explaining behavior is drawn from anthropology, sociology, and behavioral psychology. These disciplines point to the many ways the context in which people act affects their belief systems and attitudes. Different world views and values are all important, and it is too simplistic to collapse them all into a single norm of rationality. To generalize about all behavior is to omit precisely what is most interesting about people—their rich and complex diversity. In Figure 5.2, we diagram the different major determinants of behavior: values, emotions, attitudes, social structures, roles, technology, events, and the larger

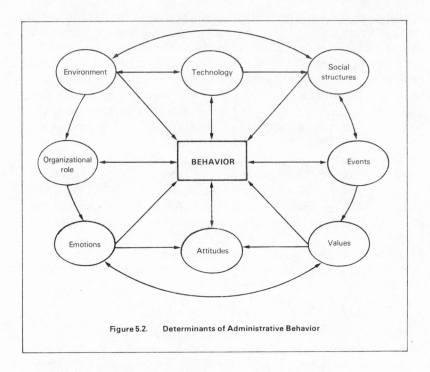

Figure 5.2.   Determinants of Administrative Behavior

political, economic, and social environment.

It is easy to see how motives and attitudes affect behavior. For example, if a farmer believes that fertilizer is inappropriate to farming, that attitude will influence whether or not he agrees to use the fertilizer. And certainly the first step for an extension agent or a local manager is to determine what peoples' attitudes are. The problem is that it is then often difficult to bring about change. An emphasis on the importance of attitudes and prior motives means that behavior cannot be changed directly, that first we have to change peoples' attitudes, admittedly a slow process. There is evidence, however, that attitudes do not always determine behavior and that in fact behavior can influence attitudes. Richard LaPiere reminds us how frequently people espouse a commonly held set of prejudices against a minority group, but that when they actually deal with a member of the minority in person, they are courteous. Perhaps there is something that happens in the actual encounter that is more important than the espoused attitude.[12]

A conversation between a development officer and an anthropologist illustrates the point. "Why do nomads believe in the nomadic life? How can that attitude be changed?" The anthropologist responds, "They believe in moving because they have always moved; therefore, it will not help to start by trying to change their attitudes." Perhaps if alternatives to their present life-style had sufficient inducements, their attitudes would gradually change. March and Simon make a similar point about behavior in organizations when they note that "the aspiration level tends to adjust to the level of achievement."[13] Peoples' values and goals are heavily influenced by what they actually do; if they are enabled to achieve more, then their aspirations might change accordingly.

Daryl Bem, U.S. psychologist, cites some evidence that indicates how the process works.

> A study of a large unionized corporation revealed that a factory worker's beliefs and attitudes changed markedly if he was elected union steward or promoted to foreman. Workers elected to the position of union steward became more pro-union on a number of pertinent issues; workers promoted to foreman became more pro-management. These attitude changes occurred soon after the *role changes*, and within three years the two groups of men had developed almost diametrically opposed sets of attitudinal positions. Furthermore, when changed economic conditions required some of the foremen to resume their previous roles of rank-and-file workers, their attitudes changed appropriately and reverted to what they were formerly.[14]

The point is that behavior and motivation comprise a system. Attitudes are only one component in that system, and they interact with values, emotions, role, social structure, and environment. The human mind is a complex faculty that adapts, learns, and processes new information. As a result, attitudes are not as permanent and fixed as is sometimes assumed. They can be, and are, changed by new evidence, new roles, different environments, new events. This concept can be graphically represented as follows:

MOTIVATION $\longleftarrow - - - - - - - - - - - - - -$ BEHAVIOR

Emotions, attitudes, values can all affect and be changed by behavior. One of the tasks of managers is to be sensitive to these various influences and imaginative about different points to intervene to bring about change.

The Environment

In the context of the social-psychological model, the term *environment* has broad connotations — economic, political, and social as well as physical. The impact of environment may be so pervasive that it is no longer considered a variable but a given. The agricultural extension agent working in a water-scarce environment incorporates that scarcity into his frame of reference. The woman whose whole life has been spent in poverty incorporates that condition into her frame of reference. Behaviors adjust and attitudes change in light of that adjustment. Those who experience abrupt environmental change know how it can affect outlooks in unexpected ways. Rapid change can even cause confusion and disequilibrium. Those who live through harsh political regimes where repression and brutality are commonplace often develop suspicious and vengeful attitudes toward others.

Technology

We choose to pay particular attention to technology because it is a central factor in the environment of people living through change. One of the reasons that the appropriate technology movement provokes so much controversy is that it challenges traditional relationships. When people feel little control over the technology they work with, changes are all the more threatening. From lower to higher levels, people work with tools—the peasant with his hoe, the extension agent with a new seed variety, the supervisor with computer-processed personnel information. Our attitudes toward these tools and techniques affect our behavior, and our comfort with this technology affects our willingness to change. Tractors free landowners from sharecropping arrangements; hence they will feel more comfortable about this new technology than those who are put out of work by its introduction. Computers allow managers to collect data on the productivity of field agents; hence managers feel more positively about computers than agents. Once again behavior influences attitudes; those with access to technology are more apt to welcome it and be willing to use it.

Emotions

Emotions, deeply rooted in the subconscious, can be harnessed to bring about change as well as repressed. Consider the effect that anger can have on the acceptance of innovation. Challenges to core values can provoke anger and resentment. An extension agent can feel angry at a peasant's rejection or ridicule of a suggested change. Feeling diminished or threatened, his anger affects his behavior, as well as his future motivation to work with that farmer. He may (1) blame the farmer for this rigidity, or (2) blame himself for apparent ineffectiveness, or (3) blame his superiors for asking him to work with such "pig-headed rascals." In any of these cases his feelings cause him to retreat from the problem at hand, rather than work at improving communication with the peasant farmer. Evidence suggests that our emotions, like attitudes, are not fixed, but that feelings about things are influenced by the reactions of others.[15] Thus in the above example, if all of the agents' peers felt compassion for the stubborn farmer, this feeling could influence the way in which the agent himself feels. Our context affects our emotions, but this influence also works the other way around.

Social Structure

This component influences an individual's political and social ties. Is one part of a minority ethnic group part of a distrusted political minority or allied with a dominant economic interest? Every collection of people, from class to village to kinship group, forms a social structure and transmits experiences and information that in turn influence beliefs and values. Each has its own culture, compliance system, and both formal and informal networks. The clerk, for example, is part of a peer group with other clerks, part of the social community within which he lives, and also part of a hierarchical group in his work place. One way in which these groups influence us is by influencing the way in which we interpret information. Most people receive their news through what are called opinion leaders. Opinion leaders are friends, community leaders, or even family members who call certain ideas and facts to our attention and influence the way we interpret them. A related concept is that of the reference group. Individuals tend to make decisions and choices with some reference group in the back of their minds, a group whose approval is sought. If an individual is placed in a new community that holds certain values, it is apt to become a reference group. When leaving that community, he may seek out a community that holds similar beliefs and values. Such situations determine social influence.[16] Social groups also have an influence when the group is very small. Research indicates that small groups can induce change by encouraging people to take risks and try out new ideas that they otherwise might be reluctant to consider. (See Chapter 10.)

Events

The model proposed here emphasizes ways in which experience and behavior affect motivations. Current events are a large part of that experience. No doubt the news learned in the morning that guerrillas have stormed the local airport will influence feelings about violent protest. Other events — natural disasters, political turmoil, staple food shortages, drought — are experiences that shape our attitudes.

Values and Beliefs

At the deepest level people hold values and beliefs that provide them with a sense of good and evil, of self-identity, and of ultimate meaning. People store these values and only seldom call them up for reexamination. On those occasions when values are challenged, the result is often great psychological stress. For example, in certain African nations, civil servants from some ethnic groups highly value authority in both public and private life, while others value leaderless groups. If people from both come together in a single group, they will experience real tension in how they interpret and respond to their work situation.

Beliefs differ according to how central they are to other beliefs and attitudes. Religious beliefs are most central and therefore most difficult to change. Others are susceptible to new evidence and are thus easier to change. The question is how closely beliefs are related to each other. If they are all related in a consistent manner, then it is difficult to change one without changing most other deeply held values. There is evidence, however, that beliefs and values are not always closely related in an entirely logical manner. Rather they cluster together in what is referred to as a "psycho-logic"; that is, they fit together in a manner that is psychologically comfortable. Moreover, it appears that people can tolerate a fair amount of inconsistency. The implication of this toleration for organizational behavior is that even if people have very traditional attitudes about authority, it may not be necessary to confront these attitudes directly in order to bring about change within an organization. Providing new experiences and evidence may generate the creation of new values and beliefs that people can live with, and act on, without having to alter their entire structure of beliefs.[17]

Attitudes

Attitudes are not as deeply ingrained as values or deeply held beliefs. Nor do people always act or behave in accordance with their expressed attitudes, much to the great frustration of those who carry out social surveys. New information and new experiences can and do affect a change in attitudes, and as discussed above they may not always be entirely consistent with other beliefs and attitudes. And yet attitudes significantly influence behavior and are thus worth examining.

Colin Leys provides an example of the importance of attitudes in his study of the Kenyan civil servants in the postindependence period. During this time of ferment, they had the opportunity to develop a variety of attitudes about their role in the nation-building process. As Leys describes, they formed a "general collective consciousness" and an "impression of themselves as primarily professionals who had a mission to expand the public sector." Without a sense of their own professional identify, he concludes, they may well have been co-opted by the economic elites in the country, instead of forming an alliance with them.[18]

Organizational Roles

A major influence on both behavior and attitudes is the role a person plays within an organization. A secretary who becomes an administrative assistant carries out procedures with which he or she previously felt very uncomfortable. The undersecretary who becomes permanent secretary discovers that old peers are not as easy to work with as before. The new role alters the relations among them. The point is that a role carries with it tasks, authority, and expectations that influence what people do. In large measure people behave as others expect.

The concept role tells us that those who have similar roles in an organization will behave in similar ways, regardless of their beliefs and values. Consider for example, a classification of roles according to their location in a hierarchy. Each level appears to have its own unique tendencies, thus indicating the problems and strengths that each group faces.

Service Deliverers. They interact with the public and deliver the products or services of the organizations. They are, for example, field agents working with farmers or staff teaching nutrition to villagers. Because they feel pressure from both the agency and external groups, they are the most vulnerable and potentially insecure members in any organizations. They are members of an organization and have responsibilities, but they also work closely with clients. They are usually the most sensitive to the demands and problems these external groups face, and often they are the sole source of information about the opinions of those outside the organization.

First-line Supervisors. Although these people have a career commitment to the agency, they are usually sympathetic to the service providers whom they supervise and thus naturally ally with them. One study of a Kenyan agricultural ministry confirms this tendency where it led to a serious problem. The supervisors "basically identify with those whom they supervise and can be counted on to report only the grossest delinquencies."[19]

Middle Management. These people are in general long-term members who maintain the organization. They are often suspicious of change and tend to rely on proper procedures and routines. The resource they provide is their considerable historical knowledge of the organization's procedures.

Agency Leaders. These people provide policy direction and control the rewards and incentives in the organization. They frequently have the power to allow change to occur or to stifle it.

Possibilities for Behavioral Change

The eight components that affect behavior provide an understanding of some of the reasons for the behavior of organization members. More importantly, they suggest the various points at which a manager attempting to bring about change can exert some influence. Efforts can be made to change attitudes or values directly, or workers can be provided with new roles or new experiences, and these in turn may alter their values and beliefs. The point is that behavior is flexible and can be affected by a variety of means. The presence of traditional and strongly held beliefs does not rule out the possibility of change. Consider the mundane example of changing the attitudes of lower-level administrators toward the poorest members of society. Robert Chambers suggests that health officials should gather nutrition data during the hungry months prior to the harvest instead of just after it.[20] This changed requirement exposes the officials to new information and in turn affects their attitudes about the poor and about their own role. Thus confronting people with new information and assigning them to explore new sources of data can affect their attitudes as well as increase their store of knowledge.

Developmental Theories of Behavior

There is a third cluster of behavioral theories that are relevant to administrative behavior. They emphasize the possibilities for members of a bureaucracy to develop their potential for growth and development. In addition to asking how people do in fact feel and behave, they ask how they might behave if the organization were changed. Individuals respond to their work in terms of their own needs; if the organization is designed to take these needs into account, it can maximize its members' contributions and elicit from them new potential. The difference between this view and the rational model is in the way in which needs are defined.

Maslow's Hierarchy of Needs

Abraham Maslow suggests that there are five different sets of needs, which form a hierarchy. The first and most basic is *physiological*; people need to eat and sleep and be sheltered. The second is *social*; people need to be accepted by others, to interact with them, and often to be part of a group or community. The third is for *self-esteem*, for self-confidence; whereas the fourth is for recognition and *approval* from others. Finally, the last is for *self-fulfillment*.

Few would disagree with Maslow's listing of different needs. The more controversial point, and also the more interesting one, is that Maslow argues that they form a hierarchical structure with the need for physiological fulfillment at the base and the need for self-fulfillment at the top. Until a lower need is satisfied, people are so preoccupied by it that they are not free to move on and satisfy the other needs. In the development context, this hierarchy means that those who are very close to a subsistence level are preoccupied with physical and security needs. As these needs are satisfied, they turn to fulfill their need for social acceptance and finally for individual achievement.

There are several implications for managing organizations. If people are to be free to pursue their need for recognition and achievement, lower-level needs must first be satisfied. Once people fulfill their lower-level needs, they are not as impressed with material incentives and rewards as they might have been. They might respond, however, to incentives that affirm their self-worth and their contribution to the organization. "At some point, economic return, for many people, has limited motivational value. The individual's motivation may have to be built upon such factors as promotion, long-term security, recognition by others, opportunities to exercise greater influence, and feelings of personal growth and contribution to the organization. These needs are higher on the hierarchical continuum and appear to have a motivational force with continuing and longer-term impact."[21]

Not all would agree with Maslow that needs are satisfied in a hierarchical pattern. Based on his experience in Mexico, Allen Jedlicka remarks that many peasants who have profound subsistence needs are indeed able to show affection and trust. Their need for self-esteem has not been diminished by their unfulfilled physical needs. Nevertheless he finds the theory useful. "The significant point of the theory, whatever the order of accomplishment, is that an unsatisfied need is a motivator of behavior and the consequences of this reality can be positive or negative depending on how that need is satisfied."[22]

Increasing Job Satisfaction

Frederick Herzberg has extended Maslow's hierarchy and applied it to actual conditions on the job. He began by studying workers to find out when they felt positive about their work. He distinguishes between two kinds of factors. The first he calls "hygiene factors" or "dissatisfiers," which include salary and working conditions. If they are not satisfactory, workers are unhappy with their jobs. Even if workers feel positive about these factors, however, they are not necessarily satisfied with their work. Thus poor working conditions can lead to discontent, but good working conditions do not necessarily evoke positive feelings.

The second cluster of factors Herzberg calls "satisfiers" because when they are present people feel positive about their work. The five satisfiers are achievement, recognition, the work itself, responsibility, and advancement. The last two, in fact, are similar to Maslow's higher levels of need. Chris Argyris expands on the argument by noting that people are more productive under three conditions: when they feel that their work is personally meaningful, when they feel important to the organization, and when they feel valued by others.[23]

Leadership and the Use of Influence

Theories that emphasize human growth and development raise the question of how to have effective leadership that can provide people with direction without stifling them. Some of the most provocative contributions of this approach lie in descriptions of and research on effective leadership. Leadership involves some sharing of power or influence. According to the traditional view, a manager who shares authority with others inevitably becomes permissive and nondirective and loses power. Behavioral theorists, however, insist that influence is not a fixed quantity. Sharing influence does not mean that a manager has less of it, for influence can grow and expand. "Rather than giving up influence, the manager needs to create circumstances under which he/she can work with others to maximize two-way influence and produce action."[24]

Douglas McGregor describes this approach as "theory Y." In contrast to "theory X" in which managers exercise control, theory Y includes the following principles:

> People are not by nature passive or resistant to organizational needs. They have become so as a result of experience in organizations.
> The motivation, the potential for development, the capacity for assuming responsibility, the readiness to direct behavior toward organizational goals are all present in people. Management does not put them there. It is a responsibility of management to make it possible for people to recognize and develop these human characteristics for themselves.
> The essential task of management is to arrange organizational conditions and methods of operation so that people can achieve their own efforts towards organizational objectives.[25]

McGregor is thus saying that managers with a theory Y style, who focus on human relations, are the most effective in the long run. Other theorists note that in reality leadership is more complex than this one dimension suggests. Leadership involves a concern both with the human element and with the tasks of the organization. This argument thus combines a human relations emphasis with the rational model. Accordingly, a leader is someone who marshals members around the goals of an organization, providing some structure and authority.

Blake and Mouton's Managerial Grid

Not only does leadership combine these two elements, but the way in which they interact determines different leadership styles. Robert Blake and Jane Mouton have placed the two dimensions in a matrix, or a "managerial grid"; each dimension varies from a low of 1 to a high of 9 (see Figure 5.3). Analytically they interact to form various styles of management. The 1.9-oriented manager, for example, emphasizes human relations, but gives much less attention to the work of the organization. Such

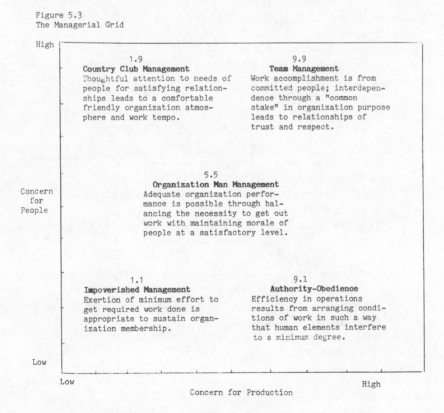

Figure 5.3
The Managerial Grid

High

1.9
Country Club Management
Thoughtful attention to needs of people for satisfying relationships leads to a comfortable friendly organization atmosphere and work tempo.

9.9
Team Management
Work accomplishment is from committed people; interdependence through a "common stake" in organization purpose leads to relationships of trust and respect.

5.5
Organization Man Management
Adequate organization performance is possible through balancing the necessity to get out work with maintaining morale of people at a satisfactory level.

Concern
for
People

1.1
Impoverished Management
Exertion of minimum effort to get required work done is appropriate to sustain organization membership.

9.1
Authority-Obedience
Efficiency in operations results from arranging conditions of work in such a way that human elements interfere to a minimum degree.

Low

Low   High
Concern for Production

The Managerial Grid figure from <u>The New Managerial Grid</u>, by Robert R. Blake and Jane Srygley Mouton. Houston: Gulf Publishing Company, Copyright (c) 1975, page 11. Reproduced by permission.

a style can create a very satisfactory work environment, but may not provide the kind of guidance and structure needed to accomplish tasks. In a 5.5-oriented style, "adequate organization performance is possible"; work and morale are in balance. In a 1.1 orientation a manager reveals an attitude of minimal concern for the task and for organization members. Some managers are able to maximize their concern for the organization and also for human feelings; in this 9.9-oriented management style, members are committed, they have a "common stake" in the work of the organization, and they share feelings of "trust and respect."[26]

Organizational Development (OD)

The human relations model known as "organizational development" (OD) prescribes ways to restructure organizations so as to encourage certain kinds of behavior. This model builds on the behavioral models and humanistic theories of organizations. It concentrates on the "solving of work problems by people. The improvement of relationships between people and work groups is not an end in itself, as it often turned out to be in human relations. Instead, interpersonal and intergroup behaviors are the focus as they are relevant to the successful problem-solving efforts of the work unit."[27]

One of its practitioners has listed the following characteristics of an organization committed to organizational development:

1. *Trust and openness.* "Trust in interpersonal and intergroup relationships is essential if full and open communication is to occur. An open and non manipulative sharing of data is required for the effective solving of work problems."
2. *Leveling.* This includes the "skill and courage to share candidly with others meaningful information about how he [a worker] thinks, reacts, and feels about work issues and co-workers."
3. *Feedback.* "Feedback is simply a communications skill for providing more accurate data on others as well as ourselves."
4. *Confronting Conflict.* "Conflict issues should be dealt with openly and problem-solved."
5. *Risk Taking.* "This refers to the ability of individuals to 'stick their necks out' in meaningful ways."[28]

Implications for Managing Development Projects

Most of the studies on which these theories are based have been conducted in the Western arena. There are, however, several applications of them in the third world that confirm their relevance to development.

Robert Chambers reports from Kenya that supervisors who consult regularly with their extension workers are much more effective than those who do not. He describes a process commonly called management by objectives. Managers and workers jointly plan what work they are supposed to accomplish, taking into account the needs of the organization and the perceptions and interests of the workers. These objectives then become the criteria by which their work is supervised.[29] (The details will be described in Chapter 9). David Leonard also finds that this perspective has value in the development context. From his experience, he has discovered that field agents feel alienated from their jobs and often perform poorly. In his diagnosis, the agents feel that their interests and contributions are ignored by management, and thus they have no stake or investment in its outcomes. Leonard specifically recommends that agents be consulted about the content of their work and given more discretion in carrying it out.[30]

Perhaps the most ardent advocate for applying human relations models to development administration is Allen Jedlicka. The problem with most technology transfer programs, he believes, is that they ignore the needs and interests of the recipients. What is needed, therefore, is a more humanistic approach to management. In fact, much of the development model is even more appropriate for working with farmers in the third world than it is for working within large institutions in the West. "Theory Y management directly addresses the fact that farmers are mature, adult, rational individuals."[31] He argues that "humanistic-democratic, participative management systems, which by definition are willing to accept the conflict and uncertainty introduced by the clients' culture, are more suited to introducing change in developing countries than are authoritative systems that rely upon certainty, and submission by clients." Jedlicka confronts the question that many administrators in third world nations (as elsewhere) are not inclined to such open, flexible procedures and relations. For this reason he says it may often be necessary to create new institutions to implement development and to train managers in human relations techniques. He stresses the importance of training for those at the top, on the theory that their priorities and influence largely shape behavior and performance throughout the organization.[32]

A variety of training exercises and manuals have been developed that apply human relations and OD concepts to development projects. The United Nations has published a most complete and imaginative collection, which covers concepts of training and descriptions of innovative training in various third world nations, as well as actual training exercises. The following example is included to illustrate both the utility and the essential simplicity of many of these exercises.[33] The exercise is designed to sensitize members of a work group to the extent to which they engage in an open discussion. It is useful after a group has already had several meetings and particularly appropriate if one or two members tend to dominate the discussion.

Two observers are selected; they draw a circle with everyone's name around the outside. Then they observe the group in action, and as they watch they draw diagrams, using lines to illustrate the directions of the discussion (see, for example, Figure 5.4). After the observers have completed their diagrams, the entire group is shown the two diagrams in Figure 5.4. The first illustrates a discussion dominated by one person; the second, an open discussion. (The arrows going to the center indicate remarks addressed to the entire group.) The observers then show the diagrams they have made, noting any similarity between the flow of conversation on these charts and the dynamics of their discussion.

The UN manual also contains an exercise that assists managers and groups in diagnosing their strengths and weaknesses and hence the kind of training they need. Tasks are divided into three categories: getting information, making decisions, and taking action. Each of these tasks involves the following kinds of skills: awareness of problems, analytical

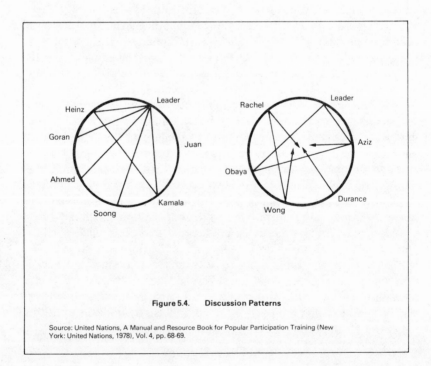

Figure 5.4.   Discussion Patterns

Source: United Nations, A Manual and Resource Book for Popular Participation Training (New York: United Nations, 1978), Vol. 4, pp. 68-69.

capacity, creative innovation, functioning as a group, technical skills, and ability to resolve conflict. Using these categories, managers or work groups can identify the areas where they need help and design a training program accordingly.[34]

Comparing the Three Models of Behavior

A model by definition simplifies reality by incorporating only those elements that a given theorist feels are most important. Thus the models we have considered are neither true nor false. Rather they are more or less useful for different purposes and in different circumstances. Their strengths follow from the variables they emphasize. The rational model emphasizes enlisting individuals to perform the work of the organization and establishing structures, formal roles, and incentives to gain their cooperation. This model is particularly valuable where organizations are trying to bring about extensive change in an often hostile and uncertain environment. A social-psychological model accounts for the variety of influences that affects individuals, shapes their perceptions, and guides behavior. Because this model focuses on those influences from the surrounding culture and political environment that motivate members of an organization, it is particularly relevant in developing nations where there is often discontinuity between the culture and the work life of an organization. And finally, the humanistic model allows for the possibilities of change and growth in human behavior and hence is appropriate in the context of development.

These differences do not necessarily mean that the models are contradictory; in fact, they can be complementary. The rational model, for example, is concerned with particular actions and choices, whereas the social-psychological model is with the context of peoples' behavior and the way behavior and attitudes interact to influence choices. The former shows how people use their values to decide what are costs and what are benefits; the latter shows the sources of these values and their distribution in the population. The humanistic model then focuses on how these values change and take shape within the organization. There are important differences, however. According to one analysis,

rational choice analysts tend to assume that different actors will reach similar conclusions when confronted with the same body of information. Social structural analysts are less likely to share this belief. They would argue that all information must be interpreted and given meaning. Because people situated differently in the social structure have had different life experiences, they are likely to interpret the same body of data quite differently. As a result, even when they share goals and information, their behavior is likely to be different because their interpretations of the data will lead to different estimates of the consequences of alternative courses of action. In addition, some social structural analysts would argue that social structures and processes inhibit the ability of many people to engage in rational calculation.[35]

Indeed a great number of studies have been written on the extent to which peasants make rational choices and on the extent to which their choices are constrained by circumstance and limited information. We return to these issues in Chapter 10 on participation and Chapter 13 on rural development.

The models can also be compared in terms of how they allow for the possibility of changing behavior. The rational model affirms the purposive quality of behavior; and because people are purposive it is possible to use incentives and rewards to alter the way they behave. The social-psychological model, however, directs us to the many influences that *prevent* people from changing and that reinforce traditional behavior. One writer even refers to the problem of "an oversocialized view of man." His concern is that by emphasizing the impact of environmental forces, the model does not allow for purposeful change.[36] As discussed here, however, the model stresses the interaction of behavior, attitudes, and motivation. By indicating the various influences on behavior, it indicates the variety of "pressure points" that can lead to behavior change. Similarly, if someone is induced to behave in a new manner, values and motivations are altered and these in turn affect future behavior. Behavior change is therefore not dependent on gradual cultural change, and it can be introduced in any of the eight variables.

The reality of the environment (political, social, and physical) nevertheless needs to be taken seriously. The human relations model allows for a greater complex of attitudes and values than the rational model and stresses organization design to unleash creative energies. Its proponents face a serious dilemma however. Although they argue that it is the only model that takes the individual seriously, critics counter that it is essentially manipulative and designed to change the individual to serve the purposes of the organization.[37] The truth is probably that both can be true depending on how the model's methods are used.

The behavioral richness of the second and third models should not obscure the value of the rational model and its emphasis on structure. Herbert Simon has serious questions about the validity of the human development model in particular.

All the evidence from the fine arts suggests that unlimited freedom is not the best condition for human creativity. The Gothic cathedrals were created not out of unlimited freedom, but out of the stern physical constraints imposed by gravity acting upon masonry walls, and the equally severe social constraints of the Catholic liturgy. Man creates best when he operates in an environment whose constraints are commensurate with the capacities of his bounded rationality. More constraint restricts his creativity, less throws him into confusion and frustration.[38]

At the same time, it seems that the rational model does not do justice to the many dilemmas people face, especially those undergoing wrenching change as they move out of traditional worlds and into more organized structures. Nor does it take into account how situations alter goals or how needs and goals constantly fluctuate. It tends to overemphasize the extent to which people pursue their own narrow interests and is less sensitive to the extent to which they may actually be committed to the values of the organization, kinship, or clan, rather than to narrowly defined self-interest. The rational model is also less apt to emphasize the importance of external constraints and the limitations that organization members face. As long as the focus is on the pursuit of their goals, it is easy to expect more of organization members than they can actually accomplish within their context. The rational model's perspective on behavior therefore needs to be supplemented with the perspectives of both of the other models in order to appreciate the full variety of constraints on individuals and the potential for increasing their capacity to work creatively with others.

In the following chapters, we draw from these models in discussing the various aspects of development administration. Our task is to incorporate the strengths of each and to avoid their limitations. The most fruitful way to combine them is to use the rational model to explore the extent to which people are able to make choices and pursue goals, the social-psychological model to sensitize us to ways in which peoples' choices are formed, and the humanist model to consider the possibilities of value change and development within the context of organizations.

Notes

1. Merrill Goodall, "Bureaucracy and Bureaucrats: Some Themes Drawn from the Nepal Experience," *Asian Survey* 15 (1975):89.

2. Richard Heaver, "The Politics of Implementation," mimeographed (n.d.), p. 39.

3. Anthony Downs, *Inside Bureaucracy* (Boston: Little, Brown, 1967), p. 83.

4. Ibid., p. 84.

5. Herbert Simon, "Organization Man: Rational or Self-Actualizing?" *Public Administration Review* 33 (July-August 1973):348.

6. Ibid.; see also James March and Herbert Simon, *Organizations* (New York: John Wiley, 1958), p. 169.

7. Simon, "Organization Man," p. 352.

8. Charles Perrow, *Complex Organizations: A Critical Essay* (Glenview, Ill.: Scott, Foresman, 1972), p. 142.

9. Amitai Etzioni, *A Comparative Analysis of Complex Organizations* (New York: Free Press, 1961), Chapter 1. For a similar classification see Kenneth Boulding, *The Organizational Revolution* (New York: Harper and Row, 1953), p. xxxi.

10. Stanley Heginbotham, *Cultures in Conflict* (New York: Columbia University Press, 1975), pp. 157–159. In his study, Heginbotham uses and describes concepts developed by Frederick Frey.

11. Simon, "Organization Man," p. 353.

12. Richard LaPiere, "Attitudes vs. Actions," *Social Forces* 13 (October 1934–May 1935):230–237.

13. March and Simon, *Organizations*, p. 182.

14. Daryl Bem, *Beliefs, Attitudes and Human Affairs* (Belmont, Calif.: Brooks/Cole, 1970), p. 66.

15. Ibid., pp. 49–53.

16. Ibid., pp. 79–83.

17. Ibid., pp. 4–13. See also Cyril S. Belshaw, *The Sorcerer's Apprentice* (Oxford: Pergamon Press, 1976).

18. Colin Leys, *Underdevelopment of Kenya* (London: Heinemann, 1975), pp. 193–198.

19. David Leonard, *Reaching the Peasant Farmer* (Chicago: University of Chicago Press, 1977), p. 201.

20. Robert Chambers, *Rural Poverty Unperceived: Problems and Remedies*, World Bank Staff Working Paper no. 400 (Washington, D.C.: World Bank, July 1980).

21. *Behavioral Science: Implications for Management* (Westport, Conn.: Systems and Designs, 1977), p. 4. See Abraham Maslow, *Motivation and Personality* (New York: Harper and Row, 1954), and *Eupsychian Management* (Homewood, Ill.: Richard D. Irwin, 1965). The argument that self-actualization is unlikely in traditional organizations is presented in Chris Argyris, *Personality and Organization* (New York: Harper and Row, 1957).

22. Allen Jedlicka, *Organization for Rural Development: Risk Taking and Appropriate Technology* (New York: Praeger, 1977), p. 41.

23. Frederick Herzberg, Bernard Mausner, and Barbara Block Snyderman, *The Motivation to Work*, 2d ed. (New York: John Wiley, 1959); Chris Argyris, "Some Limits of Rational Man Organization Theory," *Public Administration Review* 33 (May-June 1973):253–267.

24. *Behavioral Sciences*, p. 9; Rensis Likert, *New Patterns of Management* (New York: McGraw-Hill, 1961).

25. Douglas McGregor, *The Human Side of Enterprise* (New York: McGraw-Hill, 1960), p. 15.

26. Robert Blake and Jane Mouton, *Corporate Excellence Through Grid Organization Development* (Houston: Gulf Publishing, 1968).

27. Lyman K. Randall, "Common Questions and Tentative Answers Regarding Organization Development," *California Management Review* 13 (1971):46. For useful reviews of the organization development field, see Edgar Schein, *Organizational Psychology,* 2d ed. (Englewood Cliffs, N.J.: Prentice-Hall, 1970), and Warren Bennis, *Organization Development: Its Nature, Origins and Prospects* (Reading, Mass.: Addison-Wesley, 1969).

28. Randall, "Common Questions," p. 47.

29. Robert Chambers, *Managing Rural Development* (Uppsala: Scandinavia Institute of African Studies, 1974).

30. Leonard, *Reaching the Peasant Farmer,* Chapter 4.

31. Jedlicka, *Organization for Rural Development,* p. 42.

32. Ibid., pp. 47–55.

33. United Nations, *A Manual and Resource Book for Popular Participation Training* (New York: United Nations, 1978), vol. 4, pp. 68–69.

34. Ibid., vol. 1, pp. 12–15.

35. Michael Smith and Edward Jennings, *Distribution, Utilization and Innovation in Health Care* (Washington, D.C.: American Political Science Association, 1977), p. 95.

36. Dennis Wrong, "The Oversocialized Conception of Man," *Modern Sociology* 26 (1961):183–193.

37. March and Simon, *Organizations,* p. 54.

38. Simon, "Organization Man," p. 350. This article is part of a two-part exchange between Argyris and Simon; see note 20 in Chapter 2.

PART TWO
Implementing Development: Some Strategies

This section focuses on administrative processes and behavior for program and project implementation, applying the theoretical models in Part 1 to the actual tasks of development administration. Chapter 6 discusses the steps involved in designing projects. Chapter 7 explains the processes involved in data collection for the design, monitoring, and evaluation of projects. Chapter 8 discusses the ways to achieve decentralization and field responsibility, as well as to coordinate the various levels of government. Chapter 9 looks at the relationships between field staff and the consumers of extension programs and development projects. Chapter 10 focuses on optimizing participation in the administrative process by the use of incentives and social organizations. Chapter 11 discusses national planning and budgeting and considers ways to relate planning to the political and decision-making process.

6
The Process of Project Design and Implementation

Introduction

The problems of development can be overwhelming. Resource limitations mean that painful choices must be made; yet the basis for those choices is most often unclear and information woefully lacking. Preceding chapters have described the extent of the challenges and the value of designing an organization as a learning process. Such an organization is particularly relevant because the task of development is to accomplish change, seriously taking problems of equity and power distribution into account. In Chapters 7 and 8, we discuss some of the techniques that managers can use as they design possible changes and strategies. In this chapter we focus on procedures that can be used to design projects that draw on the resources in the environment, including members of the local community. Since in Chapter 7 we also look at various data collection methods and evaluation procedures that allow members of an organization to reflect on their activities and incorporate ongoing experiences into the implementation process, in both this chapter and Chapter 7 we deal with tools that enable organizations to "learn."

Those people who emphasize the importance of a learning organization, and the extent to which organizations operate under severe political constraints, frequently claim that analytic techniques are less useful than careful attention to implementation processes and political skills. Some claim that analytic and quantitative procedures are misguided efforts to impose rationality on a basically political process.[1] Others say that analytic techniques ignore the power stakes involved and the extent to which those in control can use such techniques to reinforce their own interests.[2] Those critiques have some force, but we are more impressed that the problems are real, that choices must be made, and that methods which facilitate such choices should be harnessed. Some of the design tools we describe are not always appropriate, and we indicate their problems as well as their potential. Yet it is important to be familiar with the range of tools in order to better estimate their utility and guard against their limitations. For example, it is not enough to know the cliché that cost-benefit analysis is not able to measure and compare all the relevant impacts of a project. It is also important to know the *logic* of cost-benefit analysis and the extent to which this method can help planners be explicit about alternatives. Recall the typology introduced in Chapter 4 and the different types of uncertainty it included. In this chapter various analytic techniques are used to explore, classify, and choose among the uncertainties in goals and means that managers face. The descriptions will not be sufficient to train anyone to use the techniques; rather they are intended to expand the repertoire of administrators. At the very least they may empower managers who might otherwise find themselves at the mercy of "technicos" from donor-assistance organizations.

One other caveat is in order. Data gathering and analysis need to err on the side of being simple rather than elaborate. Robert Chambers reminds us that the most effective projects are those that are designed around simple and direct procedures, ones that are easily comprehended.[3] The reason for underscoring the value of simplicity is that project outcomes depend not only on their initial design, but also on their implementation. A skillful and relatively simple project design will therefore ease the path for implementation. Too often the people who design projects are not the same people who implement them; hence little attention is paid to implementation strategies during the design stage.

In much of the discussion we apply analytic tools to project design, affirming J. Price Gittinger's claim that "projects are the cutting edge of development."[4] However, it is also true that projects should be tied closely to national programs. Programs are collections of projects, and it is a mistake to consider a project, or worse to design a project, in isolation from the program of which it is a part. David Korten and Fran Korten underscore the importance of this perspective, arguing that it is more appropriate to view projects as local expressions of broad national programs rather than as discrete activities. Projects can be designed partly to provide crucial information to program planners, can then build on other projects, and can be designed as sequential activities. The Kortens point to the National Irrigation Administration in the Philippines as an example of such an approach. Small-scale local projects were designed partly to irrigate local communities but primarily to provide the agency with crucial information about the best way to design and implement further local irrigation projects. Used this way, project design becomes the design of a process rather than an end in itself.[5] As some of the multilateral donors become more interested in program-based lending rather than project-based lending, the program perspective should command attention.[6]

There are four aspects in conceptualizing projects and programs as interacting parts of the development process. First, projects must be selected in the light of program needs; they must be designed to enhance program learning, and they should be evaluated, in part, on their effectiveness in enhancing the capacity of organizations to respond to local initiatives. In this view, projects are not judged solely on what rate of return they give, but on how much potential they have for increasing the capacity of agencies to implement development.

Second, both project and program organizations must be learning organizations open to feedback from the environment, processing that information and steadily revising their approaches. Designing a project to fit its environmental context involves assessing resources, possibilities, and political, social, and economic constraints. The difficulty comes in simultaneously insulating an agency from environmental constraints and allowing it to be responsive to the environment.

The third aspect concerns the structure of incentives for behaviors within a project. Are the behaviors that those incentives induce congruent with the project's goals and purposes? Will those incentives motivate project leaders and staff to do that which is most conducive to fulfilling project goals? Is the project organization structured to acquire and process information to maximize learning from both errors and successes?

Fourth, it is important to consider and evaluate the internal equity and efficiency of the project, the rate of return for the investment, and the impact and distribution of the proposed project benefits. As discussed in Chapter 1, development administrators have to ask, at regular intervals, Who gets what? Postmortem evaluation of the project will address who got what portion of the stream of project benefits; good design of the project lays the foundation for effective evaluation later.

Processes and Goals

The design of any project must deal with all of the following issues: organizational structure, economic and social analysis, feedback or learning systems, and balancing efficiency with equity. Project design does not, however, flow from a blueprint nor can a prescribed set of steps be followed. Rather it is a process, one that has at its core a means of learning from the environment, exploring opportunities, and evaluating different kinds of interventions. One study of twelve rural development projects in ten countries stressed the process nature of project design and listed the following components:

- improving knowledge of the social system and the environment,
- establishing a range of possible interventions,
- testing possible interventions,
- using test results to identify interventions appropriate to the local context,
- applying interventions in a way that will distribute their benefits within the project area, and
- replicating the project methodology in comparable target areas.[7]

Development analysts are paying increased attention to the process approach, and that approach is clearly an improvement over the older blueprint strategies of project design.[8] There is, however, one danger in thinking in terms of processes; it is easy to get caught up in the process and lose sight of goals and purposes. The important task, therefore, is to design a process that incorporates a focus on the goals of the project. In Chapter 4 we discussed the concept of establishing a learning process, indicating that there has to be flexibility and redefinition of the goals, but that it is still important to be concerned with purposes and direction.

The major elements or steps in project design are identification, formulation, feasibility, and implementation strategy. First, the problem that is to be addressed must be identified. Following identification, the appropriate intervention has to be formulated. The intervention must then be tested for its feasibility. And finally, there must be an implementation strategy for the project. Each of these steps can effectively use a process approach in order to improve the quality and quantity of information that is utilized in the design.

Identification

A project is an intervention that addresses a problem. Logically, then, the first step is to identify the problem, but in reality cutting a problem down to practical dimensions is often difficult. Sometimes a design team is directed to design a particular project because the donor agency has already made a determination about the problem to be addressed. When this occurs, the project that will be designed is in large part determined by the specializations that the team members bring to the exercise. Nevertheless, narrowing the spectrum of possible interventions to a small group is an exercise in problem identification. For example, suppose that a team is working in an area — region X — to design a health project that is part of a larger national health program. This team knows from existing data, interviews, scanning records, and past experience that the people within region X experience a variety of health problems that affect their productivity and diminish the quality of their lives. There are many probable causes: seasonality of available food, low income, few trained medical personnel, little information about alternative care, infection from bad water, pests, and so on. Each of these factors suggests a different kind of project. But identification of the problem that the team will tackle requires discovering much more. What is currently being done within the area to deal with the problem? What are the available resources? Local values and the social system within which health practices are imbedded must be understood so that the project can be designed to work with indigenous values conducive to change. Therefore, the first step in the design process is to carry out preliminary consultation with members of the local community to learn their perceptions, needs, and preferences.

Second, the goal of the intervention (project) must be identified. Specifically, what is the project to do? What tasks is it to perform? And third, what kind of institutional and organizational structure will enable it to accomplish its goals? Since a project organization will carry out a variety of tasks, it must be constructed in light of those tasks and of the environment in which they are performed. The design of a project, therefore, is a three-dimensional puzzle for a design team, and the key is to get components right simultaneously.

For project design teams to succeed, local beneficiaries or their representatives should be involved at an early stage in the design deliberations. Just exactly how and when this is done depends on the nature of the team membership. If the design team is from a national ministry, constraints from donor organizations may be mitigated.[9] Although local participation is sometimes avoided because of its difficulty, it is well to recall the reasons for involving local participants at an early stage. Most pragmatically, local group involvement helps the project avoid costly design errors.[10] Local women know about the pattern and incidence of childhood illness and mortality; local people can explain health practices, food customs, and food availability. They may recall their experiences with waterborne or pest-borne illness, herbal medicines, past treatments, and work-related health problems. In short, they can provide data to supplement the information available to the design team. Although local beneficiaries often know they are not technically proficient, experts unfortunately are not as frequently aware of their own limitations. Designers forget that their expertise should always be updated by listening carefully to the local people.

With local participation the project design team is also able to identify and reinforce local efforts already in place. Individual communities are often engaged in a variety of activities related to the problem a project is designed to address. How much use local beneficiaries will make of a project is related to how well they feel it does address their problem and how consistent it is with their own efforts. The acceptance and success of the Indonesian Family Planning Project are largely due to the ownership and involvement that local Indonesian women had in the project from its inception.

In those cases where projects will be eventually owned by the local community, participation affords people an investment in the project and increases the likelihood that they will choose to maintain it. Finally participation in the project's design ensures that the project fits with the social realities of the area. One design of an irrigation system, for example, might divide and polarize a community, whereas another might build and reinforce natural community ties. Participation builds important skills among the public and thus begins the process of generating more local capacity.

Tree Diagraming

Tree diagraming is a process that can be used to specify components of a problem and is particularly useful when project design is carried out by teamwork.[11] The central concept of the process, which originates in systems theory, is that the elements of a system are interdependent and are best understood in terms of a network of relationships.[12] The first step in identifying the network of components that together constitute a particular problem is to diagram these components. The problem is labeled at the top of the tree; the major parts or factors are listed on the next level, and each of these is further disaggregated. Next, the relationships among the elements of the problem are drawn in an oval diagram.

Any project design embodies a series of hypotheses. Situation A (poor health of many people in region X) exists, and so we hypothesize that it is generated by problems B, C, D, and so forth. By extension, we can also hypothesize that a project Q could affect some aspects of the situation. Any problem area suggests a multitude of such hypotheses about the key factors, and being explicit about these factors is a first step in project design.

Tree diagraming, in addition to its use in problem analysis, is functional for a team. In the construction of a diagram on a blackboard or on anything that allows for easy changes, erasures, or corrections, all the team members are encouraged to participate. It becomes apparent in the sharing of input that each member has different information to contribute, and in the process the quality of teamwork is improved.

An informal process is important in developing the tree diagram. The diagram should be revised repeatedly over a period of time to reflect the group's evolving analysis before a final consensus is reached. (Once design team members have gone through this exercise and acquired the diagraming skill, they can use it for any number of other aspects of their analysis. For example, at a much later stage they may want to diagram the organizational and political context within which the project will have to function.) The tree diagram in Figure 6.1 illustrates an analysis of the components of an area's health problems.

After completing the diagram, the team can begin identifying possible

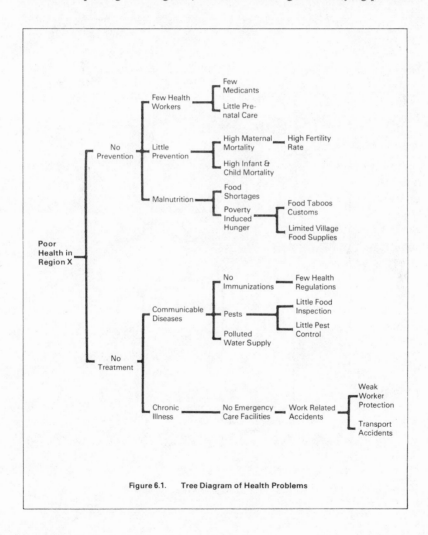

Figure 6.1.   Tree Diagram of Health Problems

points of intervention to alleviate the situation. In order to specify positive steps for each of the components, information is needed, available resources must be scanned, records searched, and people interviewed in the general search for clues as to what might be done. Figure 6.2 illustrates the further evolution of tree diagraming.

Each connecting line can be treated as a hypothesis worthy of examination in its own right, indicating what additional research needs to be done.[13] Advanced statistical techniques are sometimes appropriate to discover which factor accounts for the largest portion of the variance in each relationship.

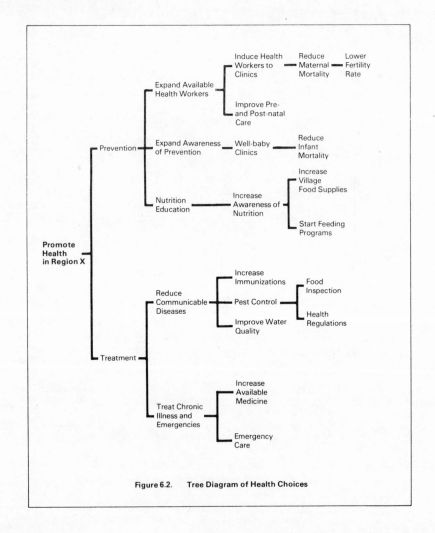

Figure 6.2.   Tree Diagram of Health Choices

Notice what the tree diagram does and does not do. The top of the tree identifies the final product of or goal for a program or project; each lower level is a further elaboration of the factors that contribute to achieving the goal. At the same time, each of these lines indicates hypotheses about what factors will bring about certain aspects of the goal. For example, in Figure 6.2 increasing immunization, controlling pests, and improving water quality are hypothesized as major factors in reducing communicable diseases. The precise extent to which these relationships hold, or are true, in a particular place is an empirical question that can only be confirmed or disconfirmed after research. Inasmuch as tree diagraming and oval diagraming clarify the interrelationships affecting the project's goal, they are useful later in monitoring and evaluating the project.

Specifying Relationships: Oval Diagraming

The limitation of the tree diagram is that it does not readily allow for greater specificity about these interrelationships. One useful device to gain some precision is the oval diagram. The major function of the oval diagram is to illustrate relationships in such a way that designers can more easily visualize the impact of one aspect of the system upon others. For example, the tree diagram above identifies four major components in health—reducing communicable disease, treatment of chronic illness, knowledge of preventive medicine, and nutritional education; common sense tells us, however, that these last two are interrelated and that the tree diagram as constructed does not depict that relationship. The impact on one element will in turn have an impact on other elements. Diagraming all conceivable interactions makes the diagram unwieldy, but the process of constructing the diagram at the very least uncovers relationships that may not be apparent initially. As one guide to this technique points out, "Oval diagramming facilitates communication between analysts and decision makers by highlighting undesirable effects and relationships that require careful attention."[14] Part of the tree diagram in Figure 6.2 can be depicted by the oval diagram in Figure 6.3.

This systems approach to project design is only one way to proceed; there are many others. Yet the key ingredients must be present in any good design effort. The problem must be identified; the goal toward which the project is to be directed must be clarified; assumptions about linkages between aspects of the problem must be specified, as well as intervening factors that can block project effectiveness. The process is rather like working out the travel route after the destination has been decided. The map indicates the terrain to be traveled as well as the potential linkages between different points. Thus if a key bridge is washed out

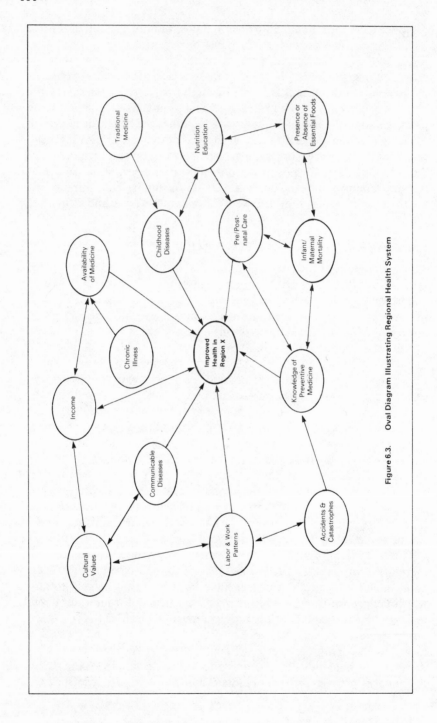

Figure 6.3. Oval Diagram Illustrating Regional Health System

on a major road, an early discovery of a vital linkage provides the option of a different route.

Consider the diagram (Figure 6.3) again. The goal is to improve the health of the population in a region. One possible intervention might be a series of clinics in different locations. But because of the web of relationships affecting health, as diagramed in Figure 6.1 (poverty-induced illness and hunger, malnutrition, and so on), these clinics might include a range of services from emergency treatment to nutrition education. Delineating exactly what functions will be included in the range of services the clinics provide is the next stage in project design — formulating the precise intervention, its scope and nature. At this point the following series of questions must be addressed:

- What functions will the clinics perform?
- Where should the clinics be located?
- How will they be funded?
- Which services will be on a fee basis?
- How should the clinics be staffed?
- Which combination of the above components has the most impact on the problem for the least cost?

Formulation

The formulation of the project requires additional information, consultations, and input from local officials, professionals, and members of the public. It is important to design procedures in the formulation stage to meet these needs.

All too often participation is taken to mean that the project's users (or beneficiaries) will help with the work of the project on a self-help basis, but not with the original planning and formulation. Yet, as we discussed earlier, crucial information is not always available to experts, and early consultation at the formulation stage can avoid unnecessary and costly mistakes. The following description of the Special Rural Development Program (SRDP) of Kenya by Uma Lele is illustrative:

In the Mbere district (Kenya) the SRDP's Cotton Block Scheme called for the construction of an 88 kilometer water pipe. The plan assumed that the digging of the pipe trenches could be done by harambee labor. However, because the pipe installation was a long range plan without immediate benefits, it was feared that any initial popular support for the pipe would soon wane. In addition, the pipe leads from a well watered area to a drier one, so enthusiasm was greater at the far end. Consequently, the project was started with contract labor. . . . Because of its high cost, however, contract labor was abandoned shortly thereafter, and efforts were made to use the self help labor originally planned. Subsequent performance on the trench was poor—only 560 meters were dug over the next two months. Whatever the initial harambee support for the project might have been, an attempt to get people to work without pay on a job for which they had previously been paid was bound to run into difficulty. Clearly if the local people had been consulted more carefully during the planning stage, these problems in sequencing could have been dealt with more effectively.[15]

Uma Lele is quite right; one difficulty is that meetings need to be held at every stage of the project process. Such meetings can be complicated and potentially controversial, and any rational administrator who is a risk minimizer will not give this task top priority. And there is another problem. Because this kind of consultation is usually not mandated, it is difficult for the design team to prove that such meetings are "cost-effective." They are cost-effective in the long run if members of the public ultimately own the project. In the short run, however, meetings are problematic at best and tend to be avoided when possible. Meetings must be held for other purposes as well. If outside funding is being sought, as it frequently is, many meetings with potential funding agencies must be conducted. Meetings must be held with interested or involved ministry officials, planning officials, and political leaders. At this point the project design team needs skills in interpersonal relationships; the field of organizational development provides guidelines for organizing effective meetings and negotiating differences.[16]

If it becomes apparent that a basis for agreement exists, despite some misperceptions blocking the path to that agreement, it is possible to address those misperceptions while also tackling some tasks central to the formulation of the project. For example, one aspect of project design calls for identifying project inputs and outputs. Breaking these into subsidiary tasks, a meeting can be called of the officials concerned with the project. They can then be subdivided into smaller task groups of five or six people, with lists of issues to be addressed by each group. Often working together on a specific task enables officials to perceive more areas of possible agreement than they had originally thought possible.

The Logical Framework for Project Design

Since project formulation requires specifying the arrangements for implementation, an organizing device can be useful. The United States Agency for International Development (AID) wanted a device that would lay out the flow of project inputs and anticipated outputs and indicate possible measures of project fulfillment. The result was the development of the logical framework for project design. This device is often referred to simply as the logframe, which is described here not because it is unique, but because it exemplifies a useful technique in the process of project design.

The technique of the logical framework has three major advantages. First, the process of working it through can assist designers in coming to some agreement about the skeletal framework of the project. Second, if a framework is established at the formulation stage, achievement can be measured at regular intervals during implementation. Third, the logframe can be used later in the project cycle to begin the evaluation process.[17] Reference to the logical framework assists in recalling project goals and purposes, indicators that can be used for verification, and assumptions made at the time of the design. (See Chapter 7 on data collection and evaluation, but these issues must be specified in the formulation of the project.) For example, at regular intervals one must ask how one will know when these objectives have been achieved. Indicators or ways to measure how far the project has come should be selected at the outset even though they may later be modified.

The logical framework for project design is a matrix that can be completed as part of the design process, then forming part of the project documentation. Essentially the framework makes sense both along the horizontal series of boxes and upward through the vertical levels. On each vertical level, for example, the questions raised are, If this factor is an input then what outputs can be expected? If those outputs result, then what purpose is achieved? The vertical questions are the "if-then" questions. Horizontally the question posed is, How will this element be known or verified? Table 6.1 gives the skeletal outline of the logical framework.

Each element of the logical framework should be filled in with the requested information in summary form. Thus the matrix, taken as a whole, reflects the project's goals, purposes, inputs and outputs, indicators by which they can be measured, data sources for those indicators, and the assumptions upon which the project was formulated. The process of completing the matrix is useful insofar as it addresses the ambiguity inherent in any design process. Care must be taken, however, that the process of completing the matrix does not become routinized, in which case the value of mutual consultation and clarification is lost. When or if the matrix is treated lightly, it can become trivialized like many such organizing devices.

Feasibility

The next step after problem definition and project formulation is to determine how feasible a project is and how it compares with alternatives. A common way to do this is to use economic analysis either to compare the costs and benefits of several projects or to determine the cost-

TABLE 6.1

Logical Framework for Project Design

Narrative Summary	Objectively Verifiable Indicators	Means of Verification	Important Assumptions
Program or Sector Goal	Measures of Goal Achievement	Examination of Records, Statistics, and Surveys	Assumptions for achieving Goal targets
Project Purpose	Conditions which Indicate Purpose Achieved	Evaluation Data	Assumptions for achieving Purpose
Outputs	Magnitude of Outputs	Measures & Observation Data	Assumptions for achieving outputs
Inputs	Implementation target	Government records and Documents	Assumptions for providing Inputs

effectiveness of a single project. The basic idea of benefit-cost analysis is straightforward—the benefits should outweigh the costs. If they do not, the government (or investor) would be better off leaving the funds to accumulate interest, rather than investing them in the project. Hence the formula:

$$\frac{\text{Present worth of benefits}}{\text{Present worth of costs}} = \text{Benefit-cost ratio}$$

Cost-benefit analysis can be used both for estimating the feasibility of a project and later for project evaluation. It is most frequently required in the first instance to attract development assistance support.[18] Three problems intrude upon the process of cost-benefit analysis: measuring the costs and benefits, determining indirect effects, and finding the discount rate.

Measuring Cost and Benefits

Both of these elements have to be measured in the same terms so that they can be compared. Attaching values to them sometimes requires creative thinking. For example, how can one measure the value of preventing disease (a benefit) with the salaries of the health workers (a cost)? Usually an effort is made to translate both of these values into money. The problem is that disease prevention is not readily translated into money, whereas increased productivity due to better health can be. Investments in human resources are usually more difficult to measure. For example, enhanced efficacy or increased local capacity is a benefit that flows from participatory strategies, but it is difficult to monetize. One way might be to consider the maintenance costs incurred if there is no local participation compared with maintenance costs with participation. These problems can be dealt with using some imagination, but there will be considerable subjectivity in many of the estimates. Often more attention to data collection can help; sample surveys can improve information about behavioral and attitudinal change. One can measure workdays gained in a region if health improves, for example. One reason that the effort should be made to translate qualitative factors into quantitative measures is that it reminds everyone to observe consequences of a project, rather than to guess at them. Although there will be subjectivity in measurements, surmises and guesses are even more subjective than asking people what has happened.[19]

Assessing Total Costs and Benefits

A second problem is measuring total costs and benefits. What is included in the total values that represent these two large umbrella concepts? Table 6.2 lays out a sample cost-benefit projection, drawn from the pioneering work of J. Price Gittinger in project analysis. The table includes three kinds of costs: capital expenditures, operating costs, and production costs. Once these costs are estimated they have to be multiplied by a discount factor to derive what is called the "present worth" of the project's costs. Consistent with usual practice, the table includes a single entry for benefits—the total value of the product. The same discount factor is applied here, and the balance between costs and benefits is determined.

Estimating these costs and benefits can often pose severe problems. The point is to be sensitive to the weaknesses in the estimates and yet be imaginative in collecting as good an estimate as is possible. Particularly troublesome are indirect or future benefits and costs. In fact, one of the concerns about this technique is that it may not appropriately account for *long-term* costs of the least easily quantified kind. For example, an irrigation scheme may have long-term deleterious consequences for the environment, soil quality, and erosion, but such costs will not appear in the short time frame of the analysis. Consider also the problem of measuring the benefits of the health clinics. The long-term effects of mortality and morbidity and consequently of productivity are difficult to estimate; some effects are further into the future than others. Consider the differences in the time involved in improving infant nutrition and in improving emergency health care for adults. Yet such trade-offs are not readily quantifiable.

Discounting

A third problem concerns the time horizon for which the investment is to be appraised. As a unit of money is more valuable to its holder today than it will be at some specified period in the future, the investment in the project has to be discounted over a period of time. The folk wisdom in the phrase "A bird in the hand is worth more than two in the bush" is precisely the logic underlying the problem of discounting the future value of money.[20] Since projects start a flow of benefits and costs over a period of time, the problem is to estimate their value over that period. Think first about the way in which interest is charged on money lended. If a farmer forgoes money today to lend it to a neighbor, he is entitled to compensation for the forgone use of that money during the time it is lent. Interest is that compensation. The concept of the discount rate simply turns that problem around to ask the reverse question—how much is a unit of money worth to you a year from now? The difference between the value of that money today and its value at some future date is the discount rate. And just as costs and benefits assessment involves

TABLE 6.2

Computing Cost-Benefit Analysis -- Hypothetical Case of Rural Health Clinics

Year	Capital items	Oper. & maint.	Production costs	Gross Costs	Discount factor 12%	Present worth of costs prod.	Total value of	Discount factor	Present Worth of Benefits
1	5000	0	0	5000	.893	4465	0	.893	0
2	4000	600	0	4600	.797	3666	1000	.797	797
3	0	600	700	1300	.712	926	5000	.712	3560
4	0	600	1300	1900	.636	1208	5500	.636	3498
5	0	600	2600	3200	.567	1814	6000	.567	3402
						12,079			11,257

Benefit - Cost

$$\frac{11257}{12079} = .93$$

ratio at 12%

NOTE: When the benefit-cost ratio works out to be less than one, as it does in this case, then we have a case where at the discount rate assumed, the present worth of the costs exceeds the benefits and perhaps the investor should not undertake the project. Notice, however, how changing the discount rate or, in this case, lengthening the number of years would have altered the ratio computed. Hence the project would be beneficial and worthwhile if one used a lower discount rate or extended it over a longer period of time.

(Table modeled after J. Price Gittinger, Economic Analysis of Agricultural Projects, Washington, D.C.: World Bank, 1972) weighing a great many factors somewhat subjectively, the discount rate is based on judgments about a variety of circumstances.

Generally it can be said that the more willing a government is to defer the earnings on money, the lower the discount rate that should be applied in analyzing the project. Conceptually, it represents the "profitability of the last possible investment in an economy given the total available capital" or, in other words, reflects the opportunity cost of capital. Once a rate is chosen, standard discount tables are available to translate that rate into multiplicative discount numbers to be used in the calculation.[21]

The same problems arise in determining the discount rate as with the costs and benefits. A project may easily appear either highly beneficial or costly, depending on the number of years that are included in discounting the values. Usually the practice is to continue the analysis for the number of years that the project requires capital financing. But consider, for example, a project that has among other effects a deleterious impact on the quality of the soil. Long-term consequences of soil loss are extremely costly; yet they may be only inadequately represented in the analysis because they are part of a very long-term process.

All of these estimates depend on the way in which projects are managed over time. Taking advantages of possibilities as discussed in Chapter 4 may increase the benefits over time. Conversely, if communication problems exist and information loss occurs, the costs of a project may increase. If rural health clinics are poorly operated, their investment potential may be lost. One implication is that organizational design and implementation considerations should be included in the cost-benefit analysis; similarly the implementers should have a part in the project design phase and in the determination of probable costs and benefits and their value over time.

Cost-Effectiveness

A brief mention can be made of a variation of cost-benefit analysis, cost-effectiveness, a somewhat simpler and often appropriate method of analysis. Cost-effectiveness is utilized whenever two different projects have the same benefits or the same costs. Thus only the differences in either benefits or costs are compared to determine which of the two projects is more cost-effective. The value is that the benefits and costs do not need to be translated into the same measures in order to compare them. For example, if there is a given sum to be spent on a project, the relative benefits of two different ways to spend that fixed sum are compared. Whichever project gives the most benefits, the more cost-effective it is determined to be.

The Uses of Cost-Benefit Analysis

In the above discussion we mention various problems that easily occur with the application of economic models to project design. Implicit in them are the weaknesses in rational maximizing models described in Chapter 4. It is erroneous to assume that we have all of the information we need to make a good decision. As Simon reminds us, satisficing is a more appropriate goal. If seen in this more modest light, cost-benefit analysis can still play a useful role to supplement and clarify other judgments. It can force analysts to be precise about their judgments and can improve the dialogue they have with other participants. The merits of these models are several. They address costs and therefore deal with competing uses of scarce resources. They can be used to examine the impacts of a project on an entire community and not just on the immediate beneficiaries. Finally, they are useful in monitoring redistribution and in determining who pays for and who benefits from such policies.

Economic analysis can provide information about the expected efficiency of capital invested in a project. But the most economically efficient project is not necessarily the most politically, or socially, efficient. Nor is it always the most effective or reliable investment to make. The political will and motivation that the project engenders is very important and can outweigh economic analysis. As was pointed out at the beginning of this chapter, if a national program can learn more from project X than from project Y, that fact must be considered in decision making. Local support for a project can also be more important than is reflected in economic analysis. As one observer comments, "In purely economic terms, it may make sense to accept a project in an area or sector which is not its highest priority, in preference to a project which has all the hallmarks of a good scheme by rural development criteria, but which will be neglected and finally fail for lack of recipient commitment."[22] For example, in a project to handle water problems in northeast Thailand, it is clear that large irrigation systems are more cost-effective than the alternative of farm ponds. However, the local government and villagers have a strong commitment to farm ponds, and thus these ponds are much more apt to be completed than are irrigation systems. Project design would therefore do well to include a "management estimate" as well as a calculation of economic return.

Managing Risk and Uncertainty

Thus far we have discussed ways of determining costs and benefits. Development, however, involves risk and uncertainty. And even if we can estimate the cost of a project, it is still fraught with many uncertainties. The problem is one of estimating how likely any of the projected costs or benefits are. One method of doing this is to develop a payoff table, which lists the likely results and the value of each. The table then can be used to estimate the probability with which each result is likely to occur. Several of the analytical devices outlined above, especially the logical framework, can be useful at this point in projecting these outcomes and their relative likelihood. For example, in a project to establish a system of rural health clinics, the following results are possible:

1. Many people (more than 65 percent) of the population will use the clinic during any one year.
2. Predominantly the wealthier population will use the clinic in any given year. (Poorer population will prefer traditional medicine or will feel intimidated by clinic staff.)
3. Some people will only use the clinics for chronic illness in the course of a year. These will include both wealthier and poorer.
4. Mostly poor people will use the clinics as wealthier population will seek services elsewhere.
5. Few people of any group will use the clinic in the course of a year.
6. No one will use the clinic.

Given these possible outcomes, the likelihood of each needs to be estimated, as well as the value each represents. The value and likelihood are then multiplied to give an expected value. These represent the possible payoffs of undertaking the project, as illustrated in Table 6.3.

The merits of this technique come in forcing planners to be explicit about the many possible outcomes. (One way in which it can be used, for example, is for estimating the likelihood of problems when the assumptions listed in the logical framework are not met.) The process of thinking out the table raises an awareness of potential problems and possibilities. Hirschman warns development administrators, for example, that we consistently underestimate the possibility of favorable outcomes just as we overestimate the possibility of unfavorable ones.[23]

Managing Implementation

Throughout the design process, the importance of management to the success of the project repeatedly surfaces as an issue. Good project management is the single most important variable affecting a project's outcome. Most design teams know this fact, but are much less sure of what to do about it. Because of its pivotal role in moving the project off

TABLE 6.3

Pay-Off Table Illustrating Value of Different Use Patterns

Event	Probability	Conditional Value	Expected Value
a	.5	+5	+2.5
b	.2	-3	-.6
c	.8	+3	+2.4
d	.6	+4	+2.4
e	.3	+2	.6
f	.1	-5	-.5

the drawing board and into effect, an implementation strategy should accompany every project design as part of the project documentation.

Management encompasses two elements — organizing tasks to accomplish a goal and motivating people to perform these tasks. It is especially easy to overlook the importance of this second factor and to be preoccupied by guidelines and tasks. Implementation, however, requires consummate skill in working with, and motivating, people; it involves patience, flexibility, and a shared sense of excitement about the nature of the work. As discussed in Chapter 5 controlling behavior frequently does not involve or motivate others. In fact there is evidence that controlling behavior, or an exclusive emphasis on production targets, can effectively cause people to disengage from their work. Managers therefore need to be concerned both with efficient organization and with motivations and feelings.

With these two principles in mind, the various aspects of the managerial task are to:

Identify recruitment and training processes; support for the project in the environment; and information gaps

Negotiate staff tasks and relationships; relationship of external supporters to staff; and conflict resolution procedures

Organize getting the project under way; communication processes; and processes for resolving bottlenecks

Supervise monitoring procedures, schedules, and budgets

Keep communication channels open

Learn from evaluation and feedback

We can pull these different activities into a single framework (see Table 6.4).[24] If design teams address these questions — the who, what, when, and how questions — a useful first step toward the rightful primacy of implementation might be taken. Space does not allow for a long discussion of each of the elements in this performance matrix; some of the concerns, however, warrant discussion.

TABLE 6.4

Project Implementation Strategy: Performance Framework

Key Tasks (what)	Responsibility (who and how)	Time Frame (when)
Identifying:		
what is recruitment process? what is training process? where is essential information? where is external support?	who is to be recruited? which authority adheres to each participating agency?	when must recruitment be completed? what is timing of support?
Negotiating:		
what will be assigned to whom? what tasks reside with project team? with outside agencies? what is process for reconciling differences?	who will constitute the project management team? how will the management team communicate with the national program? how will support be marshalled?	when must tasks be completed? when will contracts need to be renegotiated? when are external budget cycles?
Organizing:		
what is schedule for start up of project? what is strategy for maintaining project? what is the communication process? what is the budgetary process?	who will make initial start-up steps? who and how will momentum be maintained? how will budget guidelines be monitored?	what is the sequencing of initial tasks? what is the timetable for meetings, records due, budgets in?
Supervising:		
what is the monitoring process? what is the planning process? what is the evaluation process feedback?	who will work on the monitoring process? on evaluation processes? on planning processes?	what is timetable for major events? what is contingency timetable for mishaps?

Recruitment

Recruitment is more than gaining good workers; an organization "builds up an image of itself through the manner in which it recruits and selects its members."[25] For some positions, written tests can provide useful information; for others, interviews and references are important. First the criteria for the job need to be established. Is it necessary to have specific skills or can they be developed on the job? Are "capacities for growth and development" more important than skills? Whether a test is designed or interviews are held, questions need to address a worker's attitude toward the poor, concern for participation, and general flexibility. Role-playing questions, responses to films and audiovisuals may reveal some important characteristics. As an example, the Bangladesh Rural Advancement Committee (BRAC) has instituted a careful selection process; those people who pass an initial screening enroll in a "selection course," where they participate in exercises to develop communication and other skills.[26]

Identifying External Supports

Determining what support exists and what potential exists for future support is frequently termed *meta management*.[27] The system diagraming tools described earlier can help with such identification, giving specific attention to other organizations and how they relate to the project. What is the relation with the locally elected leaders, with banks and other private sector institutions, with other national agencies, with citizen representatives, and with donor agencies? (In Chapter 8 we consider ways to establish coordinating mechanisms among these groups.)

Getting the Project Under Way

Consider that the project management team involved with a network of rural clinics faces an emergency outbreak of an infectious disease. Different strategies are required to deal with this task than with the promotion of a nutrition education program. The management has to deal quickly with the delivery of large amounts of equipment and people to immunization centers, while others must be deployed to cope with the chronically ill. Speed and efficiency are essential, and motivation for short terms in these situations tends to be high, leveling off after the worst of the emergency has been brought under control. In the absence of an "emergency" (however serious the situation is), the motivation to respond might be lower. The combinations of inducements the manager can offer are therefore affected by the context and the nature of the task to be done. (The typology in Chapter 4 suggests one way to think about these different contexts and indicates relevant ways to tackle project design.)

Conflict Resolution

Conflicts are inevitable; a manager must anticipate the need for ways to resolve them. Rather than eliminating conflict, it is important to have procedures for handling it and perhaps using it as an opportunity for organizational development. If routines of appeal and negotiation are established, then conflicts are less apt to become personalized, and work can proceed during the appeals and negotiation. Routines, however, do not eliminate the pivotal role of management in guiding and controlling conflict. Are the participants in the conflict defensive and rigid or are they willing to accept conflict as legitimate? Mary Parker Follett has compiled a classic listing of guidelines.

1. Be open.
2. Search diligently for the significant rather than the dramatic features of controversy.
3. Take all demands and break them into their constituent parts.
4. Clarify all the issues and try to find ways to resolve the conflict that will allow all sides to achieve their significant desires.[28]

Establishing Communication Processes

Organizations designed around learning processes obviously have to take communication very seriously. Peter Drucker has consistently stressed the vital importance of communication within organizations, but he also reminds us that "more and better information does not solve the communications problem, does not bridge the communications gap. On the contrary, the more information the greater is the need for functioning and effective communication," in order not to be overcome by an explosion of information. He than adds that "there can be no communication if it is conceived as going from the 'I' to the 'Thou.' Communication works only from one member of 'us' to another."[29] We can think through the implications of these principles by considering different kinds of communication.

Downward Communication. According to Katz and Kahn downward communication covers five items:

1. Specific task directives: job instructions.
2. Information designed to produce understanding of the task and its relation to other organizational tasks: job rationale.

3. Information about organizational procedures and practices.
4. Feedback to the subordinate about his or her performance.
5. Information of an ideological character to inculcate a sense of mission: indoctrination of goals.[30]

The increasing emphasis on the interpersonal aspects of an organization means that special attention should be paid to numbers 2, 4, and 5. People need to be reminded of the purpose of their work and need feedback about their performance.

Upward Communication. Upward communication includes both information solicited by the management and information voluntarily supplied by the workers and clients. The latter may be complaints; they may also be innovative ideas. Frequently information does not flow upward very efficiently.[31] One reason is that it may be used as a way to control subordinates.[32] Analyses also confirm that most managers are poor listeners and that their receptivity is crucial in eliciting upward communication. "A feeble or small-minded top management, offended by any 'criticism' from within, is obviously unable to foster. . . habits of consultation, however much lip service it may pay the abstract principle. Helpful suggestions and new ideas will not come forth when they fail to find eager takers."[33]

Lateral Communication. A third form of information is that which occurs among people at the same level. It is increasingly being recognized as important for good coordination. Individuals can get support from others and may find it less threatening to share knowledge and to receive help in this manner. Managers therefore should be aware of and try to use these horizontal links.

Supervision

Managers seem to approach supervision from two extremes. Some are concerned about being too authoritarian and hence are wary of carrying out a leadership role. Others practice an authoritarian style and then are surprised at the resentment that such leadership can create. The problem is one of providing supervision that establishes clear guidelines, while allowing for negotiation and consultation.

Peter Blau and W. Richard Scott describe one way of combining these. The technique is to use general performance measures and monitoring procedures. They describe a case in which the key task was to keep written and public records of workers' performance. Records were designed to measure both the quality as well as the quantity of work. These performance records then enabled supervision to aid rather than punish when evaluating work. For example, if a person did poorly the records could be used by his supervisor to review problem areas. "In the absence of performance records, the supervisor would have to start the conference by first telling the interviewee that his performance was inadequate. The existence of public records made this opening superfluous and, consequently, transformed the supervisor's discussion from a criticism that was likely to be resented to an offer to help the subordinate improve his record."[34]

The perennial problem for supervision is establishing control while allowing for consultation. Blau and Scott suggest that in order to combine control and freedom a "flat" structure is preferable to a hierarchical one:

> A flat structure, by increasing the number of their subordinates, prevents superiors from supervising too closely and thereby alienating their subordinates. At the same time, this flat structure prevents them from leaning too heavily on their own superiors and thus losing their independence and the respect of their subordinates. Further it makes it less likely that superiors become over-involved with their subordinates, simply because there are so many of them, and consequently promotes detachment.[35]

Summary

A project design is not a blueprint; rather it is a process for gathering information, for formulating plans, specifying tasks, and for implementing them. It is also a process involving a variety of people: managers, field personnel, public representatives, national-level personnel. In implementing the design the manager faces a tension between maintaining some control and being open and flexible. In this chapter we suggest various tools and strategies that can provide some structure to the design and implementation process, but that also encourage flexibility and learning to occur. In large part, their success depends on the style and leadership capacity of the project manager and his or her ability to deal with the various components of the managerial task. Another aspect of effective management is the information system developed and the use of monitoring and evaluation. These concern us in Chapter 7.

Notes

1. Aaron Wildavsky, *Speaking Truth to Power: The Art and Craft of Policy Analysis* (Boston: Little, Brown, 1979); and Charles Lindblom and David Cohen, *Usable Knowledge* (New Haven, Conn.: Yale University Press, 1979).

2. James Rule, *Insight and Social Betterment* (New York: Oxford University Press, 1978).

3. Robert Chambers, *Managing Rural Development* (Uppsala: Scandinavian

Institute of African Studies, 1974), p. 14. See especially the documents in the appendix for some very useful suggestions regarding supervisory forms that Chambers used in Kenya's Special Rural Development Program. Later we discuss a performance framework that was inspired in part by Chapter 2 of his book.

4. J. Price Gittinger, *Economic Analysis of Agricultural Projects* (Boston and London: Johns Hopkins University Press, 1972). His emphasis on projects has found wide acceptance within the World Bank and is also taught by Dr. Gittinger in the Economic Development Institute at the Bank.

5. Fran Korten and David Korten made this point at a series of seminars held on July 1–3, 1980, at the U.S. Agency for International Development, in which they reported on some of their Philippine experience.

6. The World Bank is considering adopting more program lending to supplement its project lending.

7. Donald Mickelwait, Charles F. Sweet, and Elliot R. Morss, *New Directions in Development: A Study of U.S. AID* (Boulder, Colo.: Westview Press, 1979), p. 153.

8. For a comparison of blueprint and process approaches, see David Korten, "Community Organization in Rural Development," *Public Administration Review* 40 (Sept.-Oct. 1980):480–511.

9. For a discussion of the problems of designing participatory projects within a donor development-assistance agency, see Coralie Bryant, "Organizational Impediments to making Participation a Reality: Swimming Upstream in AID," *Rural Development Participation Review* I (1980).

10. For a more detailed discussion of the possibilities in organizing participatory projects, see Coralie Bryant and Louise G. White, *Managing Rural Development: Peasant Participation in Development Projects* (Hartford, Conn.: Kumarian Press, 1980).

11. Peter Delp, Arne Thesen, Juzar Motiwalla, and Neelakantan Seshadri, *Systems Tools for Project Planning* (Bloomington, Ind.: PASITAM, 1977).

12. Jay Forrester, *System Dynamics* (Cambridge, Mass.: MIT Press, 1968); Geoffrey Gordon, *System Simulation* (Englewood Cliffs, N.J.: Prentice-Hall, 1969).

13. As this approach is also the first step in modeling, it is used by some prior to undertaking their regression analysis. Many statistics textbooks can be used to assist the reader in this respect; one of these is George W. Snedecor and William G. Cochran's *Statistical Methods* (Ames: Iowa State University Press, 1968). For an example of an application of this approach to rural to urban migration, see Lorene Yap, *International Migration in Less Developed Countries: A Survey of the Literature* (Washington, D.C.: International Bank for Reconstruction and Development, Staff Working Paper no. 215, 1975).

14. Delp, Thesen, Motiwalla, and Seshadri, *Systems Tools,* p. 83.

15. Uma Lele, *The Design of Rural Development* (Washington, D.C.: Johns Hopkins Press, 1975), p. 148.

16. See Edgar H. Schein, *Organizational Psychology,* 2d. ed. (Englewood Cliffs, N.J.: Prentice-Hall, 1970). One of the major sources in the organizational development field is Christopher Argyris's *Integrating the Individual and the Organization* (New York: John Wiley, 1964).

17. See *Evaluation Handbook*, 2d ed. (Washington, D.C., Agency for International Development, 1975).

18. Much of this section is drawn from Gittinger, *Economic Analysis of Agricultural Projects.*

19. A good source book on survey techniques is Donald P. Warwick and Charles A. Lininger, *The Sample Survey: Theory and Practice* (New York: McGraw-Hill, 1975). A good source on other measurements that can be added to those of the survey is E. J. Webb, D. T. Campbell, R. D. Schwartz, and I. Sechrest, *Unobtrusive Measures: Nonreactive Research in the Social Sciences* (Chicago: Rand McNally, 1971).

20. Ibid., p. 52.

21. One particularly valuable source is *Compounding and Discounting Tables for Project Evaluation,* edited by J. P. Gittinger and published by the World Bank (1972); the tables were compiled with project analysis in mind.

22. Richard Heaver, "The Politics of Implementation: Management and Motivation for Rural Development," mimeographed (1980), p. 56.

23. Albert O. Hirschman, *Development Projects Observed* (Washington, D.C.: Brookings Institution, 1967).

24. Part of this performance matrix was inspired by Robert Chambers, *Managing Rural Development,* Chapter 2, and by comments made by Marcus Ingle on Richard Heaver's paper, *The Politics of Implementation.* See also Marcus Ingle, *Implementation: The State of the Art* (Washington, D.C.: Agency for International Development, Office of Rural Development and Administration, 1979).

25. Schein, *Organizational Psychology,* p. 29.

26. Korten, "Community Organization."

27. John C. Ickis, "The Management of Rural Development in Central America: Structural Responses to New Strategies," Instituto Centroamericano de Administracion de Empresas (INCAE) Occasional Study (Managua, 1978).

28. Henry Metcalf and Lyndall Urwick, eds., *Dynamic Administration: The Collected Works of Mary Parker Follett* (New York: Harper and Row, 1940), pp. 38–45.

29. Peter Drucker, *Management* (New York: Harper and Row, 1973), pp. 481, 491.

30. Daniel Katz and Robert Kahn, *The Social Psychology of Organizations,* 2d ed. (New York: John Wiley, 1978), pp. 440–443.

31. Anthony Downs, *Inside Bureaucracy* (Boston: Little, Brown, 1966), pp. 112–131.

32. See discussion in Harold Gortner, *Administration in the Public Sector* (New York: John Wiley, 1977), pp. 168–192.

33. Fritz M. Marx and Henry Reining, Jr., "The Tasks of Middle Management," in *Elements of Public Administration,* ed. F. M. Marx (Englewood Cliffs, N.J.: Prentice-Hall, 1959), pp. 378–379.

34. Peter Blau and W. Richard Scott, *Formal Organizations* (San Francisco: Chandler, 1962), pp. 176–179.

35. Ibid., p. 238.

7

Data Collection, Monitoring, and Evaluation

Introduction

Development is in many respects an empirical issue. It involves very specific and down-to-earth questions such as how much people have to eat, how much food is produced, what basic needs have been met. All of these questions require the collection of data, the handling and absorption of information about people, their situations, and their environments. This data gathering can be a liberating process. Asking farmers about problems or mothers about health needs can raise the consciousness of administrators. The process may help them to be more perceptive and effective. Sending field agents to survey the perceptions of landless peasants puts them in touch with a previously unrecognized sector of the community.

The process of collecting and using information is central to the purposes of an organization. Systems theory emphasizes the ways in which organizations learn from their environments in order to adjust over time to new problems and demands. And the greater the uncertainty the more organizations need to learn and adapt. The central component in this learning process is establishing an information process that *collects* and uses data in the initial project design stage, *monitors* processes and outcomes to provide feedback, and finally *evaluates* what has occurred. The form that the process takes will vary with the particular task of each project. Sometimes there is a need to gather information on the appropriate goals, other times on the best means to achieve these goals. These tasks may require taking surveys, or they may involve more or less interactive processes; the procedures emerge out of the particular nature of each project.

The information system is thus integral to the work of any project or-

135

ganization. Because it involves special skills, administrators may be tempted to create special task forces or turn to external groups. The design of data procedures, however, is an administrative rather than a technical problem and should be closely integrated into the management process. A learning approach to organizations and a process approach to project design mean that the data need constantly to inform and reshape the project itself, as well as the perceptions and attitudes of those people administering it. The problem is that most organizations are not structured either to gather or to use information effectively. One management task then is to insure that the data are relevant to those who will *use* it, rather than selected by what is technically feasible. Besides the project leadership, users may include social or participants' organizations, regional and national sponsors, political leaders, and donors. The information also needs to be *integrated* into the procedures of the local organization and any sponsoring agencies. Or in the words used in Chapter 4, the administrative task is to "fit" together the kind of information used in a program or project, the way in which decisions are made, and the tasks that its members perform.

General administrators, rather than technical experts, should take charge of designing data gathering activities. Collecting usable, appropriate, and relevant data involves *judgment* as well as technical skill. Researchers will always want to collect more data than managers do, and their respective interests will have to be negotiated.[1] The most rigorous methods will not always be appropriate, and trade-offs will frequently have to be made between formal procedures and those that allow the organization to learn and change most effectively. How much time and resources are available, on the one hand, affect how sophisticated the data will be, on the other. Given scarce resources there will always have to be trade-offs. These trade-offs create both a management problem and a political issue. In order to involve the local community in the process, simple procedures may be in order. Satisfying the requirements of donor groups or coping with political opposition may require more elaborate procedures. One study suggests that the competing demands for data may indicate that a hierarchy of users needs to be established, with project level needs coming first and the interests of national agencies second.[2] As discussed in Chapter 6, however, not all would agree. The Kortens, for example, suggest the reverse, that the primary users are those at the national levels where the information can influence the overall program. In any case, deciding on which users have priority is an important administrative decision and needs to be made at the management level.

A judgment about the purposes of information will suggest how sophisticated the data process should be. It is tempting to design elaborate methods, which in the end may reveal more than is necessary and waste valuable time and resources. Even more troublesome, such techniques multiply the complexity of a project and may only be useful to experts and not to project participants. Robert Chambers refers to the common tendency for collecting "mounds of unused data," echoing the concern of Herbert Simon that we function with "bounded rationality." The time spent in information gathering is a "scarce resource, and in complex situations activities should be optimal not maximal. It requires experience and imagination to know what is not worth knowing, and self-discipline and courage to abstain from trying to find it out."[3] A project design might, for example, require collecting only data that are specific to those problems the project identifies, excluding a lot of demographic information on population characteristics. Conversely, a project evaluation might want to include demographic data in order to determine how broadly project benefits have been distributed.[4]

This chapter is based on a highly pragmatic assumption — information systems should vary with the circumstances. We lay out various alternatives, introduce the logic behind each, and compare the trade-offs among them.[5] Our descriptions will not create data experts, but should suggest to administrators some of the possibilities they can explore. Their choices will vary with the nature of the task, the funds available, the extent to which a project is controversial or apt to be replicated, and the capacity of those involved in implementing it. In many cases, those choices will require further study of quantitative techniques; thus the following description in intended to lay out possibilities and suggest when each is relevant.

Deciding What Kinds of Questions to Examine

There are two questions of relevance to development administrators. One concerns information about the community and the impact of a project on that community; the second concerns information about the political and administrative processes. More precisely these questions are two aspects of a single issue, since the nature of the process will influence the impact of the project.

An emphasis on impacts is fairly recent in public administration. During the 1960s observers noted that many well-intentioned policies were not having the intended results. For example, it was evident that many development policies were actually increasing inequality in a community. Administrators therefore needed to look at the results of their activities, at the *output, impact,* and *outcome* of what they do.

Output is the amount produced or the resources expended. How many packets of seeds were supplied, or how many nurses were trained? These data are the simplest kind of information to acquire; often records are automatically kept or expenditure data can be used.

Impact analysis asks what immediate results these outputs have. The seed may or may not have been used; the nurses may or may not have been placed in communities where they were needed. Again it may be possible to use existing records to learn this, or one can simply ask people what happened.

Outcomes and consequences are a more long-range estimate of what difference was made by the output. What happened to farm production and the income of the community over time? Was infant mortality or malnutrition reduced by virtue of having more nurses?

Applying these to the data needs of a project to increase farm production, data can be collected about the *output,* the number of farmers visited; the *impact,* the number of farmers who adopted new methods; the *outcome,* the actual changes in production and in the welfare of the farming community. The design of the information system or evaluation would begin by deciding which level to focus on or whether all three were relevant to the concerns of the project.

Such attention to the results of a policy is only part of the story; it is also essential to examine the process of designing and implementing policy. This concern deals with such questions as how the policy was made, whether the beneficiaries were included in the process, and whether the learning achieved is institutionalized in the continuing processes of the organization. An example may be useful. Administrators of a project in the Philippines were having difficulty including members of the local community in the project implementation. The problem was that the local people wanted to work part-time with flexible hours, while the project administration was using complicated personnel procedures designed for full-time civil servants. Clearly, the administrative procedures needed to be changed to accommodate the needs and interests and availability of those in the area.[6] A useful evaluation process would collect data on these kinds of practices as well as on the actual outcome of the project.

Both impact and process questions are implicit in the definition of development described above. Because development includes a concern with equity, it matters what physical goods are produced and who receives them. Since development also includes a concern with peoples' capacity for increasing their ability to determine their own future, it also matters whether the organization has developed the kinds of structures that facilitate its work and its processes. Briefly, any data collection should cover the following questions:[7]

1. Why are the data needed, and how do they fit into the overall design?
2. What kind of information is wanted at the end of this process?
3. What approach is desirable, and what level of quality is necessary?
4. How should the data be gathered?
5. Who will use the data, and in what form do they need the data?
6. What skills are necessary to gather and analyze the data?
7. When are the data needed?
8. How should the data be reported?

Approaches to Acquiring Data

Using Existing Records

Often data collected for other purposes can be used for a project. Examples include records of births, deaths, weather conditions, marketing information, bank records on loans, zoning applications, government budgets, clinical records on patients, media reports. It is an understatement to say that projects never make sufficient use of already existing information; partly this neglect is because it often requires considerable imagination to find out what exists and where to get it.

The two major criteria in using such data are whether the data are accurate and whether or not they are reasonably objective; data collected for political or public relations reasons or collected carelessly should probably not be used. A recent study of housing needs and resources in Swaziland made an effective use of existing government documents, budget figures, consultant reports, wage and employment data, land use records, and water and sewage data.[8] Caution is sometimes indicated. The Danfa project in Ghana wanted to use census data on births and deaths; in order to check data accuracy, project administrators recruited volunteers in local villages to keep their own records. On the basis of an independent estimate, however, they found out that the census had a success rate of only 60 percent, and the village volunteers a success rate of 47 percent. The project directors changed their system and used full-time salaried registrars, significantly improving the accuracy of the information.[9]

Surveys

Often the most appropriate way to gather information is simply to ask people what happened or how they feel about a project. Surveys can be used to gather descriptive information about people—the number of children, their health problems, their use of public facilities, where they get their water, the conditions of their housing, the skills they possess. Surveys are also useful to find out attitudes and opinions, whether people feel that field agents are helpful, how they feel about family planning, with which specific needs they most want help. Because surveys use a previously determined set of questions and sometimes require people to select among specific answers, they are useful to establish profiles and compare large numbers of people. They can compare the living conditions and attitudes of different groups—landless with small landowners, migrants with those who remain in rural villages—and can describe a total population in terms of a few important characteristics.[10] (For more details see below.)

Interviewing

Whereas surveys usually limit the possible answers that can be given, interviews can be open-ended and allow people to state their own experiences and feelings and to put their answers into their own words. Anthropologists prefer this approach because interviews can do justice to the varieties of behavior, to their context, and their meaning. Two farmers may each reject the adoption of a new kind of fertilizer, but they may do so for very different reasons; it may be crucial to future efforts to know these reasons. Interviews can also elicit information about the problems that people encounter and about the various ways people are involved in trying to deal with them. In fact, much of the information used for the social profiles described in Chapter 6 could only be gained in this manner.[11]

Direct Observation

Attitudes do not always indicate how people will actually behave; where possible it is often preferable to observe them.[12] Examples include sitting in a market and noting what people purchase and at what prices, or *observing* the kind of maintenance being done on a local irrigation system, or the ways in which people build their huts and organize to put on roofs. Health specialists in Ghana provide an imaginative example of the value of direct observation. They became suspicious that polio was a common occurrence in rural villages even though it was almost never reported. They asked teachers to provide a list of any children who limped. Not satisfied with the results, they had the school-age children simply walk by them and found that many more limped than the teachers had reported. Neurological tests indicated a high incidence of polio among those who were observed limping, and as a result, polio vaccine was included as part of the routine health care.[13]

Multiple Methods

Most projects combine several of these sources. For example, interviews and direct observation may be used initially to develop a profile of a community and several hypotheses about the reasons for any problems that exist there. Then a broader survey might be used to determine how general the problem is and what resources exist to deal with it. Finally, existing documents might be checked to review past activity in this area and what commitments have already been made. Or records might be used to determine how many farmers have been visited (output), a survey might be made to determine if the visits were effective (impact), and direct observation might be used to see what eventual results these had on the agricultural production (outcome). To take one more example, changes in crops could be studied by surveying farmers and by looking at marketing data in the area, by open-ended interviews in a few cases to consider special problems, and by direct observation of the harvest on randomly chosen plots.[14]

The Special Problem of Sampling

In countries where the public sector has very inadequate or rudimentary collections of information, surveys of existing conditions can be particularly enlightening. They are particularly helpful when there are broad segments of the population that might be largely invisible. Chambers reminds us of the many invisible poor who live in remote areas; their invisibility only increases during the rainy season when their needs may actually be the greatest.[15] Another study confirms that women are often invisible also; agriculture agents, for example, are more apt to pass by farms owned by women.[16]

Sampling the population is one way to acquire basic information about all members in a community. Samples vary by their size and randomness; the larger and more random they are, the more accurate they will be. It is intuitively easy to see that the larger the number of people included in the sample, the more apt it is to reflect the nature of the larger population. Randomness means that every member of the population has an equal chance of being included, thus maximizing the chance that the sample will represent all segments. Randomness is hard to achieve however; if you select the first ten farmers you meet at random, you are not likely to meet those who remain at home. A truly random sample would begin with a list of everyone, from which names are picked at random, but such lists almost never exist.

The two most commonly used sampling procedures are a "stratified random sample" and a "cluster sample." The first divides the population into groups such as men and women, or farmers, tenants, and landless.

A random sample is then drawn from each group. A cluster sample is based on geographic areas rather than on groups of individuals — a group of huts within a village or an areal division within a squatter settlement. Once the clusters are specified, several are selected at random, and finally a sample of residents within each of these clusters is chosen randomly. The following case illustrates one imaginative way to deal with the sampling problem and carry out a survey.

A Case Study: Sampling and Interviewing
in a Squatter Settlement

The task assigned to the researchers was to survey migrants in Gaborone, Botswana. They wanted to be able to generalize their findings to all of the migrants in Gaborone and to make distinctions among different income groups. The logical way to study different income groups was to stratify by income. There were no listings of people either in toto or by income. The team therefore decided to stratify the city's population by housing types, on which they could get information, on the assumption that the type of housing a person lives in reflects his or her income group. Then within each stratum they would identify clusters of houses and sample among these.

A problem arose, however, in drawing a sample for Old Naledi, a large squatter settlement on the edge of the city that had mushroomed in the past few years as an unauthorized settlement. No one was sure how many lived there; in fact, very little at all was known about the area. There were no street maps, no hut numbers, and no estimates of the total population. Council members and administrators alike tried to pretend the settlement did not exist. With persistence the team found some aerial photographs from the lands and surveys branch of the government. Fortunately they had been taken from a low enough altitude so that most of the self-built huts were discernible.

First the aerial photographs, which served as maps, needed verifying. So members of the team used them to walk through the labyrinthian pathways of the settlement, noting their congruence with the map. Working off a room-sized blowup of the map, they divided the area into clusters of huts and gave each cluster a number. These numbers in turn were used along with a table of random numbers to select the actual sample.

The next problem was to locate those people chosen to be interviewed, a difficult task because of the absence of street names or hut numbers. The team used their ingenuity to agree on the names of pathways and gradually laid out the geography of the area. Interviewers on bicycles soon became accustomed with the newly named pathways, and the need for bicycle repair kits emerged as the next logistical problem. Student interviewers had originally been reluctant to get involved in this aspect of the survey; but what initially appeared as insurmountable or at least uncomfortable was found to be difficult, but "doable." Stereotypes were replaced with information and some new data were collected about the reasons for migration and the current conditions of the migrants. This information was then combined with surveys of other strata, or income groups, to provide a picture of the entire city.[17]

Deciding What to Measure

Indicators or Operational Definitions

Choosing any or several of the above approaches to data collection is closely tied to the nature of the data you want to collect. Deciding what to measure is not as obvious as it might appear. A project might be designed to increase the welfare of a community, to improve the health in the region, or to increase crop production. None of these can be directly observed, and the problem then is to find *indicators* of each. The technical term is to make the goal of a project, or the issue you are investigating, *operational*. This means that you define an issue in terms of the operations that can measure it. For example, an operational definition of a person's wealth is the salary he or she receives or the amount of money he or she accrued from crops last year, plus all other assets, such as land.

Trade-offs in Selecting Indicators

Several examples will illustrate problems that can arise in deciding on indicators and possibilities in getting around them.[18]

Income. As mentioned above, income can be measured by payments received. But it must include the value of any goods a farmer produces for personal use, and this requires a procedure for evaluating monetary value.[19]

Nutrition. Nutrition can be measured by counting caloric intake. Since people have different needs, however, it is hard to specify what is adequate nutrition. Another approach, therefore, is to measure not what people consume, but what results that consumption has. For example, measurements of the upper arm or records of illness can both be used as indicators of nutrition.

Health. A third example is finding data on a person's health. Obvious measures include birth and death rates, life expectancy figures, infant mortality. These measures, however, reflect a very long time horizon and do not tell us much about the immediate results of a single project. A more immediate indicator is access to health services, rather than health itself.

Multiple Indicators

Indicators need to be *valid*—they must measure what you want them to. Indicators must also be *reliable*—if someone else does the measuring, he/she should produce the same result. In almost all cases it is desirable to select multiple indicators; these will correct any validity or reliability problems that single measures may have. Being close to the situation and knowledgeable about it and having imagination are often the keys to establishing useful indicators. Consider the following examples:[20]

Credit. In order to determine how successful a project has been in increasing the availability of credit in a region, the following indicators have been proposed:

- increase in field staff,
- number of rural banks established,
- number and value of import and distribution loans, and
- number of loan applications received, processed, approved.

Land Reform. Indicators of land reform can include:

- number of titles registered,
- percentage of farmers on their own land,
- necessary legislation passed,
- average size of landholding, and
- number of hectares aerially photographed.

Institutional Capacity. Measures of a government's capacity for handling development problems are

- time in existence,
- professional status recognized,
- technical competence proved,
- survival capacity demonstrated,
- ability to attract financial resources shown,
- capacity to innovate demonstrated,
- linkages established with community groups, and
- services being used in community.

Although the indicators listed under credit and land reform can actually be measured, the indicators of institutional capacity have to be further specified. For example, "linkages established with community groups" can be measured by numbers of personnel involved, by number of meetings held, by impressions of those meetings, and so forth.

The choice of indicators can have an interesting effect on the implementation of the project. If lower-level personnel know that data are being collected on a specific output, they have an increased incentive to work on that. For example, in Thailand, evaluators were trying to measure the impact of a project on community development. They selected a proxy measure of the number of co-op stores that were opened in the area. This measure subsequently influenced the work of the local staff, who now had a special incentive to establish co-ops.[21]

Monitoring

It is important to distinguish monitoring from actual evaluation studies. Monitoring involves the collection of information about the project while it is in progress. The emphasis is on continual feedback about the ways in which resources are used and the manner in which implementation is being conducted. These data are constantly fed back to those people involved in the project so that immediate changes and adjustments can be made. For example in the Danfa rural health project in Ghana, records of those who used a new health center indicated that 70 percent lived within three miles of the center. The project staff quickly decided to set up satellite centers in order to reach a wider group.[22] Feedback can either consist of formal reports and memorandums to all staff, or it can be more informal. The BRAC project in Bangladesh follows a fairly informal process; it holds regular staff meetings to share observations about what works and what does not. According to one observer, part of the strength of this approach is that it makes use of all the information possessed by regular staff rather than of only that fed into a formal report.[23]

One other informal process is worth describing more fully because it is so often overlooked. It is variously called "storytelling" or "process documentation" and uses observation methods to describe the actual process of carrying out a project. The director of an irrigation project in the Philippines reported that when she arrived and needed to catch up on what had been done, the most useful information she found was anecdotes or personal accounts of the project. They described the actual problems and conflicts that had occurred and the anxieties that people faced. Because these accounts proved so useful, the project management adopted a new research strategy that they call process documentation. It is based on monthly reports that "tell the story" of what has been occurring.[24] In addition to quickly zeroing in on problems, such an approach can document success stories by providing a rich narrative in such a way that others can learn from it and then be more fully equipped to devise their own project. Used in this manner, to facilitate replication, process documentation also becomes a form of evaluation.[25]

The monitoring process also is necessary to examine the management system and specifically the kinds of incentives that exist for managers and other project members to carry out their work. Do the incentives encourage them to facilitate the goals of the project? The researcher needs to get information about the pressures the administrators face and which pressures provide the most incentive for them. The most appropriate approach is usually informal interviews. According to one source, "The need is for open-ended rather than predisposing questions, e.g., 'What do you see as the chief problem in this area?' rather than 'What have you done to improve extension water management in this area?' Perception, priorities and pressures tend to emerge rather clearly if the evaluator does not betray his interest in getting a particular type of response, and does not impose his own a priori perceptions of the project on the interviewee."[26] Other questions can cover how various officials spend their time, what pressures they feel, what aspects of their tasks are most difficult to accomplish.

Evaluation

Evaluation is an effort both to document *what* happened and to determine *why* it happened. Ideally a project will be designed to determine these causes and effects, and therefore thinking ahead about evaluation is an integral aspect of the original design. As described in Chapter 6, any program or project design is essentially an hypothesis. It represents a "hunch" or good guess that the program will actually bring about the desired goal. Implicitly, it hypothesizes that there is a relation or a connection between the project and a certain outcome.

By this reasoning, evaluation is an effort to find out if these connections do in fact exist. The simplest evaluation collects before and after information; for example, data on crop yields can be collected before and after a fertilizer demonstration. It is not enough, however, to know if farm production has increased; the point is to find out if the specific fertilizer project brought about the increase. Perhaps it is due not to the program to increase the use of fertilizer, but to changes in the weather conditions, to the influence of neighboring farmers, or to a new credit program. Considering all of these other possible factors, the question then is, How significant was the fertilizer project in increasing crops? Thus evaluation not only needs to determine the results of a project, but also to demonstrate that these other factors were not responsible; in other words it needs to control for alternative explanations.[27]

Attention to cause and effect questions is particularly important in rural development projects that are trying several interventions at the same time. Analyses of the evaluation component in the PIDER project (Programa de Inversiones para el Desarrollo Rural) in Mexico came to this conclusion. Its original research questions were too general and did not focus on finding relations between specific variables of relevance and management decisions. One conclusion was that "definitions for a restricted list of key independent variables should have been worked out and their relationships tested."[28]

Evaluation with Controls—Experimental Design

The best way to separate the effects of a project from those of other factors is to select two or more groups or communities that are similar in most respects—socioeconomic level, soil conditions, or whatever factors might influence the results. Selecting similar groups means that all of these other factors are experimentally controlled; since they are present in both, they cannot cause any differences that might occur. Therefore, if changes occur only in the community where the project is located, it can be assumed that the project probably caused them.

The logic and some of the pitfalls of experimental design are illustrated by the Danfa rural health project in Ghana. The basic hypothesis being tested in this case was that the best way to reduce the birthrate was to improve health care for children and mothers through health services, nutrition, and education. The program was designed to provide variations of health services in four similar areas: the control area where nothing was done, one with only family planning, one with an educational campaign about health, and one where actual health services were provided. The logic was to compare birthrates in each community before and after each program was established and to use these results to determine which was most effective.

The design, however, failed to anticipate implementation problems. As it happened, workers carried out an extensive information campaign about birth control in the control area, and so it could not be used in the evaluation. Then in the middle of the project, it was decided to combine family planning and health services in all of the areas. The administrators in effect rejected the original design because they felt that too much data would have to be collected and that it was too complex for the existing situation.[29] It would be very misleading to suggest that experimental designs are never relevant; the point here is only that any evaluation design needs to grow out of the context of the specific project or program being studied.

Quasi-Experiments

Most efforts to evaluate development projects have devised less rigorous models. Since they do not include controls in the same manner, they are called "quasi-experiments." Two examples are cited below.

Time Series. Here evaluators try to collect data for several periods before and after a project, instead of only immediately before and after. If fertility had been increasing in three prior observations, then declined after a family planning project and remained lower over time, there is evidence that the project made a difference.

Control Series. Sometimes it is too difficult to find two similar areas in order to control for other factors; it may be satisfactory then to compare several areas that are not the same, one of which received the project.

Example of a Quasi-Experimental Design. The Upper Volta Women's Project is an effort to promote small enterprises in villages. One of the enterprises it encourages is a grain-milling business owned and run by women's groups. The project has been designed to determine under what conditions such a business is most apt to succeed. Two hypotheses were suggested. One was that year-round access to water might be important; the second was that the presence of a cash crop in the community would help to get the grain-milling project off the ground. To test the importance of these two factors, project members are establishing a grain-milling business in three types of communities: one where both water and a cash crop are lacking; one where both are present; and one where there is water, but no cash crop. The project is still under way.[30]

Several recent studies of the development process recommend evaluation methods that are essentially quasi-experiments. One of the studies concludes that even when the evaluation falls short of being a quasi-experiment, or of explaining exactly why the result occurred, learning can still take place. "Given the urgency of the problems confronting small farmers in many of these project situations, identification of techniques that work may justify full-scale application even if the reasons that they do are not fully understood. For example, a great deal can be learned in a post hoc analysis of a 'treated' population by investigating why some small farmers adopted a particular intervention and others did not." The authors of this study make an additional and very significant point. They note that a less formal process approach to evaluation is often much more suited to the abilities of local participants than formal evaluations. Thus it may equip communities to practice their own "exploratory testing and adaptive research" instead of requiring social scientists.[31]

Criteria for Evaluation

The most frequently used criteria for judging a project positively or negatively are to determine how closely it accomplishes the original goals of the project and whether it does so in an efficient manner. Obviously it makes sense to be concerned with efficiency and whether the resources of a project are better used in one place than in another. It is also true that efficiency is often used as a criterion because of external pressure from political leaders or donors and because economic measures are often the easiest kind of information to acquire. The cost-effective use of resources is a crucial aspect of any evaluation, but for several reasons efficiency needs to be supplemented with other concerns.

First, consider some of the problems with the norm of efficiency. A study of the Lilongwe Rural Development Project in Malawi emphasizes that like many such projects this program specified efficiency criteria from the outset. In project documents it is stipulated, "We must make sure that when money becomes available: (a) it is spent on the best and most rewarding development programs; (b) the particular program is executed in the most efficient way." One observer of the program has argued that these two aims may in fact be contradictory; "best" and "most rewarding" are not necessarily "most efficient." As an example he describes the use of ditchdigging machines in the program. The machines were incredibly efficient in the sense that a great quantity of ditches were dug quickly and inexpensively. He continues, however, by challenging this definition of efficiency, suggesting that it might have been more efficient if the local people had built the roads and ditches themselves. This tactic would have given them a cash income, it would have included them in assuming maintenance of the ditches, "and more importantly still, it would have given them an essential sense of participation in and identification with the activities of the Program."[32]

Judith Tendler confirms that labor-intensive programs may well be more efficient in the long run. She also indicates that efficiency criteria often have strong political backing. To continue the example of capital-intensive road building projects, she notes, "The results of the past neglect of labor-intensive techniques still exert a strong influence today: equipment lasts many years, a contracting industry has grown up around this type of business, many engineers have been trained in these techniques, and donors still finance many equipment-purchasing or equipment-intensive construction projects."[33]

Efficiency criteria will continue to be both useful and politically necessary; however, it is possible to supplement them with others such as the following:

1. The extent to which a project develops *institutions* that will be able to organize and maintain the new services over time.
2. Its effectiveness in reaching specific *target groups.*[34]
3. The amount of *behavioral change* that occurs. Do the farmers adopt the new technology, or do they agree to adjust their traditional practices?
4. Whether the organization has *learned from* the project experience and altered its decision processes to fit with the development task.
5. Whether the project succeeds in *mobilizing the public* and expanding their awareness of their capacities.[35]

Constraints on Evaluation

In spite of all the attention given to evaluation, organizations do not necessarily welcome or facilitate it and will often downplay or fail to use the information that monitoring and evaluation produce. One review of evaluations of development projects funded by the World Bank found that in 1977 only one-third had detailed costing and less than 20 percent had staff specifically for evaluation. And even these projects usually failed to think through the evaluation process systematically or determine what its uses would be.[36]

The reasons for the neglect of evaluation can be traced back to some of the issues raised in Chapters 3 and 4. Evaluations are one way to enable organizations to function more effectively and to choose projects on the basis of their success in meeting their goals. But because organizations have other purposes in addition to accomplishing their goals, evaluation studies can create tensions. We can define four kinds of constraints.[37]

1. *Psychological.* Evaluations can be threatening. They are easily seen as means of criticizing or gaining power over others. This fact alone is one reason for having the monitoring and evaluation system part of the overall project design, approved by the project management. Otherwise a manager will probably remain unaware of what evaluation can do for him and how it can serve his purposes.

2. *Economic.* Good evaluation is costly in terms of time and money, and "more data" are not always worth the cost.

3. *Technical.* Data handling often requires trained staff and data processing capacity. Time is a factor; information that cannot be available when it is needed is wasted. Finally, managers can only absorb and use so much information; if a study does not serve their immediate interests, it may well be consigned to a dusty shelf.

4. *Political.* Results may not only be threatening to administrators, they may also be politically embarrassing. Rights to the data and restric-

tions on data use need to be carefully outlined. Beyond this, administrators may find it helpful to adopt a different approach to "their" projects. Rather than identifying themselves with any specific policy or project design, they would be more willing to incorporate evaluation if they were to take a problem-oriented focus. Evaluation then is conceived as part of an ongoing learning process rather than a threat.[38]

Conclusions

Development by definition requires that projects be closely tied to the needs and resources in any given area; therefore collecting data about the area and evaluating the impact of the project are central to the entire process of administering development. Data have a way of breaking us out of stereotypes, of putting us in touch with new possibilities, of suddenly revealing to us errors in the original design. A learning model of organizations in fact centers on the production and use of information. Much of the actual implementation of data collection and evaluation is done by experts, but it is crucial for managers to understand the potential of data analysis as well as the problems that can occur. Then they are most apt to design an information system that is both creative and relevant to the purposes of the project and to the needs of the organization.

Notes

1. Uma Lele, *The Design of Rural Development Projects: Lessons from Africa* (Baltimore: Johns Hopkins, 1975), p. 147.

2. Guido Deboeck and Bill Kinsey, *Managing Information for Rural Development: Lessons from Eastern Africa,* World Bank Staff Working Paper no. 379. (Washington, D.C.: World Bank, 1980), p. 7.

3. Robert Chambers, *Managing Rural Development* (Uppsala: Scandinavia Institute of African Studies, 1974), p. 153. At the Workshop on Rapid Rural Appraisal, Institute of Development Studies, Sussex, England, October 1978, the following papers were presented exploring efforts to make data collection as simple as possible: D.G.R. Belshaw, "Village Viability Assessment Procedures in Tanzania"; George Honadle, "Rapid Reconnaissance Approaches"; and Robert Chambers, "Shortcut Methods in Information Gathering for Rural Development Projects."

4. A project that emphasized a limited amount of data was the Indonesian Family Planning Project. James Heiby, Gayl Ness, Barbara Pillsbury, "AID's Role in Indonesian Family Planning" (Washington, D.C.: AID, July 1979). A project that designed a broader data base, but that took care not to overload its system, was the Tanzanian Village Development Project. U.S. AID Tanzania,

Tanzania: Village Development Project, Project Number: 621-0143 (Washington, D.C.: AID, September 1977).

5. A variety of studies cover data collection for development projects; the following were used as background for this chapter: Glynn Cochrane, Molly Hageboeck, Gerald Hursh-Cesar, "Information and Decision-Making," mimeographed (Washington, D.C.: Practical Concepts, n.d.); and Samuel Daines, *An Overview of Economic and Data Analysis Techniques for Project Design and Evaluation* (Washington, D.C.: AID, 1977).

6. We are grateful to Fran Korten for calling this situation to our attention.

7. This listing is adapted from Cochrane, "Information and Decision-Making," Chapter 2.

8. Rivkin Associates, *Swaziland Shelter Sector Assessment* (Washington, D.C.: Rivkin Associates, August 1978), Chapter 3.

9. Gene B. Peterson, *A Case Study of the Danfa Comprehensive Rural Health and Family Planning Project, Ghana* (Washington, D.C.: AID, June 1978), pp. 61-69.

10. Michael Cernea and Benjamin Tepping, *A System for Monitoring and Evaluating Agricultural Extension Projects* (Washington, D.C.: World Bank Staff Working Paper no. 272), Chapter 6. Deborah Freedman and Eva Mueller, *A Multi-Purpose Household Questionnaire* (Washington, D.C.: World Bank, 1977). Gerald Hursh-Cesar and Prodipto Roy, eds., *Third World Surveys: Survey Research in Developing Nations* (Delhi: Macmillan Co. of India, 1976).

11. An example of the effective use of interviews is found in Wendy Izzard, *National Migration Study: Rural-Urban Migration of Women in Botswana* (Botswana: Central Statistics Office, August 1979).

12. Richard LaPiere, "Attitudes vs. Actions," *Social Forces* 13 (October 1934-May 1935):230-237.

13. Peterson, p. 72.

14. Cernea and Tepping, *A System for Monitoring and Evaluating.*

15. Robert Chambers, *Rural Poverty Unperceived: Problems and Remedies,* World Bank Staff Working Paper no. 400 (Washington, D.C.: World Bank, 1980).

16. Kathleen Staudt, "Agricultural Productivity Gaps: A Case Study of Male Preferences in Government Policy Implementation," *Development and Change* 9 (1978).

17. Coralie Bryant, Betsy Stephens, and Sherry MacLiver, "Rural to Urban Migration: Some Data From Botswana," *African Studies Review* 21 (1978).

18. Daines, *An Overview,* pp. 4-19.

19. Michael Cernea goes so far as to recommend that income not be used as an indicator because of these measurement difficulties. Cernea and Tepping, *A System for Monitoring and Evaluation,* p. 16.

20. AID, *Evaluation Handbook,* 2nd ed. (Washington, D.C.: AID, Office of Program Evaluation, September 1976), Appendix C.

21. Richard Heaver, "The Politics of Implementation: Management and Motivation for Rural Development," mimeographed (1980), p. 63.

22. Peterson, *A Case Study,* pp. 70–71.

23. David Korten, "Community Organization and Rural Development: A Learning Process Approach," *Public Administration Review* 40 (September-October 1980), pp. 480–511.

24. Fran Korten discussed her success with this technique in a series of seminars at the Agency for International Development, June 1980.

25. Michael M. Patton recommends a similar approach to evaluation in *Utilization—Focused Evaluation* (Beverly Hills, Calif.: Sage, 1978).

26. Heaver, "Politics of Implementation," p 44.

27. There are many works applying evaluation techniques to development. See G. W. Edward Schuh and Helio Tollini, *Costs and Benefits of Agricultural Research: The State of the Arts,* World Bank Staff Working Paper no. 360 (Washington, D.C.: World Bank, 1979); and Michael Cernea, *Measuring Project Impact: Monitoring and Evaluation in the PIDER Rural Development Project—Mexico,* World Bank Staff Working Paper no. 332 (Washington, D.C.: World Bank, 1979).

28. Cernea, *Measuring Project Impact,* p. 27.

29. Peterson, *A Case Study,* pp. 26–30.

30. Donald Mickelwait, Charles Sweet, Elliot Morss, *New Directions in Development: A Study of U.S. AID* (Boulder, Colo.: Westview Press, 1979), p. 169.

31. Ibid., p. 162.

32. Brian Phipps, "Evaluating Development Schemes: Problems and Implications: A Malawi Case Study," *Development and Change* 7 (1976):469–484.

33. Judith Tendler, "Rural Infrastructure Projects: Roads," mimeographed (Washington, D.C.: AID, Bureau for Program and Policy Coordination, October 1978).

34. Two articles that examine impact on target groups are John Montgomery, "Food for Thought: On Appraising Nutrition Programs," *Policy Sciences* 9 (1977):303–321; and John Montgomery and Martin Katzman, "Cui Bono? Measuring Income Redistribution Effects of Capital Projects," *Administration and Society* 10 (1978):235–255.

35. Cernea, *Measuring Project Impact,* Annex 3. The PIDER project emphasized the criterion of citizen participation in its design and evaluation.

36. Rural Operations Review and Support Unit, "Monitoring and Evaluation of Rural Development Projects: A Progress Report" (Washington, D.C.: World Bank, 1978), p. 3.

37. These distinctions were made in ibid., pp. 11–13.

38. Deboeck and Kinsey, *Managing Information,* p. 16.

8
Decentralization and Coordination

Introduction

The task of development administration is to marshal resources to bring about substantial change in an uncertain and fragile environment. Because governments in most developing nations have limited capacity, it is natural for them to conclude that centralizing power is their only recourse. The temptation is even greater when development is defined to include redistribution of power and resources—it is assumed that only a broadly based authority could accomplish this kind of change. Compelling as this argument appears, it has generated its own critique. If development is also about sharing power and being responsive to popular interests, it is easy for strong central authority to overwhelm the process and become heavy-handed and unresponsive. The cry "let a hundred flowers bloom" is often echoed, albeit in less colorful terms, suggesting that some degree of decentralization is necessary to ensure responsiveness and variation and to mobilize the public around development opportunities. Nation building may require centralization, but development requires some local control.[1] The dilemma cannot be resolved ideologically; regimes of both the Right and Left have struggled with the premise of decentralization, and the solution is as perplexing to Western industrialized nations as it is to the third world.

The problem raised in this chapter is where responsibility for designing and implementing development projects, programs, and policies lies. It is immediately apparent that there are no either/or solutions. The question is what combination of decentralization and centralization "fits" various development tasks. How can institutions coordinate the various levels of government and the different participants in the process? Before turning to these organizational questions, recall existing patterns in third world nations.

Center-Periphery Issues in Developing Nations

In spite of recent interest in decentralization, the prevailing bias clearly reinforces the dominant role of central authority. This central bias is based on three factors. Structurally, the central government retains most of the formal powers in third world nations. Politically, the problem of developing a nation and optimizing scarce resources has reinforced the powers and visibility of the central government. Finally, in many states the public accords much more legitimacy to the central government than to local or regional levels.

With few exceptions, most of the formal powers in these nations are located at the national level. In some cases colonialism encouraged this phenomenon, particularly when the home government was centralized, as was the case with French and Spanish rule. British colonialists saw more possibility in local government and officially espoused "indirect rule," or working through indigenous leadership. However, their efforts to develop local power were usually opposed by nationalists, who tended to see any form of decentralization as a scheme for deflecting national sentiment. In several nations central authority was reinforced by military or other authoritarian leadership. More recently, it has been encouraged by the practices of donor nations, who prefer to negotiate directly with a single source of authority, partly because it appears less risky and partly because loans and aid can be used to deal with balance of payments gaps. Although there was more flexibility in the 1970s, at least more than in the 1960s, donors concentrated on granting loans to central governments.[2]

By contrast, local governments have relatively few responsibilities or resources. In Mexico, for example, many issues clearly of a local nature are decided in the capital. Consider the case of the Mexican city of Japala. "Even 'local' matters such as the electrification of a new area or the installation of drainage pipes may depend on administrators who are independent from — if not disdainful of — the local scene."[3] A review of events in Tanzania over the past decade confirms a similar momentum there. In a nation with a strong ideological commitment to local control, even "what would appear to be the minutiae of village life are subject" to central control.[4] Similar patterns are evident in Brazil, where recent changes have strengthened the role of the central government. Prior to 1964 the country had a municipalist form of government and had clear and specific roles for local governments. In 1965 the new constitution was passed to strengthen the national government on the assumption that it was the best vehicle to carry out economic development. The change meant that the cities lost most of their tax resources to the national government. As a result, "municipal finances became dependent on na-tionally directed grants and shared revenues, with a host of directives and prohibitions governing their use."[5]

A third example of the weight attached to central government is in India. Unlike the French and Spanish, the British colonialists formally encouraged local government, but in practice the central government continued to make most of the decisions. Although the 1950s witnessed a strong ideological commitment to decentralization and participation, it waned over time. Throughout the 1960s and 1970s there was an increasing centralism in Indian politics, with village government—the panchayati raj—as well as the states, becoming more and more subservient to the national government. At present local resources are meager and local decisions are frequently overruled, eroding any vestiges of local authority. "Many of the tasks expected of local government are simply not done. Especially noticeable is the lack of activity in physical planning for urban expansion. With no operational plans for new neighborhoods and no advance provisions for new streets, water sewer, electric lines and market areas, newcomers set up wherever they can."[6]

These examples illustrate not only the structural realities in developing nations, but also their political rationale. Scarce resources and manpower create pressures to concentrate both at the center, where they presumably can be used most efficiently. Ethnic diversity creates tensions giving national governments an additional reason for expanding their power and maintaining control over regional and local bodies. In many nations these tendencies are reinforced by a strong national party operating out of the capital and distributing political rewards at the local level according to national agendas.

Central dominance is also encouraged by bureaucratic politics. "It is in the political and personal interest of most civil servants to centralize their activities. At the personal level, a base in the capital or provincial centre brings the advantages of city living. . . . All major allocational decisions are taken in the capital, as are all decisions about promotions. The goals of both empire building at the departmental level and career advancement at the personal level are thus best served by continued centralism."[7]

This center bias holds true even for those bureaucrats assigned to line agencies at the local level. "In case of conflict of interests between local and national objectives, bureaucrats tend to side with the latter in order to enhance their career prospects regardless of the merits of the situation. Where careers depend exclusively on national agencies rather than some elements of local approval, central planners should be especially attentive to structural causes of poor 'receptivity.'"[8] This conclusion appears generally true; in socialist Tanzania, where bottom-up planning is officially emphasized, bureaucrats find that their job descriptions encourage them to "bring the thinking of Dar es Salaam down to the village level" rather than the reverse.[9] The incentives and internal rewards an agency establishes can thus have the indirect impact of enhancing the authority of those at the center.

These organizational and political realities are reinforced by popular perceptions of national power. Local governments have much less legitimacy and are often viewed as wasteful and ineffectual. Citizens frequently expect little of them beyond red tape and corruption. The total effect of all these pressures is that local political systems have very little capacity for effective initiatives and creative change.[10]

National Governments and Development

Given these several dynamics, the responsibility for designing and implementing development has often been carried out at the national level. Central control can take one of four forms. First and most common, a project or program is handled by a regular line agency or ministry, of agriculture or forestry for example. The problem frequently is that bureaucrats within these agencies have important vested interests in maintaining their positions as elite corps of civil servants and also in competing with other agencies for resources.[11] They are therefore reluctant to disperse power, either to the periphery or to special project units.

A second possibility is to establish semiautonomous institutions or special project units controlled on the national level. Sometimes the manager operates directly under the authority of the prime minister (for example, regional and district agricultural development officers in Tanzania).[12] In such cases an agency's strength varies with the amount of support it receives from the head of state. In other instances, several agencies will jointly administer a project through a special committee. Tunisia, Indonesia, and Jamaica have all experimented with this arrangement. The problem is that often the project readily lapses into being the second or third priority of each agency involved, and no single authority has a vested interest in seeing project implementation through.[13]

A third form of project management is the integrated rural development project; its purpose is to reintegrate functions that have become highly fragmented and specialized under line departments. During the 1970s it became apparent that rural poverty is a seamless web of interrelated problems, and that projects that address only a single aspect of development are less successful than integrated projects that can address multiple aspects at the same time. For example, integrated rural development projects may simultaneously involve seed and fertilizer distribution, new and appropriate technologies, literacy programs, nutrition, and health clinics.[14]

Instead of relying on cooperation from the several agencies, integrated projects involve the creation of a new integrating structure, usually at a regional level. For example, river basin development boards are often created with broad functional powers, to avoid having to get departments to work together. Another example is the Puebla Project in Mexico where a single integrated authority was created due to a suspicion that none of the existing agencies was sufficiently innovative. It has reportedly worked in this case because it has the resources to operate independently of other groups. The more common pattern is for integrated projects to have difficulty gaining the cooperation of regular line agencies; members "borrowed" from the agencies tend to maintain their original agency loyalties. Another objection is that it is more difficult to build on and institutionalize the learning from developmental experience if it is administered by an autonomous unit rather than a traditional agency.[15]

There are various reasons for using one or another of these centralized organizations to plan and implement a project. The national government has a preponderance of a country's resources and can operate with "economies of scale." If one wishes to pursue a fast rate of growth, central control over key sectors appears to be a very direct and logical route. This choice makes especial sense where the policy goal is to increase income and productivity, a goal of many national policies.[16] It is also true that the central government has most of a nation's managerial skill and a greater ability to solve internecine intergovernmental battles. A third reason is that empirically much of the impetus for reform and change has come from national bodies; they are in fact often more committed to development than are local governments and may be able to prevent powerful local economic interests from co-opting a project's benefits. Finally, if a project is assigned to a permanent national line agency, it is more likely to be institutionalized over the long run; the government has the opportunity to learn from its experiences with the project and repeat the successes elsewhere.[17] For all these reasons, it can be argued that centralization is more viable, effective, and development oriented than decentralized approaches.

In spite of these several claims about the strengths of centrally directed development, there is increasing evidence that such organizational arrangements are not as appropriate for the newer range of developmental goals as they were when states focused almost wholly on keeping order and encouraging economic growth. The problem is that centrally directed projects are often very ineffective; frequently they are wasteful and ignore local interests and contributions. Centrally controlled projects also tend to be "showcase efforts." "The progress of higher officials, particularly national officials, can be traced by the trail of newly graded roads, newly painted buildings, functioning water systems, and projects hurriedly completed."[18] In addition, central control often neglects the poor. A review of six rural development projects funded by the World Bank concluded that "those [systems] with top-heavy power appear to work less effectively than those with power concentrated at the local and intermediate levels. Top-heavy power systems tend to stifle motivation and commitment and have difficulty obtaining valid information from lower levels, especially of a negative nature. Systems with balanced power or more power at the lower levels tend to be more highly motivated and have better flows of information from the lower levels, and so are better able to change."[19]

Case Study of an Indonesian Fishing Village Project

In a brief digression, we may indicate some of the problems that arise when local communities are not involved in planning and designing projects. In the case we present as illustration, the information the local community had to offer was so much a part of the social structure that it was easily overlooked. Indonesian officials designed a project to increase the daily catch of fish in several small villages. Since national planners perceived that the fishermen were being exploited by the local lenders and boat owners, the project was designed to loan money directly to small collectives of fishermen to enable them to buy their own boats and equipment. The local community was not included in defining the problem, in designing the project, or in selecting the members of the collectives. If it had been, the designers would have learned some crucial information. The existing system of borrowing money and working for the boat owners is central to the entire social fabric of the community. Loans, for example, cement a relationship in which each party has obligations; the borrower promises loyalty, and the lender guarantees the borrowers support in any crisis. Since the project overlooked these intricacies it ended by disrupting the social patterns within the village and arousing violent opposition from the villagers.[20]

Approaches to Decentralization: Deconcentration and Devolution

Because of the apparent weaknesses with central control, decentralization is increasingly seen as an important factor in development administration. There are actually two forms of decentralization—administrative and political. Administrative decentralization is commonly called *deconcentration* and means the delegation of some implementing powers to local levels. Officials at the local level work within a plan and budgetary resources; however, they have some element of discretion and responsibility over the nature of those services at that level. Their discretion can vary from pro forma rulings to more substantial decisions. Political decentralization, or *devolution,* means that some decision-making authority and control over resources is assigned to regional and local officials. One example is a federalist system where different levels of government have specified powers and taxing authority.[21] Otherwise instances of devolution are uncommon; and most frequently when decentralization is discussed, or tried, it comes as some form of administrative delegation of responsibility and involves different levels of government dividing and sharing power among themselves.

The organizational perspectives we have developed in prior chapters suggest several principles for assigning responsibility among levels of government. First, a project or program should be assigned to whatever organization has an *incentive* to carry it out. Second, the *political environment* of an organization should support project implementation. Hence, the question arises, Which organization is best able to consolidate resources and counter opposition? Which is most apt to provide access for the public? Third, most projects involve several organizations rather than single ones; *relations among organizations* and the ways in which organizations interact with each other are therefore important. Finally, choices should be made not only with reference to the existing capacity of organizations, but in terms of developing their *institutional capacity.*

Arguments for forms of decentralization derive from these criteria. There is a vast communication gap between the capital and the rural villages. The national leadership does not, and perhaps *cannot* from its vantage point, understand rural problems. At the same time there is often a bottleneck in the transfer of technology because local area officials fail to realize what alternatives they have. Given this gap, there are limits to the ability of the central government to design appropriate projects and to their incentives to carry them out.

There is also ample evidence that local input can improve project design and implementation.[22] It is easier to respond and adapt to new opportunities if there is room for discretion and flexibility at the local level. For example, a "lack of authority at the field level can delay action until a point where the problem has changed and the authorized remedy is no longer appropriate."[23] Local input also permits adaptation of general directives to local conditions. Studies of soils can be made by national research groups, but they usually need to be adapted by local farmers to the particular conditions in the local areas.[24]

Decentralization is also one way to develop local level capacity. Power and influence gravitate to resources. If a local body is given responsibility and resources, it will be better able to expand its authority. Where local governments are solely charged with following national policy, leaders and public will both have less investment in them.[25] But note that if a local unit increases its power, it does not automatically follow that the national government has less. The central government may receive some credit for assigning projects and resources, and thus it increases its influence and legitimacy.

Some argue that decentralization generates more benefits to poorer groups in the society. John Montgomery reviewed twenty-five case studies of rural development in 1970 and concluded that decentralization had a major impact on their success in distributing benefits. Central control usually benefited the the agency rather than the peasants. Decentralization also benefited the bureaucracy, but at the same time it reduced the concentration of power. The most successful approach, he found, was to devolve power to local political leaders; this tactic is more beneficial to the local peasants than using professionals in either a decentralized or centralized system.[26] A study of the Comilla project in Bangladesh by Harry Blair supports the value of giving discretion and power to local officials. In this case, it was found that excessive supervision caused local administrators to favor the local elites. This surprising conclusion is based on the following reasoning. When local bureaucrats are faced with being supervised by officials above them, they feel they have to produce tangible measures of success and hence gravitate toward working with the more experienced and wealthier farmers.[27]

Decentralization is very appealing as a strategy; however, there are numerous case studies that document its unseen and often damaging results, challenging what Naomi Caiden and Aaron Wildavsky call the "myth of decentralization."[28] In contrast to the two studies by Montgomery and Blair described above, their consistent theme is that when responsibility is dispersed, local elites reap the benefits of a project. The problem is that decentralization often erodes administrative and political power. Resources and supports are diluted, and projects become more vulnerable to external interests. Organizations simply lack the power to carry out their policies as intended. The dilemma is a difficult one. Where there is little authority to begin with, there is room for various levels of government simultaneously to expand their authority. But it is precisely under these conditions, when the state is perceived as "soft," that officials husband and protect any authority they do have. Dispersing it they feel will deplete rather than enhance their capacity.[29]

On the face of it, there are severe inconsistencies in the literature; while some writers offer evidence that decentralization is valuable, others are equally convinced that it creates severe problems. One way to resolve these differences is to consider three kinds of circumstances: (1) the political climate and the extent to which other groups are supportive; (2) the nature of the policy itself; (3) the kind of linkages and means of coordination that exist between the various levels of government and among agencies. As each of these varies so do the importance and value of decentralization. To the extent that the political climate is supportive, the policy appropriate, the linkages with the central government effective, and activities coordinated, decentralization is most apt to be successful and its benefits realized. We will consider each of these circumstances in turn.

Contingency Theory and Decentralization

While organizations generally are vulnerable to the uncertainty and conflict in their environments, decentralized systems are particularly so. Whenever power is dispersed, special interests may be able to assert themselves with one or another authority, or the agencies may need to turn to external groups to expand their resources. The story of the Chilalo Agricultural Development Unit project in Ethiopia is only one of many instances where an effort to organize a project at a regional level was undercut by external groups. CADU, an autonomous unit within the Department of Agriculture, was designed to stimulate agricultural production by providing access to a variety of resources from seed to technical assistance to marketing. Although national authorities were very supportive, local political leaders felt threatened and were very hostile to the project. As a result they refused to cooperate, withheld support, and severely undermined the project's efforts.[30] Because of this vulnerability, political factors were able to have considerable influence on CADU. A study of decentralization strategies in Kenya and the Sudan concluded that "little was done in any of the three countries to anticipate and cope with political opposition, or to build political support for decentralization, until after political problems rose."[31]

The lesson is that decentralization strategies need to be appropriate to their political environments or contingent on the resources and constraints that are available from others. Two variables that seem particularly significant are the support that is available from local political leaders and organizations and the extent to which the public has any influence. First, local political units may or may not support the goals of a project. In the case of CADU, the project threatened the power base in the community. In general, the preoccupation of local units with their political needs may make them more interested in distribution issues — who gets what — than in overseeing a development project.[32]

Second, the extent to which the public is organized and can exert some influence is relevant to decentralization. As discussed above, in some projects local elites benefit from local political control; in others they benefit most when national bodies retain control. One possibility is that the extent to which the public is organized makes the difference. In Montgomery's research the public's role is pivotal: "Local and administrative procedures could protect the program against such takeovers more easily *when the public participated* in the process than *when the decisions were left to the discretion of central ministries.*"[33] And referring to CADU, David Korten found that the absence of any effort to organize the landless tipped the balance toward the landowners and elites.[34] Presumably when poorer farmers are organized, local political leaders are able to form an alliance with them and resist the incursions and demands of the wealthier farmers.

These dimensions give us four types of decentralization strategies (see Table 8.1). In the first instance, there can be a greater degree of decentralization than in the others, with some actual devolution of power. The second case suggests a developmental model. The national body takes the initiative, but uses a project assignment to develop local power, such as providing services as a stimulus to institutional development. The stimulus may be given to either a public or a private group. For example, the Bicol River Irrigation Project in the Philippines was designed not

TABLE 8.1

The Political Context and Types of Decentralization

Influence by	Attitudes of Local Politicians	
the public	Supportive	Opposed
Public is organized and potentially influential	I. Greater local responsibility.	II. National level can use projects to develop a local capacity.
Public has little access; only local elites have influence	III. Local responsibility is possible; should be used to organize public; retain national controls.	IV. Central authorities need to maintain control and design projects to both develop local capacity and organize the public.

only to deliver water, but also to create a viable farmer organization to take over the project.[35]

The third type of design is an instance where local responsibility is appropriate with a continuation of controls and guidance from the central agency. Only then can local elites be prevented from "hijacking" its benefits. The third and fourth types of design include efforts to organize the public. More than likely the result of such organizing efforts will be some form of co-optation or effort to use the public for the support of the program.[36] Whether co-optation eventually leads to more legitimate forms of participation is an open question.

Nature of the Policy

Another way to consider when decentralization is appropriate is to examine the nature of the policy. The implementation of certain policies is more appropriately decentralized than others. Some of the dimensions that may be relevant are the following:

The amount of information that is needed. To the extent that the policy is based on a well-developed body of knowledge and certainty about procedures and outcomes, there can be a greater degree of central direction and control. To the extent that a policy operates in a context where information is incomplete, where the preferences and needs of beneficiaries are unclear, where the tasks of administrators are ambivalent, then some degree of decentralization is desirable. The amount of information needed may not be immediately apparent. It may seem that all the necessary information exists, that an engineer, for example, can determine where to put a small dam. Local farmers, however, are apt to know more about water flow and hence have valuable advice to offer.

Manner of supply. Some goods rely mainly on capital-intensive methods and are usually produced on a large scale. Others involve contacts between individuals, such as the delivery of health care. The latter kinds of projects are much more difficult to monitor; they may need to vary with the locale, and they depend on how people respond to them. "The more face to face contact that is required, the more difficult it will be to manage a large organization because of the difficulties in controlling the quality of interpersonal relationships and of measuring outcomes."[37] Under any of these circumstances, some manner of decentralization and local monitoring becomes more important.

The relative importance of regulation and responsiveness. Regulation means imposing equitable standards; frequently equity is best served when regulation is handled at the national level. When responsiveness is the major concern, however, it may be useful to decentralize tasks so that local agents can adjust programs to local conditions. A 1975 official study of the panchayati raj system in India distinguished between regulatory functions that should be retained by the central government and developmental functions that it argued needed to be decentralized to the panchayati raj. The report also recommended greatly strengthening the powers of local governments and then added that the district level should expand its monitoring and regulatory role in order to assure that benefits go to the poor.[38]

Central Local Linkages

The extent of political support and the nature of the policy suggest that there are some occasions when decentralization is more appropriate than others. The solution is almost always to decentralize some functions and not others; therefore the key issue concerns the linkages or means of coordination that exist between local, regional, and central bodies. CADU examplifies a project that was greatly affected by its lack of linkages. Previously, CADU was described as a project that was subverted by local elites, who were able to gain such influence in part because CADU had few if any linkages with the national government, or ways to involve local officials in joint decision making.[39] Two other projects, by contrast, the Comilla project in Bangladesh and the Joint Commission on Rural Reconstruction (JCRR) in Taiwan did have such linkages and were able to draw "a wide collection of actors into project decision-making. By establishing a variety of links to the power setting, these projects generated the support necessary to carry out their program."[40]

One other example of the role of linkages illustrates their importance in facilitating innovative organizational structures as well as in distributing benefits. The Special Rural Development Program in Kenya established an imaginative program for designing and implementing its projects at the local level—programming and implementation management (PIM). Although it has been well received at the field level, it has reportedly had problems over time. One observer traces the problems to the fact that PIM was never effectively integrated with agency decisions at the national level. Specifically, he writes that "on the one hand we have scheduling upset by the load of demands from above; and on the other by bottlenecks in the release of financial resources to execute projects." Its problems can thus be traced to the fact that it was never integrated into budgetary and planning decisions.[41]

Although most agree that linkages are important, there is less agreement as to what form they should take. The major organizational issues focus on control, accountability, interorganizational relations, incentives, coordinating mechanisms, learning processes, and overlapping memberships.

Central Control

The anomaly may be that decentralization requires strong central authority, not an authoritarian rule, but a sure and certain central structure of authority. The next question is what this means in practice. One argument is that it means "control over the rewards or the penalties necessary to elicit compliance with program goals."[42] Others, however, suggest the need for caution in the use of controls. A study of decentralization in the Sudan concludes that financial control can be overdone. In this case the central government supplemented local budgets; however, "reimbursements for deficits could only be obtained after an item by item review by central ministries, and this left the provinces with little flexibility or discretion in using funds and virtually no capacity to plan ahead."[43] And based on the experiences of the PIM system, an observer concludes that "centralized fiscal control and decentralized project decision-making are incompatible."[44] Local governments not only need some control over resources, they also need to be given sufficient power to carry out the tasks assigned to them. For example, in the Sudan, "without corporate status for local government, administrative officers were rendered powerless to perform their previous duties."[45]

One model distinguishes between control and influence relationships. A line agency at the national level that gives orders to regional offices exercises *control*. A coordinating body, however, can only *influence* its members and thus has less power. With these concepts, observers can study an organization, its formal and informal powers, and come up with an estimate of its power, influence, and control.

After analyzing and comparing various linkages and coordinating mechanisms using these concepts, the authors conclude that a learning model is more likely when units are linked by "influence" rather than by hierarchical or controlling relationships. In such cases, "the relationship is more one of coordination between semi autonomous levels. The output (objectives, goals, action plans) of any level becomes information rather than directives to adjacent levels. This information is processed through the adjacent level's own information system. . . . It is a political process of confrontation, negotiation and compromise."[46]

Accountability

If tasks are decentralized to local groups, but links are maintained to central authorities, the problem of accountability occurs. To whom are the local administrators responsible? The organization of the Nan Tan Irrigation System in western Laos illustrates a useful resolution to the problem; it also illustrates the point that authority can by decentralized to private groups as well as public bodies. In this case regional units retain final authority, but rely on traditional leadership to manage local irrigation systems. Local headmen are designated to oversee maintenance of the system and also to monitor the distribution of the water. The authority to monitor the water gives the headman some small degree of actual power. In one respect the Nan Tan system is fairly unique. Frequently, such local personnel are accountable only to the bureaucracy, and in consequence they lose any legitimacy with local farmers. In this case, however, it is the farmers who hire them and can replace them, and it is the farmers who pay them; as a consequence the headmen are accountable to the farmers and not the irrigation agency. The headmen therefore have an incentive to be responsive to the farmers' needs, rather than the interests of the water authority.[47] The example suggests that whatever linking arrangements and control procedures are established, the "lower" levels in any decentralized system need to be accountable to their immediate community, as well as to higher levels. Otherwise most of the advantages of decentralization are unlikely to materialize.

A Case Study of Effective Decentralization

As described in Chapter 4, one of the challenges of development is to design organizations that are flexible enough to take advantage of new possibilities and also to handle problems that emerge during the course of a project. Often this adaptability can be accomplished by decentralizing a program. The part played by the village of Nabagram in the Thana Irrigation Program (TIP) in Bangladesh is illustrative. The village cooperative society applied to TIP for a tube well and pump, a form of technology suitable for control at the village level. A formal group is elected to manage the system; in addition the thirty-two family members of the co-op meet weekly to discuss the co-op's affairs, much of their conversation centering around water and irrigation. Over a period of years, the group has designed several innovations. For example, they decided the system needed a person to distribute the water fairly, and thus created the role of a *panichalak*. The group also decided to hire private mechanics to repair the pump rather than those TIP would provide for a fixed fee. The villagers felt that this arrangement would allow them to negotiate the specific contract they wanted and hold the mechanic accountable. The arrangement means that irrigation management is "in the hands of individuals intimately familiar with local engineering, agronomic and socio-economic conditions" and that there is a "mobilization of locally provided and locally controlled resources."

The irrigation agency continues to provide resources and guidelines, but wisely permits variation and encourages flexibility. At the same time they are available if a village is unable to assume responsibility.[48]

Learning Processes

A learning model of coordination is based on the assumption that no single level of government has sufficient information to design and execute a project. A top-down system means the loss of considerable information from local units, and a bottom-up system means that local units will not be aware of changes and pressures outside of its immediate purview. Decentralization designed as a learning model can incorporate information. Linking mechanisms need to be structured to encourage learning and feedback as well as to generate control. As an example, individual projects can be used by an agency to design its broader programs, rather than vice versa. Korten argues that a project-by-project approach is unlikely to promote development or build administrative capacity. It is far more useful to enable agencies to use single projects as a basis for designing programs. The National Irrigation Administration in the Philippines has followed this sequence. Initially the agency began with two pilot projects and used these experiences to learn what processes, organizational changes, and strategies are useful elsewhere. A central committee, made up of project and agency representatives and outside support groups, has served as a coordinating committee to monitor the projects and recommend changes in the agency.[49]

The Lilongwe project in Malawi is a second example where linking structures have encouraged learning. Initially the project manager, a regional officer, controlled all of the project's resources. When it became apparent that the project needed close ties with participating agencies at the national level, a liaison committee was set up under the secretary of agriculture. The next question was how to coordinate the work of the various agencies.

The district level solved the problem of coordination by creating a dual reporting relationship whereby drilling and survey teams continued to work for their respective ministries, but their schedules were approved by the project manager. . . . The District Development Committee had a strong base of power and influence. It was chaired by the District Commissioner and was attended by key party members and the heads of line agencies. . . . It was also the primary vehicle for coordination of line agencies. The Committee initially functioned as a learning center where members discussed the program and its effect. Later its role developed to become the primary vehicle for use of influence on line agencies, setting priorities and planning activities.[50]

The point is simply that learning occurs at higher as well as lower levels.

Coordinating Mechanisms

There are a variety of ways to carry out coordination, some more formal than others and some encouraging more learning than others. The following list of means, ordered from weaker to stronger, was developed after reviewing a series of development projects:

1. Ad hoc meetings to coordinate as problems arise.
2. Training seminars (support understanding).
3. Transfer of staff between divisions.
4. Development of task forces (temporary coordination across divisions).
5. Part-time membership in team/committee (ensures knowledge of other divisions and activities).
6. Participation in a regular planning meeting.
7. Development of liaison positions (e.g., coordinator role).
8. Written working agreements.
9. Full-time membership in a committee (e.g., development committees).
10. Development of a liaison group.
11. Participation in a structure that has dual reporting relationships.[51]

Interorganizational Relations

Several of the above mechanisms establish relationships among agencies. Organization theory has tended to focus on internal procedures or on relations with the environment. Only recently has it begun to look more specifically at interorganizational relations. The point is that other organizations are not *just* a part of one's environment, but are bodies with very similar interests and dynamics. Consistent with this interorganizational focus is a realization that project implementation and coordination is a highly political process. It is important to take into account the career needs of other bureaucrats and to appreciate that organizations will want to control a project if, and only if, it helps them achieve their original purposes. Understanding the political field entails an "understanding of the purposes of the project or organization in terms of who is promoting it and why; an understanding of how the purposes of those involved in implementing the project, including beneficiaries, will be affected by any proposals."[52] The importance of political factors is especially great with development projects. "The vagueness of development goals and the difficulties of measuring success will allow and encourage the pursuit of political goals within the system, which may in practice be a greater significance to managers than the official [goals]."[53]

Organizational Incentives

It follows from the above that there must be incentives for officials to work with other organizations. Consider the case of a project involving cooperation between several agencies. A special project committee is often created with the power to recruit personnel from the line agencies. However, if the committee has no influence over the rewards or career paths of these borrowed personnel, their loyalty remains with their original agency rather than the project.[54] An irrigation project in Thailand provides another example. "The project uses the talents of engineers as well as of members of the agriculture department. Because of different incentives it has been difficult to get both groups to work together. Bureaucratic rewards go to the engineering fraternity involved in visible and politically important construction work and only minimally to the agriculture department, responsible for the extension services in the newly developed area." Because there were few rewards, it is not surprising that the agriculture department invested little effort in the project. Incentives are important, and projects must be designed with these in mind.[55] Sometimes the incentive is simply to have a role to play in a policy. For example, national authorities in Tanzania took over the rural training centers from district authorities. Appreciating the resentment caused by this change, the national authority gave the task of selecting those who would receive the training to the local councils. As a result the councils have continued to feel a sense of ownership for the centers.[56]

Dealing with Redundancy

Most of these procedures are ways to improve communication and regulate activities. Coordination can also be defined as an effort to eliminate duplication, or what is referred to as redundancy. Martin Landau, however, stresses that redundancy may be useful at times and perfectly functional. Similar approaches to the same problem, or having two different groups perform the same task, will turn out to be useful if one or the other breaks down. As an example, an engineer from the department of irrigation and a field agent from the ministry of agriculture might both be assigned to maintain a community's irrigation system. These are redundant efforts, which some would argue should be coordinated so that only one is responsible. If either the engineer or field agent fails to do an effective job, however, it may be very functional to have both assigned to the work.[57] It is basically a question of how disastrous or costly a breakdown would be. In general, the greater the cost or possible damage, the more functional redundancy becomes. (Jet airplanes do not need all their engines. But their redundant engines are a safety factor.)

Overlapping Memberships

Another model for linking different levels of government relies on team meetings and overlapping memberships to provide coordination. In this case learning is done through the role of key personnel. One version was developed as part of the Puebla Project in Mexico. The organizational problem was how to increase communication with other village units and at the same time coordinate policy among several levels. The particular model is based on one developed by Rensis Likert and represents an effort to combine historical efficiency with local needs. A series of groups of farmers and bureaucrats have overlapping members; those who overlap are the "linking pins" who connect different levels in the hierarchy. Because the links are members of both "lower" and "higher" groups, they are able to represent the interests of each to the other and provide feedback (see Figure 8.1).

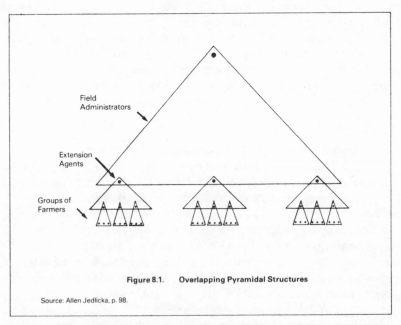

Figure 8.1.   Overlapping Pyramidal Structures

Source: Allen Jedlicka, p. 98.

The Puebla Project is based on a series of small working groups; each has an elected leader who shares the leadership with an extension agent. Both of these individuals act as "links" and are included in the next level of decision making. In practice some of the information that moves between the levels is straightforward and can move down the hierarchy easily and rapidly (e.g., "Loans should be processed in the following manner"). Other information is more complex and requires more feedback and more opportunity for comments by work-group members (e.g., "Adopt this new hybrid seed"). Overall, the system is able to incorporate leadership and influence from those at the local level and is also able to coordinate and provide guidance and resources from higher levels.[58]

Conclusions

There are many real and continuing pressures for developing nations to emphasize the role of national authority and to curtail the influence of local bodies. Recent attention to a model of development that both enhances participation and increases equity has led many to look at the value of decentralizing some of the responsibility for development to regional and local governments and to local nonprofessionals. This pressure has come from political groups within third world nations, as well as from international agencies.

One theme of this book is that organizational theory brings us to a similar conclusion. In a previous chapter, the model of a learning organization was presented, one that is open to its environment. It is apparent that decentralization increases the possibilities for such openness, for taking advantages of local opportunities, and for learning from mistakes. Recall that organizations also need to protect themselves to keep from being consumed by their environment and need resources to enable them to pursue their goals. Most often this necessity requires some central direction, some coordination with other organizations, both vertically and horizontally. Several models of coordination were presented, each of which represents an attempt to take seriously the importance of providing incentives to all the relevant parties, rather than relying solely on persuasion and commitments.

Notes

1. The issue of central control versus local control and their relationships to nationalism was widely debated through the 1950s and 1960s. The British Colonial Office views can be found in Lord Hailey's *An African Survey* (London:

Oxford University Press, 1957), which is also a general reference work. Among the economists who differed from the view that rapid growth required centralization, the best known is Ursula Hicks, *Development from Below* (Oxford: Clarendon Press, 1961). The central-local debate reached a zenith in Nigeria where the Nigerian contributions proliferated. See Chief H. O. Davis, Q.C., *Nigeria: The Prospects for Democracy* (London: Weidenfield and Nicolson, 1961); Obafemi Awolowo, *The People's Republic* (Ibadan, Nigeria: Oxford University Press, 1968); Raph Uwechue, *Reflections on the Nigerian Civil War* (New York: Africana Press, 1971). On the other side of the continent, Uganda's kingdoms raised this issue as well. See L. A. Fallers, *The King's Men* (Nairobi: Oxford University Press, 1964). There are many articles on this issue written by African participants and officials in the *African Review* published by the University of Dar es Salaam, Tanzania.

2. Not only did the reaction to colonialism tend to have a centralizing thrust, the practices of most donor development assistance furthered the pressures on centralization. Yet even more than development assistance, the stabilization agreements of the International Monetary Fund mandated, and still continue to do so, a highly centralized system of planning and control. Given the increasing rates of third world indebtedness, this issue will have to be addressed by those in the IMF.

3. Robert Lineberry and Ira Sharkansky, *Urban Politics and Public Policy*, 3d ed. (New York: Harper and Row, 1978), p. 30. See also Richard Fagen and William Tuohy, *Politics and Privilege in a Mexican City* (Stanford, Calif.: Stanford University Press, 1972).

4. Louise Fortmann, *Peasants, Officials and Participation in Rural Tanzania: Experience with Villagization and Decentralization* (Ithaca, N.Y.: Cornell University, 1980), pp. 79, 72-93.

5. Lineberry and Sharkansky, *Urban Politics*, p. 31. See also Ivan Richardson, *Urban Government in Rio de Janeiro* (New York: Praeger, 1973).

6. Ibid., p. 32. For further discussion of local issues in India see A. Avasthi, ed., *Municipal Administration in India* (Agra: Laksn mi Narain Agarwal, 1972); and Shriram Maheshwari, "New Perspectives on Rural Local Government in India," *Asian Survey* 19 (November 1979):1110-1125.

7. Richard Heaver, "The Politics of Implementation: Management and Motivation for Rural Development," mimeographed (1980), pp. 23-24. Other writers who examine the tendency of bureaucrats to be oriented toward the center are Richard Symonds, *The British and Their Successors, A Study in the Government Services in the New States* (London: Faber and Faber 1966); and David E. Apter, *The Politics of Modernization* (Chicago: University of Chicago Press, 1965).

8. John Montgomery, "The Populist Front in Rural Development," *Public Administration Review* 39 (January-February 1979):62.

9. Joel Samoff, cited in Fortmann, *Peasants, Officials and Participation*, p. 78.

10. The implications of the low capacity of local government for urban and

rural issues will be examined further in Chapters 12 and 13. See also Fred G. Burke, *Local Government and Politics in Uganda* (Syracuse, N.Y.: Syracuse University Press, 1964); and Rupert Emerson, *From Empire to Nation* (Boston: Beacon Press, 1960).

11. The literature on the elite nature of the bureaucracy is vast. See Myron Weiner, "India: Two Political Cultures," in *Political Cultures and Political Development,* ed. Lucian Pye and Sidney Verba (Princeton: Princeton University Press, 1965); and B. B. Schaffer, "Deadlock in Development Administration," in *Politics and Changes in Developing Countries,* ed. Colin Leys (Cambridge: Cambridge University Press, 1969), pp. 177–211.

12. Fortmann, *Peasants, Officials and Participation,* p. 27.

13. John Thomas and Richard Hook, *Creating Rural Employment* (Washington, D.C.: AID, 1977).

14. Integrated projects were frequently modeled after the Tennessee Valley Authority (TVA) experience in the United States; for a discussion of TVA, see Philip Selznik, *TVA and the Grass Roots* (Berkeley: University of California Press, 1949).

15. Allen Jedlicka, *Organization for Rural Development* (New York: Praeger, 1977). Several studies confirm the problems that arise when personnel are controlled by several agencies; see S. N. Dubey, "Organizational Analysis of Panchayati Raj Institutions in India," *Indian Journal of Public Administration* 18 (1972):254–269, as one example.

16. M. S. Bell, "Political Framework," in *Redistribution with Growth,* ed. H. Chenery et al. (London: Oxford University Press, 1974); and Donald Mickelwait, Charles Sweet, and Elliott Morss, *New Directions in Development* (Boulder: Westview Press, 1979), p. 183.

17. See Vernon Ruttan, "Integrated Rural Development," *International Development Review* 17 (1975).

18. Fortmann, *Peasants, Officials and Participation,* p. 36.

19. William Smith, Francis Lethem, and Ben Thoolen, *The Design of Organizations for Rural Development Projects—A Progress Report* (Washington, D.C.: World Bank Staff Working Paper no. 375, 1980), p. 24.

20. Donald Emmerson, "Orders of Meaning: Understanding Political Change in a Fishing Community in Indonesia," mimeographed (Madison: University of Wisconsin, 1975).

21. The literature on federalism has been enriched by all the reports, symposia, and constitutional conferences held in Nigeria, India, and Uganda on federalism in the past two decades. Both India and Nigeria have endeavored to use federal structures to contain ethnic tensions; states that are approximately coterminous with ethnic populations are sometimes able to ameliorate ethnic rivalries.

22. For example, see David Leonard, *Reaching the Peasant Farmer: Organization Theory and Practice in Kenya* (Chicago: University of Chicago Press, 1977).

23. George Honadle, "Anticipating Roadblocks in Organizational Terrain," mimeographed (Washington, D.C.: Development Alternatives, 1977), p. 2.

24. For example, see Jedlicka, *Organization for Rural Development,* p. 81.

Leonard also presents a strong case for adapting research to local conditions, *Reaching the Peasant Farmer,* pp. 160–161.

25. Fortmann, *Peasants, Officials and Participation,* p. 60.

26. John Montgomery, "Allocation of Authority in Land Reform Programs," *Administrative Science Quarterly* 17 (1972):62–75.

27. Harry Blair, "Rural Development, Class Structure and Bureaucracy in Bangladesh," *World Development* 6 (January 1978):65–82.

28. Naomi Caiden and Aaron Wildavsky, *Planning and Budgeting in Poor Countries* (New York: John Wiley, 1974), p. 82.

29. The soft state dilemma is discussed in Gunnar Myrdal, *The Challenge of World Poverty* (New York: Vintage Books, 1970), pp. 208–252. Fortmann reminds us that decentralization does not necessarily lead to participation; *Peasants, Officials and Participation,* p. 75. Problems that occur when decision making is decentralized are described in a case study by Irene Rothenberg, "Administrative Decentralization and the Implementation of Housing Policy in Colombia," in *Politics and Policy Implementation in the Third World,* ed. Merilee Grindle (Princeton: Princeton University Press, 1980).

30. Derick Brinkerhoff, "Participation and Rural Development Projects" (Ph.D. diss., Harvard University, 1980), p. 215. For one of many studies on CADU, see John Cohen, "Rural Change in Ethiopia: The Chilalo Agricultural Development Unit," *Economic Development and Cultural Change* 22 (July 1974):580–614.

31. Dennis Rondinelli and Marcus Ingle, "Administrative Decentralization and Local Participation in Development Management," (Paper delivered at annual meeting of the American Society for Public Administration, April 1980), p. 2. Numerous cases document that projects will be replicated only if they fit the political agendas of political elites and not solely if they are effective. See cases by Gerald Sussman and David Pyle in Grindle, *Politics and Policy.*

32. Stanley Heginbotham, *Cultures in Conflict: The Four Faces of Indian Bureaucracy* (New York: Columbia University Press, 1975), p. 169.

33. John Montgomery, *Technology and Civic Life: Making and Implementing Development Decisions* (Cambridge, Mass.: MIT Press, 1974).

34. David Korten, ed., *Population and Social Development Management: A Challenge for Management Schools* (Caracas: Population and Social Development Management Center, Instituto de Estudios Superiores de Administracion, 1979), pp. 24–25.

35. George Honadle, "Farmer Organization for Irrigation Water Management," mimeographed (Washington, D.C.: Development Alternatives, 1978).

36. For further discussion of co-optation, see Chapter 10.

37. Robert Bish and Vincent Ostrom, *Understanding Urban Government* (Washington, D.C.: American Enterprise Institute for Public Policy Research, 1973), pp. 26–32.

38. *Report of the Committee on Panchayati Raj Institutions* (New Delhi: Ministry of Agriculture and Irrigation, Government of India, 1978); see analysis in Maheshwari, "New Perspectives on Rural Local Government."

39. Brinkerhoff, "Participation," pp. 166–205.

40. Ibid., pp. 213–215. It seems that national support is a necessary but not sufficient condition for the ability of a project to benefit peasants rather than local elites. Of the three projects CADU, Comilla, and JCRR, only the latter had enough authority to influence national policy.

41. E. Philip Morgan, "Rural Development Management," *International Review of Administrative Sciences* 45 (1979):167.

42. Grindle, "Introduction," in *Politics and Policy*. Also see the article by Susan Hadden in this same volume.

43. Rondinelli and Ingle, "Administrative Decentralization," p. 16.

44. Morgan, "Rural Development Management," p. 167.

45. Rondinelli and Ingle, "Administrative Decentralization," p. 16.

46. Smith et al., *Design of Organizations,* p. 44.

47. E. Walter Coward, Jr., "Indigenous Organization, Bureaucracy and Development: The Case of Irrigation," *Journal of Development Studies* 13 (1976):92–105.

48. E. Walter Coward and Badaruddin Ahmed, "Village, Technology, and Bureaucracy: Patterns of Irrigation Organization in Comilla District, Bangladesh," *Journal of Developing Areas* 13 (July 1979):431, 400.

49. David Korten, "Community Organization and Rural Development: A Learning Process Approach," *Public Administration Review* 40 (September-October 1980):480–511.

50. Smith et al., *Design of Organizations,* p. 18.

51. Based on a list in ibid., p. 26.

52. Ibid., pp. 16–17.

53. Heaver, "Politics of Implementation," p. 17.

54. Honadle, "Anticipating Roadblocks."

55. Heaver, "Politics of Implementation," p. 25.

56. Yussuf Kassam, "The Folk Development Colleges Programme in Tanzania," mimeographed, n.d.

57. Martin Landau, "Redundancy, Rationality and the Problem of Duplication and Overlap," *Public Administration Review* 29 (1969):346–358.

58. Jedlicka, *Organization for Rural Development,* pp. 92–108.

9
Lower-Level Administrators and Field Agents

Introduction

Development decisions are usually associated with international financing and national plans, making it easy to forget that development happens in the "mere encounters of everyday life."[1] Indeed the development process depends on the involvement of people at the grass roots and on the choices that they make. In part, whether or not they are caught up in developmental change is in turn dependent upon the actions of officials at the local level. The daily activities of extension agents, teachers, and local administrators in clinics become crucially important. In the first place, these people help determine how efficiently and equitably services are provided. Since local-level administrators are the most visible link between government and public, they also affect public perceptions about the quality of those services. Attitudes toward agents influence a wide range of responses to government plans and public life. Research on fertilizer, for example, is of little use unless agents share the information and unless farmers value it and are willing to take such advice. Therefore if an organization is going to establish links with its environment, particularly with prospective clients, these agents are of central importance in its structures and processes.

In the last chapter we focused on trade-offs among alternative structures for administering development; in this chapter we examine the role of local-level administrators, those who interact directly with the public—extension agents, health workers, teachers, those organizing cooperatives and credit unions. We examine development and its management problems from the perspective of local administrators, their incentives and roles. In the next chapter we reverse this perspective and look at development management from the view of the public—why,

when, and how they choose to become involved in development projects
and programs.

The Behavior of Local Bureaucrats

In Chapter 2 we described the variety of tensions and problems that
arise within organizations, problems that are all painfully evident as one
moves into the lower levels of an organization. Most studies of local-level
administrators in fact present a bleak picture. The three charges most
frequently made are that agents are lazy, corrupt, and favor well-to-do
farmers.[2] There are essentially three ways to respond to these problems.
One is to think of fieldwork as a traditional manpower problem. This
approach reasons that field agents are poorly equipped for their work
with the public, they require more training, and the training should be
fairly extensive. "An effective field agent should not only be technically
proficient, but should have a somewhat above average understanding of
human behavior as it relates to decision making on unknown, risky matters such as the adoption of a new and different technology. . . . Fortunately this behavioral understanding can be taught to just about
anybody if the commitment for such training exists within the agency
and the government."[3] This approach has merits, for field agents do need
more training. The major problem with the diagnosis, however, is that
even where qualified people are out in the field, their performance is frequently very poor.[4]

A second approach looks at the role of field agents within their
organizations and at the ways in which organizations reward them. According to this view, the poor performance of bureaucrats is often due to
poor organizational support. For example, they may be "reacting rationally to a situation in which it is not clear what is expected of them but
in which it is clear that the exercise of initiative in development matters
is at least as likely to be penalized as deviant behavior as rewarded for being good work."[5] In such a setting they are unlikely to be creative, and
the only recourse is to try to change the situation or the rewards and
sanctions that an organization offers.

A third perspective emphasizes the political context within which the
field agents work, the attitudes of the public, the extent to which the
public is organized, and the availability of other political support. It
holds that this external environment is an important resource and constraint and that the agents' behavior is something more than a response
to organizational incentives.

In this chapter we draw from preceding arguments and elaborate on
these latter two perspectives — the links that bureaucrats have with their

organizations and their relations with the public. Organizationally, local field staff are in fact in a unique position and illustrate the importance of the ways in which organizations relate to their environment and also protect themselves from being overwhelmed by their environment. Field staff function on the boundary of the organization, which means they are directly caught up in two conflicting pressures, from the organization and from the public.[6] On the one hand, for example, they are part of a project team, a program agency, or a health unit. Their job descriptions and rewards if any are given by this organization. Therefore they have to be attentive to their organization, taking account of how they are expected to function. On the other hand, they are assigned to work with a community of people, or a group of squatters, or a list of farmers. To all these people, local bureaucrats may be the most visible contacts with the government. Hence they will often bear the brunt of the public's frustration with the government. Inevitably they experience conflicting demands and pressures, all of which affect how they do their work.

Local Bureaucrats and Their Environments

Recent studies in the United States have looked at the unique role of what are called "street-level bureaucrats," the teachers, policemen, service deliverers, community planners.[7] Most typically they have too few resources to do their work and satisfy the public—too few books, seed packets, welfare payments, or available time and energy. They also are not clear about exactly what is expected of them, how demanding they should be, or how lenient and supportive. These competing pressures undermine their job satisfaction and induce insecurity rather than confidence.

Part of the dilemma is that their work is not only dependent on how well they perform their tasks, but also on the receptivity of the public. How does the public view them? Does it value their service? Clients after all play a large role in determining how effective the agents are. They can exert their own influence; they can ignore services such as new grades of fertilizer or new information on nutrition. All these possibilities set very real limits and constraints on the agents. Studies indicate that citizens vary greatly in their attitudes toward local agents. For example, a survey of bureaucrats and citizens in India documented several different perceptions of the role of these local agents. Interestingly, rural respondents were far more positive about local administrators than urban residents were. This same survey also confirmed that agents assume they are seen much more positively than they are in reality. While local officials view their relations with the public as predominantly "good," the public is much more divided and is more apt to rate it "fair."[8] (See Table 9.1).

In many respects, therefore, the environment of the local agent is hostile territory and fraught with problems. And studies find that agents everywhere tend to adopt a variety of coping patterns: projection, stereotyping, controlling, distrust, retreat to rules. Local bureaucrats for example tell themselves they are not responsible for what happens; instead they *project* the responsibility onto others. If crime escalates, it is not their fault; if students continue to perform poorly, it is not because of what teachers do; if farmers do not use new seed varieties, it is not the extension agent who is at fault. A health worker running a greatly overcrowded clinic in which it is impossible to respond to all demands tries to escape these pressures by *stereotyping* clients, deciding ahead who will and will not get services, rather than responding to each person on an individual basis.[9]

Another coping technique of local agents is to *control* the kinds of demands being placed on them, by not asking for information they do not want to hear or do not feel they can handle. And they may depersonalize clients, keeping them at a social distance. Similarly, they convince themselves that their clients are untrustworthy; hence they do not have to take their demands seriously. Finally, they cope by establishing a series of *routines* that clients must follow: filling out certain forms, making requests for supplies in a specific manner, dealing with problems only during office hours.[10]

The above coping patterns have been found among local agents in in-

TABLE 9.1
Citizen-Administrator Perceptions of Relations with Each Other

Relations are:	Urban		Rural	
	Official image of relation with public	Public image of relation with officials	Official image	Public image
Poor	0%	18%	2%	15%
Fair	0%	41%	2%	15%
Good	86%	24%	96%	55%
Very good	12%	3%	3%	3%
Don't know	2%	14%	-	9%

Source: S. J. Eldersveld, V. Jagannadham, and A.P. Barnabas, The Citizen and the Administrator in a Developing Country (Illinois: Scott, Foresman, 1968), p. 92. Reprinted by permission.

dustrialized as well as developing nations. One other coping technique is particularly apparent in the development context. A great number of studies of field staff relations in developing nations emphasize the tendency of staff to ally themselves with the more elite sections of the community. We would argue that this is not so much a form of corruption as it is a way of coping with pressures. Consider the community in which there is a small group of citizens with some resources and some access to the government and a larger group with few resources.[11] Agents will perceive each group very differently according to their economic position, their political access, and their life-style.[12] (See Table 9.2)

Clearly these two groups appear very different to the local agent. Those relatively well-off have more resources to contribute to development projects and more willingness to take risks. Hence they are easier to organize and more rewarding to work with, both personally and professionally. Members of the general public, by contrast, composed of subsistence farmers, urban laborers, the landless, migrants, and squatters are more difficult people with whom to work. Their needs are greater and their resources fewer. This group Robert Chambers describes as essentially "invisible" to administrators. They live in remote areas, are hard to reach and communicate with, and suffer from what Chambers calls the "urban and tarmac" bias, referring to the tendency of officials to stay on paved roads when they make their rounds in rural areas. Even those who do have some contact with officials remain invisible during the wet seasons when contact is most difficult and their needs are greatest. Poor rural women are especially likely to be treated as invisible by male administrators. To the extent that local officials are aware of them, they

TABLE 9.2

Characteristics of the Public From the Perspective of Local Administrators

	Elites	General Public
Economic Position	Resources to invest in change	No extra resources
Political Access	Easier to organize since few in number and have specific interests.	Harder to organize and lacking in access to policy-makers.
Life style	More self-assured, open to change. More rewarding to work with.	Less self-assured or achievement oriented. Less rewarding to work with.

tend to rationalize that rural women are too hard to work with and that it is more sensible to work with citizens with more potential. In economists' terms, the agents are calculating that the opportunity costs of working with the poorest, and especially with poor women, are too high.[13] The dilemma is that the official could be overlooking the most effective entry point for meaningful change; often women are the food producers as well as change agents within their communities.

This emphasis on the work environment of local agents demonstrates the unique constraints they face and the ways they cope with pressures and tensions. The literature on local-level agents assumes that they function in a hostile environment and tends to emphasize that we need to set up appropriate incentives and methods to control and supervise them. But it is also important to stress the extent to which their work is a political task and to see that supervision and efficiency criteria need to be moderated to take the role of these environmental pressures into account. Because of this environment, effective management is more complex than merely increasing efficient administration. These issues we discuss next.[14]

Local Administrators and Their Organizations

Supervision

Those who worry about the role of field agents usually define the major problem as one of more effective supervision or control. The more lower-level staff are seen as unreliable and unskilled, the more attention is focused on ways to increase their efficiency. Part of this emphasis goes back to the colonial tradition, but it is generally true of any system that has to rely on untrained and poorly educated workers. Under such conditions, those in power do not trust their subordinates to work effectively or to handle discretion.[15] And in situations that are highly politicized, supervisors may be more concerned with loyalty than with efficiency. Local agents are perceived as untrained, dishonest, lazy, or some combination of all these characteristics. For any of these reasons administrators often establish elaborate structures to supervise local officials and routinize their work. In its classic form it has been called the "hub-and-wheel" approach to administration. "The center-post man sets up a circle of subordinate workers each capable of doing one limited aspect of the total operation. Thereafter it is always quicker for the center-post man to perform the difficult task himself than it is to train someone else each time a special skill is required. The subordinates soon become accustomed to relying on the center-post man for all inputs of a supervisory, planning, and coordinating or decision-making nature."[16]

Although colonial practices have been modified, their characteristics are still part of the supervisory process. After observing extension work in East Africa over a period of years, Robert Chambers concluded that the same problems kept recurring and that all of them evoke ingrained habits of heirarchical control. His list of problems includes authoritarian management, wasteful meetings, excessive reports, top-down targets, and inadequate resources. In addition to these he adds "departmentalism," referring to competition among various departments, and "ineffective programs," suggesting that sometimes programs themselves are so inadequate they are difficult to administer.[17]

Studies of relations between field agents and their supervisors confirm that these patterns are very common. The supervisors follow formal and authoritarian methods, passing down orders; promotions and evaluations are based on education or certification. One survey described supervisors as "often erratic, almost non-existent, or poor."[18] For their part the staff are usually deferential to such hierarchical control and find their own ways to adjust to the system rather than to challenge it. Often the result is that the productivity of staff declines and they provide little feedback to administration.

Many of these problems can be traced to information gaps and communication processes. One scenario illustrates a common chain of events. Supervisors have a difficult time knowing what their field staff are doing, particularly when the geographic area is extensive. Because it is difficult to get accurate information, work plans and targets are assigned with little sense of what is realistic to accomplish. This same lack of information means that supervisors have to rely on the reports given to them by staff in order to evaluate their work. However, when field staff see that their reports are often turned around to serve as a means to evaluate them, they are less willing to pass on information about problems. They fear that if they give their supervisors feedback about problems they are having in the field, these will be attributed to their own incompetence, and so their reports are greatly distorted. The result is that little useful information passes from the agents back to the decision makers.

Organizational Incentives

Another way to understand the activities of these bureaucrats is to examine the incentives provided by their organizations. The actual incentives that exist may not even be consistent with the aims of the organization. For example, a study of teachers in rural Thailand conludes:

> Educational administrators send at least two messages to teachers simultaneously—one overt and the other covert. The essence of the overt message is that an important part of the duties of a rural primary school teacher is to involve himself and participate actively in community affairs. The covert message says that teachers will be rewarded on the basis of their performance in the classroom and the school and that community participation means little in terms of career advancement. . . . Because formal education, the ability to pass examinations and time in service are the "requisites of bureaucratic survival and advancement," it would appear that there is little reason for civil servants to respond to needs or pressures emanating from outside the bureaucracy in order to secure the rewards of the bureaucratic system.[19]

As this example from Thailand indicates, promotion and advancement are more likely to be based on training and certification than on actual job performance. One reason this occurs, as noted above, is that the work of the local bureaucrat is often very difficult to supervise directly. The goals are not always clear, and the way to achieve them is often equally unclear. Therefore the temptation is to turn to behavioral measures. How many farmers have agreed to buy new fertilizer? How many have been visited? How many loans have been processed?

The problem is that such incentives are often perverse; that is, they often encourage activity that works against the goals or that is only marginally related to them. Agents may log a lot of visits to farmers if that is the criterion for the work, but they may spend little of that time actually teaching those farmers about new methods or listening to their problems. And when staff are evaluated by amount of seed dispensed or loans made, they focus on pushing these commodities rather than engaging the farmers in discussions about their needs and problems. Finally, incentives based on training and certification are perverse in that they serve to raise the expectations of low-level personnel and to encourage them to want to change their jobs.[20]

Congruence

The studies mentioned thus far examine ways in which bureaucrats cope with their work environments or focus on organizational incentives or on supervision. According to contingency theory, described in Chapter 4, the way in which decisions are made internally influences the way in which an organization relates to those outside of it. Because of this influence, there will tend to be a congruence, or fit, between internal and external relations. For example, if an agency is hierarchical, then it will relate to those outside on a hierarchical basis. If field agents are heavily controlled within an agency, they are unlikely to develop give-and-take relations with their clients. If bureaucrats are trying to establish a learning process in the community, it will be a very difficult task unless they are also part of a learning process within their agency.[21]

Congruence occurs because of the role the local field agent plays. Organizations socialize their members into appropriate roles which reflect the values or norms of the organization. (Recall the discussion of roles in Chapter 5). To the extent that they succeed, the members internalize these roles, and they become part of their own self-image. If they are treated authoritatively, then they will internalize this style into their way of relating to others. One study of the possibilities for participatory development programs concludes that "the probability of 'Top Down' administrators recognizing the legitimacy of a 'Bottom Up' approach to clients is low."[22]

Bureaucrats need to participate in decisions within their organizations, if they are to be expected to enhance the capacity of the public to participate in development. Others have come to this same conclusion for somewhat different reasons. For example, David Leonard argues that field agents need to participate in decisions in order to give them more of a stake in the work of the agency.[23] Rosabeth Kanter has developed a theory to demonstrate the linkage between such participation and productivity. When an administrator is given a chance to participate, she "identifies more strongly with the goals of the organization, applies job skills more efficiently, focuses on reaching goals, rather than adhering to routine, and is less concerned with territorial protection."[24]

Convictions

A final influence on the behavior of local bureaucrats is their own value commitments and convictions about the development task and about the role of the public. For example, field workers in India have been influenced by the ideology of the community development movement in that country, and to some extent this commitment shapes their role. Convictions often vary by agency. The Eldersveld survey of administrators in India in 1964 asked whether the agents thought it was "necessary to relax procedures" in working with the public. The percentage saying no among the line administrators were: police—63 percent; health—59 percent; community development—24 percent.[25] This striking difference suggests that it is useful to try to talk about attitudes within various agencies and the nature of their tasks, instead of generalizing about all officials. There is very little data that permits such distinctions, however.

Multiple Pressures

The various influences on bureaucratic behavior are summarized in Table 9.3. Frequently these influences will interact to create considerable pressure on local bureaucrats. In addition, the demands by their organization and the demands from the environment can work against each other. When this occurs, field agents temper their commitments and redefine their jobs in order to adjust to these multiple demands.[26] Although their adjustment will vary with each situation, the following case study illustrates two characteristics of such redefinitions. The agents usually sacrifice the demands of their clients in order to meet the demands of the organization, and they usually are diverted from their primary task.

Stanley Heginbotham describes the work of field agents (Gram Sevaks) in the state of Tamil Nadu in India. The agents are multipurpose workers, assigned to local villages to implement the programs of a variety of government agencies. They see themselves as promoters of community development, responsible for bringing technical assistance to the farmers and for helping them. From the perspective of the agencies, however, their task is to promote the work of each agency. The Ministry of Agriculture, for example, might demand that a certain number of farmers use a new kind of seed; another agency might require that a certain amount of equipment be rented out. All of these demands taken together create great pressures for the Gram Sevaks. At the same time they know that they are being judged on their effectiveness in mobilizing others to meet these goals. The villagers add a further complexity to the demands on the Gram Sevaks. Because of their own past experiences

TABLE 9.3

Influences on Field Staff Behavior

Personal Convictions	Their Environment	Organizational Relations
Values about development	Resources	Extent to which agents
Convictions about their own	Pressures and demands from	share an identity of
role	their clients	interests
Extent to which these values	Extent of public support	Methods of supervision
are reinforced by their		Incentives
organization		Congruence of incentives
		with their relations to the public

with government agents the villagers view Gram Sevaks as rigid, impersonal and controlling, and insensitive to their interests. The Gram Sevaks therefore find that their job as community developers actually conflicts with the expectations held by both government officials and villagers.

Heginbotham notes that the Gram Sevaks are able to make certain useful adjustments in their role, but in the end the situation prevents them from carrying out any significant community development. They find that they are unable to follow through on extension and development work, and instead they concentrate on getting the farmers to meet all the targets imposed by the government. They essentially become administrators and brokers rather than extension workers. A sample of the ways in which they spend their working days indicates that only 18 percent of their time is spent on extension work. Interestingly enough, in the process of adapting, the farmers and villagers find they need each other, and certain relations have been built up. Farmers need supplies and information from the Gram Sevaks, and the latter need the farmers' cooperation in trying new programs and introducing new seed. Official rigidity and formality have gradually been replaced by a willingness to accommodate one another. On the one hand, the system has been moderately effective in moving commodities such as fertilizer and seed. On the other hand, the commercial role of the Gram Sevaks severely limits the kind of agricultural extension work they can perform and means that agricultural development is far more limited than it should be.[27]

Designing More Effective Supervision

Some of the most creative work in development studies in recent years has gone into designing more effective systems to supervise field agents. Three alternatives are discussed next.

Supervision Through Management by Objectives (MBO). Robert Chambers describes a supervisory system for extension agents used in Kenya that links supervision "with a clear specification of the work to be done and then with fair evaluation of the performance of that work." It includes a detailed work plan for each agent, staff participation in preparing the plans, and an insistence that useful information be collected. There are five components:

1. Daily activities record by each staff member. This lists target accomplishments for each month. The agent then plans what should be done each day and records progress in meeting targets.
2. Location planning sheet. The supervisor keeps this record of the total staff time available in each location. The supervisor and the

agents use this as a basis for discussing together how to set realistic work targets for each of them.
3. Small register. Each agent keeps a list of all the farmers visited and the dates.
4. Daily diary. Each agent keeps a list of daily activities.
5. Farm visit book. This record is kept by farmers in the area and is used to record visits from agents and what advice was given.

The focus of the system is a monthly meeting. First the supervisor meets with each agent, going over the above material, discussing problems and accomplishments. A general discussion and a planning session follow. During this planning meeting, the supervisor begins by listing the target activities for the month, and then he/she works with the staff to plan the best way to carry these activities out. The purpose of the system therefore is to give supervisors more control over their staff and more awareness of what they do. It also can serve as a mechanism to make sure that agents do not spend all of their time with the wealthier farmers. Finally it can begin to stimulate farmer demand by giving them record books to keep.[28]

The Use of Group Demonstrations. David Leonard's system, which was also developed in Kenya, is very similar to the work of Chambers described above. He adds, however, an emphasis on the use of group meetings of farmers. The two key elements are first to have the junior staff participate in setting their work targets and second to have agents meet with farmers in groups instead of on an individual basis. He presents evidence that participation in goal setting usually produces fair targets. In using group methods, the agents design experiments and then convene groups of farmers to whom they demonstrate the results of the experiments. He demonstrates that such meetings can stimulate more innovation, reach more people, and allow for more effective oversight. A large part of the rationale is to provide a convenient means for supervisors to oversee what the agents are doing. "From the supervisory point of view, the advantage of demonstrations and group meetings is that they represent an inspectable, relatively infrequent, final product of a considerable amount of extension work and the observation of them is likely to tell one almost everything one would like to know about one's junior's performance."[29]

The Benor Method. Daniel Benor has developed a training and visit system of extension that has been widely used by the World Bank.[30] The Benor Method is highly intensive; workers focus on a fairly small cluster of farmers and visit them frequently. Similarly, the extension service itself concentrates solely on the single function of working with the farmers. The workers do not operate alone; a whole cadre or network of village workers live in the villages and work directly with the farm families. A system for visiting, record keeping, and supervision on a regular basis is used to provide a structure for the agents. The method also emphasizes the importance of periodic training for the agents. Much of this training is designed to inform the agents about recent research and to involve them with subject-matter specialists who can keep them up to date and deal with their problems in some depth.

Because each of these three systems includes careful attention to defining goals and also involves the agents to some extent in goal definition and feedback, they exemplify the management-by-objectives approach described earlier in Chapter 4. It includes designing specific procedures and structures to establish goals and tasks, as well as incentives for agents to carry them out. David Leonard describes why this approach to extension workers is actually very creative. All too often, he notes, workers feel that their actual work is unrelated to the organization's demands. "Employees either have ceased to believe that their careers depend on their task performance or feel that their promotion prospects are based on only a small portion of their total task. In these circumstances a reaffirmation of the sanctions governing the civil servant's behavior and a promise to apply them to the wider definition of his task are likely to increase and broaden his task orientation."[31] Essentially he is agreeing with those theorists described in Chapter 4 who emphasize ways to make organizations more efficient in achieving their goals.

The Context of Extension Work

A Typology of Work Environments

The above methods provide structure and routinization to make supervision of field agents more effective and to make their work more predictable. Not all observers would agree with this approach. David Korten, for example, reviewed several efforts in community development and concluded that organizations that were responsive to their environments and incorporated direction from those in the community were the most successful. By contrast, projects that relied on central guidance were sometimes able to accomplish their immediate goals, but were less creative and flexible in building on a project's experience. What are needed, he concludes, are "learning laboratories" to experiment with a variety of techniques.[32] Too much structure or routinization might well interfere with such learning by preventing sufficient flexibility.

It is most likely that each of these approaches has merit and utility,

depending upon the specific circumstances within the environment. The
different work situations of field agents require them to assume different
roles and determine how much flexibility is possible. Adapting the
typology used in Chapter 4 (Table 4.2, p. 74), affords us the opportunity
to think in more detail about the nature of the field agent's work.

One aspect of the work situation is the extent to which the public ac-
cepts the goals of the program or project. People may, for example, accept the goal of establishing an irrigation project more readily than the
goal of a family planning program. In each instance, the administrator
has a very different relation with the public. A second distinction is the
extent to which the organization is able to define a clear set of tasks for
the agents. For example, in a campaign for literacy, is there clarity about
the way to proceed? If there is, then the agency can lay out more specific
guidelines for the bureaucrats to follow than in cases where the tasks are
harder to define. Whether or not guidelines exist then will have a major
influence on the kind of organizational incentives that are appropriate
and the nature of the supervision which is possible. These two dimensions give us the typology in Table 9.4.[33]

Service Delivery Role

In the first type, called the service delivery role, there is either an explicit agreement between the agents and their beneficiaries that their efforts are of value or a clear consistency between the goals of each. In addition, the technology or task is clear enough that it can be defined ahead

TABLE 9.4

Roles of Local Administrators in Different Work Environments

Extent to which agency can clearly define tasks of the agent	Concurrence by public beneficiaries that the goals of bureaucrats are valid	
	YES	NO
YES	I. SERVICE DELIVERY: dispensing goods, services, information	II. NEGOTIATION/MOBILIZATION: stimulating demand, bargaining over goals
NO	III. FEEDBACK: research and development experimentation	IV. MUTUAL LEARNING: goal setting

of time in consultation with the agent. In such cases the agents can assume that the public will use their services if there is effective communication and timely supply. The role of the organization is to provide effective support and supervision and to assist the agent in laying out his tasks. Rewards can be designed to fit with the task performance and specific criteria and efficiency standards can be established. Under such circumstances it is appropriate to use management by objectives or some similar rationale to establish routines and formal procedures. Because the technology can be defined, reporting can be routinized, and hence supervison will not be as difficult or as costly as under other circumstances.

The supervisory and monitoring procedures for field agents described above are consistent with this type — for example, the systems developed by Chambers and Benor. Another example of this model being used is the Masagana 99 project in the Philippines, an effort to increase rice production. According to one observer the success of the project can at least partially be traced to organizational decisions. In one particular area the regional director defined the work of the agents in fairly narrow and technical terms. The agents were charged with processing loans to those who would make best use of them and with improving the marketing system. "Bureaucrats up and down the line only had to perform their carefully defined duties for the Program to function smoothly. From the local community the Program required nothing more than submission to the authority of the officials. Even the process of forming the associations which farmers had to join to participate in the Program could be reduced to a matter of following the rules."[34] Not only was there general concurrence among the farmers that increased rice production was a valid undertaking, but the director felt that he could establish the essential steps to carry that out.

This type is subject to several problems. We know from studies that top-down task descriptions and close supervision can lead to "passive resistance, general dissatisfaction, and slow-down."[35] Describing the role of field agents in India, Rudra Singh writes, "Policies and plans were made at the top of the official hierarchy, with little participation by the men in the field. . . . Orders were passed down and the men in the field were expected to show results. . . . Targets and steps were not modified in accordance with the local situation. The local worker (extension representative) was given little opportunity for initiative, and since the plans he had to execute often had no logical relationship to the local situation, he found it difficult to achieve the target set for him."[36] Because of these tendencies, any monitoring must be sensitively designed to allow the local managers to participate in designing their tasks, and in laying out criteria by which they are to be evaluated. In addition, there must be incentives and rewards established to encourage them to carry out their work conscientiously.

Another potential problem is that an emphasis on internal routines and procedures can lead to a neglect of the political dimensions of a project. E. Philip Morgan suggests that in the case of Chambers' effort to establish a monitoring system, it was not institutionalized as effectively as it might have been. The reason he suggests is that attention focused on supervising the field agents and ignored the necessity for building political support at higher levels in the bureaucracy. The problem was that "the complexity of a multi sector rural development program could not be managed simply by rationalizing the information flow."[37]

This approach views an organization as an incentive system that manipulates incentives and rewards to induce the desired performance. The point of the typology is that it is a valid model under certain conditions—when the beneficiaries agree on the value of what the agent is doing and when his tasks are not dependent on interactions with the public and can be specified ahead. Under other circumstances routinized supervision is less appropriate. Either tasks cannot be routinized, and supervision becomes very costly, or the task of the field agent is more dependent on how the clients respond. The typology suggests three alternative roles, each of them according greater flexibility and discretion to the field agent in order to increase his ability to allow or enhance public participation.

Feedback

In this type of interaction there is agreement on goals, either implicit or explicit, but it is not clear how best to accomplish them. If the goal is economic development, for example, it may not be clear whether the best means is to organize the farmers into cooperatives or to stimulate the most prosperous to try new seeds and hope for a diffusion effect. When means are not clear, agents will need to have some flexibility to adjust plans and strategies as they work with farmers or villagers. They will have to spend more time collecting information, talking with people, maintaining and comparing records.

Efforts in Peru to encourage local subsistence farmers to adopt well-water systems illustrate the importance of feedback. The project failed and had to be abandoned because, according to one analyst, the agents had neglected to consult with the farmers about the drilling. "If the change agency had allowed them to discuss the matter with local officials and villagers, allowed them to participate in the location and drilling of wells (since many of the people already had practical experience with well drilling), and gone along with the villager's magico-religious beliefs and practices with respect to water, all of the difficulties could have been averted and a success made of the project."[38]

The appropriate role for agents is to do research, to gather information from the farmers, and to try experimenting. The Puebla Project in Mexico illustrates a feedback role. "Preliminary studies were done in the project area on what production methods were being used, and interviewed farmers were allowed to give feedback on what kinds of technical approaches were most feasible. Then extension agents were, to the degree possible, selected for their degree of empathy with their clients and willingness to allow them to participate in the planning and decision-making processes, as well as for their technical ability in a particular agronomy and communication area."[39]

Supervisory systems can still maintain some of the formal procedures as in the service delivery model. However, the supervisor will need to work with the agents on research strategies, on monitoring, on data collection, rather than solely on service delivery strategies. Thus more attention will have to be paid to the role of agents as listeners, as information collectors. The feedback will work both ways, for the agents will have to communicate with beneficiaries about the relation between the information they collect and the goals they share. Farmers may identify their major problem supplies and indicate that farm production would increase if supplies were timely. Agents than might transmit this information, at the same time that they explain to the farmers that changes in fertilizer usage would also increase production. The information exchange therefore is two-way, and the learning involves techniques and means-end relationships.

The potential problem with this approach is that an experimental method requires granting a fair amount of discretion to the agents at the local level, which in turn will most likely produce failures as well as successes. Administrators find it hard to cope with uncertainty and are seldom receptive to negative results. They may try to control the experiments, to filter out negative information, and to halt prematurely the experiments. A feedback approach therefore requires sustained commitment. Reports on the Indonesian Family Planning Project attribute its success precisely to this kind of commitment. There was great uncertainty about the best means of accomplishing family planning. As a result, the project granted discretion for local staff to carry out small-scale experiments, many of which did not work. "The willingness of the mission to suppport unconventional projects with a significant risk of failure has been essential in the rapid evolution of the overall program."[40] The local staff were given the discretion necessary to try out new methods in their areas, at the same time that the central office rapidly provided funding and supplies.

Negotiation-Mobilization

When the technology is clear, but beneficiaries do not concur that the goal of a given program is a priority for them, or perhaps even desirable, the appropriate role is for the agent to negotiate with public beneficiaries over the goals of a project. Such bargaining over the project's aims should continue during implementation, since the initial policy formulation stage is not final. "Policy goals may be lacking in clarity because public feeling is ambivalent, and a certain amount of goal modification is inevitable as abstract policy ideas are converted into concrete programs of action."[41]

Organizations, however, may find it unnatural to bargain over goals. They are far more apt to try to reduce the uncertainty they confront and control the demands with which they choose to deal. Thus it is very likely that instead of negotiating, organizations and their agents will try to mobilize the public around predetermined goals. Similarly supervision will tend to encourage agents to enlist the public to support the organization and its programs. One example is provided by the Danfa Comprehensive Rural Health and Family Planning Project in Ghana. An analysis of the program found that the extension workers were given the task of convincing residents to "abandon traditional and customary modes of behavior and adopt new patterns of life, on the advice of an outsider. Some areas of behavior required only the motivation of individuals; in other areas group cooperation and sometimes the commitment of relatively scarce physical or monetary resources was required."[42]

Mutual Learning

In this final role, administrators are involved in negotiating with the public about their work and its purposes, and at the same time they need to collect information on how to accomplish it. Their role is therefore to organize the public and involve them directly in the process of accomplishing the task. But since there is no basis of agreement, they are not organizing the public to accomplish certain clearly defined goals as much as they are engaging beneficiaries in defining development and involving the community in self-development. The emphasis is on interaction between agents and the public, on mutuality and learning together.

The Bangladesh Rural Advancement Committee (BRAC) exemplifies a highly successful organization that has institutionalized ways to learn from its environment, particularly from its errors. For example, its first ambitious attempts at teaching adults did not sustain local interest. A review found that teaching materials appeared irrelevant to the peasants. A special unit was therefore set up to develop new materials based on interviews with the villagers. In yet a later phase, the project shifted away from all efforts to design tasks centrally and instituted a people-centered approach. The goals were also changed by the groups. The purpose of education shifted from a focus on literacy to consciousness raising and group skills.[43]

Although the BRAC project is a fairly sophisticated example of group decision making, requiring a very open-ended process, it is possible to add some structure to a mutual involvement role. Jedlicka describes the Puebla Project in Mexico, where a concerted effort was made to involve clients in selecting their goals as well as the technology to accomplish them. The method chosen was to have the extension agents organize the farmers into work groups. Once formed, the groups used consensus processes to determine whether to actually use the technology the agents proposed and, if they chose to use it, how to adapt it to their circumstances. It is obvious that this fourth mode demands more of the extension workers and requires considerable training and education. It is also clear that supervision is a much more complex task and must be consistent with the need to accord these agents flexibility and discretion in implementing their development assignments.[44]

The major problem is that this fourth type of situation has so many implicit uncertainties that a vacuum may be created. Because there is no initial agreement on either goals or means, a stalemate can result; agents might then be tempted to define the situation narrowly, avoiding opportunities for dialogue and interaction. In effect this fourth type of situation might readily be treated as an instance of the service delivery mode where goals and means are both clear, and routinization is an appropriate response.[45] David Korten notes the political volatility that surrounds any efforts to engage in a mutual learning process. From his several case studies it appears that interaction is most apt to occur when the public is already organized and project directors or agents can work with social organizations.[46]

Implications

Local bureaucrats or field agents are appropriately viewed as functioning on the boundary of an organization. They are part of an organization with its rewards and incentives and also part of a political environment that exerts its own pressures on them. Most studies suggest that on balance agents are not very effective in dealing with these tensions, a finding that has led to various efforts to strengthen the way in which they are supervised and to use structural incentives and rewards. These measures are appropriate when there is agreement and shared expectations between the government agency and its clients. When this is not the case, supervision needs to be integrated with more fruitful and open-ended ways of linking bureaucrats to their political environment and particularly to the public. When agreement is lacking, then relations marked by feedback, negotiation, or mutual learning are more appropriate.

In these last three types of relations among agents, organizations, and clients, supervision and incentives will need to be less structured than in the first type. Supervision will need to allow for goal changes and for open-ended dynamics to occur. Agent evaluation cannot be based solely on efficiency in achieving results for it needs to also include the extent to which the process of consultation and interaction has occurred. Similarly, agents need to know that they have some discretion and can modify their tasks and respond to the preferences of the public. The model of an organization based on economic exchange is thus not as appropriate here as the sociological model in which the administrator is viewed as an actor in a political setting. To ignore the role of this political setting is actually to place too much responsibility on the local agents. Indeed, much remains beyond their control and influence.

The typology also clarified that organizations frequently will not use these opportunities, but that in each case they will be tempted to foreclose their options and try to exert some control over these environmental pressures. Thus in the second type, where means are unclear, they will try to limit the kind of research that occurs and constrain the kind of information that agents collect. In the third type they will frequently try to mobilize groups rather than negotiate with them. And finally, they will tend to avoid open-ended learning models where change and uncertainty will clearly abound.

Relations with the Public

The above typology describes four different ways of relating to the public: serving, mobilizing, encouraging feedback, and mutual involvement. It also indicates that organizations frequently try to avoid open-ended interaction with the public and attempt to control and structure their relations with external groups. And yet there are cases where organizations do work creatively with the public. Next we examine the potential trade-offs that development administrators face in deciding whether to collaborate with the public.

To the extent that administrators are governed by efficiency, relations with citizens will take on a very pragmatic character, and citizen participation is acceptable to the extent that it contributes to program effectiveness. There are essentially three ways in which the public can enhance a program. They can provide information, they can offer political support, and they can contribute resources. The public, for example, can inform administrators about the best way to improve nutrition and help it avoid costly mistakes. The public can also provide a constituency for administrators who are trying to promote change. If an affected public has participated in designing goals and strategies, it will have a stake in the project and may provide administrators with crucial political support. Similarly, the public can find ways to contribute to efforts to improve nutrition or housing on its own.[47]

All of these results of participation can facilitate the work of the local adminstrators, and it appears reasonable that if agents are aware of these benefits they will make the effort to encourage participation. Benefits can be of two kinds. They can be fairly certain and immediate, or they can be uncertain and remote. If a field agent estimates that by working closely with farmers he is fairly certain to improve agricultural yield in the next growing season, he is likely to invest the effort. However, if the benefits will only be forthcoming in the long run, he is less likely to be impressed with participation. Costs have the same characteristics. Some are immediate and certain; these include time and energy negotiating with suspicious citizens who have a very marginal commitment to development. Or costs can be remote and thus not salient to the adminstrator; future demands of the public as it gains more political experience are an example. Table 9.5 lays out the four options that result from different combinations of costs and benefits and indicates the circumstances under which bureaucrats will be most apt to choose to work with the public.

TABLE 9.5

Circumstances Under Which Bureaucrats Will Encourage Participation

| COSTS | BENEFITS | |
	Certain	Uncertain
Certain	A. Will work with the public if benefits outweigh costs	B. Least Likely to work with public
Uncertain	C. Most apt to work with the public	D. Highest risks: working with public unlikely.

When public participation provides certain and immediate benefits such as better information or contributions of support and resources, administrators will support it. Then they are operating under either Type A or C conditions. Under Type B circumstances, agents are less likely to mobilize the public unless they are given specific incentives. Extension agents for example could be rewarded for being available to farmers or for meeting with them in groups, as in several of the cases described throughout this chapter. Under some circumstances, particularly those characterized by Type D, participation is less apt to be supported unless citizens are already organized and demand a role. These are occasions when the risks are very great because the benefits are so uncertain. Milton Esman notes that administrators in several countries have been willing to assume such risks; the determining factor does not appear to be ideology, but rather a "willingness to risk the political consequences of a mobilized peasantry."[48] One can only assume that these uncertain costs are balanced by an intuitive appreciation for the potential benefits.

Conclusions

Lower-level administrators are strategically important in determining the success of development programs and projects. Yet they are often caught in the cross fire between members of the public and their own organizational hierarchy. The ways in which they resolve these pressures will vary with their own preferences, with organizational incentives, and with the way in which they estimate the results of working with the public. Thus far we have only told half of the story however; we have only looked at the way in which administrators and extension agents view their tasks and the role of external groups. It is also important to consider how members of the public view their opportunities and under what circumstances they elect to get involved in the development process. In Chapter 10 we examine participation from the public's viewpoint.

Notes

1. Bernard Schaffer and Huang Wen-hsien, "Distribution and the Theory of Access," *Development and Change* 6 (1975):13-36.

2. David Leonard, *Reaching the Peasant Farmer* (Chicago: University of Chicago, 1977); Allen Jedlicka, *Organization for Rural Development* (New York: Praeger, 1977); Harry Blair, "Rural Development, Class Structure and Bureaucracy in Bangladesh," *World Development* 6 (1978):65-82; David Gould, "The Administration of Underdevelopment," in *The Political Economy of Underdevelopment,* ed. Guy Gran (New York: Prentice Hall, 1979). See also

Robert Chambers' analysis of this oft-repeated criticism in *Managing Rural Development* (Uppsala: Scandinavia Institute of African Studies, 1974).

3. Jedlicka, *Organization,* p. 24.

4. Chambers, *Managing Rural Development,* p. 23.

5. Ibid.; see also David Leonard, *Reaching the Peasant Farmer,* p. 155.

6. Daniel Katz and Robert Kahn, *The Social Psychology of Organizations* (New York: John Wiley, 1978), pp. 65–66.

7. Jeffrey Prottas, "The Power of the Street Level Bureaucrat in Public Service Bureaucracies," *Urban Affairs Quarterly,* 13 (1978):285–311; Michael Lipsky, "Street Level Bureaucracy and the Analysis of Urban Reform," *Urban Affairs Quarterly,* 13 (1971):391–409; Yecheziel Hasenfeld and Richard English, *Human Service Organizations* (Ann Arbor: University of Michigan, 1974), pp. 1–24.

8. S.J. Eldersveld, V. Jagannadham, and A. P. Barnabas, *The Citizen and the Administrator in a Developing Democracy* (Illinois: Scott, Foresman, 1978). Data for this exploratory study were obtained from interviews with citizens and administrators in Delhi state between January and May 1964. A two-stage sampling procedure was used in order to obtain a random probability sample of 400 adults from rural areas and 400 adults from urban areas. In addition 220 administrators from five agencies were interviewed. J. N. Khosla was director of the Indian Institute of Public Administration when this study was done. In a two-volume collection in honor of Professor Khosla, *Dynamics of Development,* ed. S. K. Sharma (Delhi: Concept Publishing, 1978), there is an empirical study building on this earlier survey by V. A. Pai Panandiker and S. S. Kshirsagar, "Bureaucratic Adaptation to Development Administration", vol. 1, pp. 309–337, and generally confirming its results.

9. Lipsky, "Street Level Bureaucracy"; Hasenfeld and English, *Human Service Organizations;* Clarence Stone, "The Implementation of Social Programs," *Journal of Social Issues* 36 (1980):13–34.

10. Lipsky, "Street Level Bureaucracy."

11. Jedlicka, *Organization,* p. 34.

12. Stone, "Implementation."

13. Robert Chambers, "Rural Poverty Unperceived," mimeographed (Brighton: Institute of Development Studies, 1980).

14. Stone, "Implementation."

15. For example, see Stanley Heginbotham, *Cultures in Conflict, The Four Faces of Indian Bureaucracy* (New York: Columbia University Press, 1975).

16. See the discussion of Jon Morris's work in Leonard, *Reaching the Peasant Farmer,* pp. 197–198.

17. Chambers, *Managing Rural Development,* pp. 49–51.

18. Ibid., p. 60.

19. Robert Gurevich, "Teachers, Rural Development and the Civil Service in Thailand," *Asian Survey* 15 (1975):840–851.

20. Chambers, *Managing Rural Development,* pp. 67f; Leonard, *Reaching the Peasant Farmer.*

21. Paul Lawrence and Jay Lorsch, *Organization and Environment* (Cambridge, Mass.: Harvard Business School, 1967).

22. Derick W. Brinkerhoff, "Participation and Rural Development Project Effectiveness: An Organizational Analysis of Four Cases" (Ph.D. diss., Harvard University, 1980). Coralie Bryant, "Organizational Impediments to Making Participation a Reality: 'Swimming Upstream' in AID." *Rural Development Participation Review* (Ithaca, N.Y.: Cornell University Press, 1980).

23. Leonard, *Reaching the Peasant Farmer*, p. 217.

24. See Rosabeth Moss Kanter, *Men and Women of the Corporation* (New York: Basic Books, 1977); see also Jedlicka, *Organization*, p. 36.

25. Eldersveld, Jagannadham, and Barnabas, *The Citizen and the Administrator*, p. 79.

26. Carolyn and Martin Needleman, *Guerrillas in the Bureaucracy* (New York: John Wiley, 1974).

27. Heginbotham, *Cultures in Conflict*, Chapter 7.

28. Chambers, *Managing Rural Development*, Chapter 3.

29. Leonard, *Reaching the Peasant Farmer*, pp. 201–209.

30. Daniel Benor and James Q. Harrison, *Agricultural Extension, The Training and Visit System* (Washington, D.C.: World Bank, 1977).

31. Leonard, *Reaching the Peasant Farmer*, p. 220.

32. David Korten, "Community Social Organization in Rural Development," *Public Administration Review* 40 (September–October 1980):480–511.

33. James Thompson, *Organizations in Action* (New York: McGraw-Hill, 1967), p. 134. The four modes that he derives are computation, bargaining, majority judgment, and inspiration.

34. Edilberto DeJesus, "Local Linkage Building in a Small Farmer Development Program," mimeographed (Manila: Asian Institute of Management, 1979).

35. Prottas, "Power of the Street Level Bureaucrats," p. 296; Schaffer and Wen-hsien, "Distribution."

36. Singh, cited in Jedlicka, *Organization*, p. 46.

37. E. Philip Morgan, "Rural Development Management," *International Review of Administrative Sciences* 45 (1979):165–168.

38. Jedlicka, describing a study by Allan Holmberg, in *Organization*, p. 59.

39. Ibid., pp. 52–53.

40. James Heiby, Gayl Ness, Barbara Pillsbury, "AID's Role in Indonesia Family Planning," mimeographed (Washington, D.C.: AID, 1979), p. 18.

41. Stone, "Implementation." For a discussion of mobilization from the public's perspective see Coralie Bryant and Louise G. White, *Managing Rural Development: Peasant Participation in Rural Development Projects* (Hartford, Conn.: Kumarian Press, 1980).

42. Gene B. Peterson, "A Case Study of the Danfa Comprehensive Rural Health and Family Planning Project, Ghana", mimeographed (Washington, D.C.: AID, 1978). Also see the discussion on "mobilizing capacity," John Montgomery, *Technology and Civic Life* (Cambridge, Mass.: MIT, 1974), p. 216.

43. Korten, "Community Social Organization."

44. Jedlicka, *Organization*, p. 82.

45. E. Philip Morgan called this point to our attention.

46. Korten, "Community Social Organization." See also John Montgomery, "Development," *Public Administration Review* 39 (1979):58–65.

47. John Turner, "Housing in Three Dimensions," *World Development* 6 (1978).

48. Milton Esman, "Development Administration and Constituency Organization," *Public Administration Review* 38 (1978):166–172.

10
Managing Participation

Introduction

Development as a process of increasing people's capacity to determine their future means that people need to be included in the process — they need to participate. Participation, or empowerment (as discussed in Chapter 1), is part of the process and definition of development. In previous chapters we have referred to participation by the public, or by beneficiaries, in project design or in implementation. Managing participation, however, is more than including the public in one stage of the design process or in evaluation of the project. Rather participation informs the meaning and integrity of the entire process. It is an attitude of openness to the perceptions and feelings of others; it is a concern for what difference a project makes in peoples' lives; it is an awareness of the contributions that others can bring to an activity. The techniques and strategies for eliciting participation that we describe in this chapter are means and not ends. More basically, we explore the various dimensions of participation in development in order to suggest its potential and possibilities.

As a starting point, consider some actual examples of participation:

A program to train health workers in Guatemala:

We have found it is of vital importance to select trainees with care. At first we generally accepted those who were recommended to us by a local priest or a Peace Corps volunteer. We have since learned better. Our approach now is to encourage each community to set up a community betterment committee, which . . . selects the person whom we are to train . . . . The man we train represents his community and the community is responsible for him and can discipline him, retain him, or recommend his dismissal.[1]

A development of farming cooperatives in the Ivory Coast:

Farmers belonging to block planting groups would own individual plots, but would undertake important group obligations. The farmers would be mutually responsible for all project-related debts incurred by group members, and would agree to undertake mutual assistance in the implementation of block planting and maintenance.[2]

A squatter settlement in Lusaka:

Several nights a week there are community meetings, in which leaders and citizens explain, talk and listen to each other. There is a conviction that talking together can resolve any misunderstandings and problems which have occurred. . . . The groups on one of their planning weekends will work through a whole series of issues—issues they themselves generate.[3]

These examples suggest the variety of forms that participation can take. Each response emerged from the particular needs of the project or activity and out of an appreciation for the potential contributions of the public. And each assumed, at least implicitly, that people can develop and grow in the process and therefore that the design of participatory processes should not be totally constrained by people's existing capacities and preferences. Next we consider various approaches to participation and then examine participation from the perspective of the public. Finally, we suggest what implications these approaches and the view of the public have for participation; what they suggest for organizing, designing, and managing participatory processes and for increasing the effectiveness of such processes.

Varieties of Participation

Participation in Political and Administrative Processes

Traditionally, participation has been identified with partisan or political behavior—voting, campaigning, interest group activity, lobbying. These activities are what Joan Nelson calls horizontal forms of participation; people get involved collectively in efforts to influence policy decisions. A second arena of participation Nelson refers to as vertical participation. Vertical participation includes any occasions when members of the public develop particular relations with elites or officials, relations that are mutually beneficial. Examples include patron-client networks and political machines. In both these cases the public is not as concerned with influencing the government as it is with developing the particular relationship and receiving benefits from it.[4] Nelson's distinction is a useful reminder that these individual alliances are pervasive and may either interfere with, or substitute for, more direct involvement in the political process.

Participation in administrative processes, a third arena for participation, can overlap with either of the above. It may take the form of interest group activity to shape administrative decisions, or of a particular exchange between patron and client; but usually it is more inclusive than either of these forms. It includes decisions by farmers whether to adopt a new technology, squatters meeting together to plan communal efforts to put roofs on their huts, joining a collective to plan ways to market farm produce, taking part in a nutrition education program. In this chapter we focus on this third type of activity.

Changes in the Meaning of Participation

These different perspectives on participation are part of a broader debate, one in which development theorists, donor agencies, third world leaders, and citizen groups themselves have all participated. And just as the concepts of both development and administration have been given new meaning over the years, similar and related changes have occurred with the meaning of participation.

With a few significant exceptions, the dominant concern during the 1950s and 1960s was controlling the amount and type of participation. Military regimes, for example, were efforts to foreclose participation at the national level. Elsewhere participation was feared as a disruptive influence. Even where participation was encouraged in a community development program, it was usually very limited in its scope.[5] This preoccupation with the dangers inherent in participation was consistent with definitions of development as capital intensive and growth oriented and with administration as a hierarchical top-down structure.

During this period, participation was defined in purely political terms; it meant voting, party membership, activity in voluntary associations, protest movements, and so forth. As modernization proceeded, it was assumed that the benefits of growth would trickle down to the public and gradually stimulate their involvement in these political processes.[6] In the meantime it was important to provide institutions to channel participation so as to prevent its potentially unstable results. Parties were particularly encouraged as a means to harness and manage the political energies and demands of the public.[7]

By the 1970s, the meaning of participation in the development context began to be redefined. Rather than being identified with political and electoral processes, it became associated with the administrative process. According to John Cohen and Norman Uphoff, this change in attitude was initially spurred by politicians, and "had a notable counter insurgency quality about it." Participation was valued as an alternative to revolutionary movements and the green uprising.[8] The reasoning was that if people could be mobilized to be part of the development process, they would be less available to revolution.

Another reason for this changed meaning was the realization that the political process was too undeveloped to elicit preferences or involve the public, and therefore participation would have more impact within the implementation process. "The implementation process may be the major arena in which individuals and groups are able to pursue conflicting interests and compete for scarce resources. It may even be the principal nexus of the interaction between a government and citizenry."[9] A related argument was slightly more pessimistic. The work of economists such as Kenneth Arrow implied that democratic political processes had fatal flaws even at their best and except in special circumstances were unlikely to reflect accurately public sentiment.[10] Thus for a variety of reasons, attention was turned to ways to involve the public in the implementation phase of development and particularly in administrative processes.

Those involved in development projects picked up this new emphasis and talked about the practical values of involving farmers or peasants in the development taking place in their villages. For example, Uma Lele reviewed African rural development projects and found that participation had been a significant and positive component. "Participation in planning and implementation of programs can develop the self-reliance necessary among rural people for accelerated development."[11] A similar study of thirty-six projects tried to explain why some were more successful than others. Success was measured by benefit-cost ratios, the number of new agricultural practices, the extent to which the projects increased the farmer's capacity for self-help, and the project's capacity to be self-sustaining. They found that the best predictor of success was the extent of local action in the project. They defined participation as involvement by the farmers in project design and implementation and as commitment of either labor or money.[12]

As a result of similar studies and actual experience in the field, participation came to mean being a part of the process of project design and implementation. Instead of being equated with electoral politics, it took on the more pragmatic meaning of involving people in those administrative actions that directly affect them. Participation was usually valued for very pragmatic reasons — it could provide useful information and it often could improve project design.

The Community Development Model

The meaning of participation was also informed by the approach termed *community development*. Its influence was primarily felt during the 1950s when it spread to over sixty nations, although it was most systematically introduced in India.[13] Poverty was primarily attributed to deficiencies in individuals, and thus considerable attention was paid to the necessity for first changing attitudes in order to stimulate participation. "The core of the community development movement and method is to help people help themselves improve the material and non material conditions of their lives because the assumption is that 'there, in the long run, lies the salvation of the community.'"[14]

The ideology of community development was seldom translated into reality. For some it was seen as a method to expand agricultural production rather than as an end in itself.[15] One study found that in spite of its participating rhetoric, "time and again programs were formed and targets set from above" in an essentially top-down process.[16] A more serious indictment was the claim that the community development approach had a simplistic view of the development process and ignored conflicting interests and the need for structural changes in the community. By focusing on the local community, it ignored the larger economic and political context that frequently subverted its impact.[17]

In any case by 1965 the community development model had been largely abandoned. Reasons for its decline include its uneven performance, the ease with which benefits were skewed to the wealthier, and conflicts with existing bureaucratic agencies.[18] The new major thrust was to use central planning, to focus on the urban sector, and to encourage centrally directed economic growth. And participation was not seen as relevant to these emphases, except the urban sector.

It would be a mistake, however, to forget the contributions of the movement and the lessons it offers for expanding participation. One study lists the following: (1) participation should not be a separate program, it is a process and hence should be integrated with other activities; (2) participation has to be based on local organizations; (3) more equitable distribution would encourage more participation; (4) instead of basing development on isolated efforts, linkages between various levels need to be created.[19] In summary, participation needs to be part of a broader conceptualization of development, with much more attention to organizational structures and linkages.

Receiving Benefits

Although participation is generally defined in terms of "influence" or "being part of" a process, participation is sometimes defined in terms of the benefits received from development. This perspective is based on the contributions of economists and has been picked up by other development analysts.[20] Defining participation solely in terms of received benefits is restrictive and alters what is generally publicly understood as participation. If participation in the benefits is used to *supplement* other definitions, however, it is a useful addition. Definitions that focus solely on political and administrative processes too easily ignore the issue of benefits. It is possible, after all, for the public to invest itself in the political process and yet not gain any additional benefits from their contributions.[21]

Power Versus Co-optation

Participation should be considered in its relationship to power. The basic point is that unless the public has power to back up its preferences and demands, these demands are unlikely to be met. Participation is then a way both to generate and to express power, through elections and interest groups or through cooperatives and tenants' groups. Those in authority are likely to co-opt these processes and use the public to support their own ends. That is the nature of politics. Participation in administrative processes is particularly vulnerable to co-optation and to being used to reinforce the influence of managers. In fact, it has repeatedly been stressed throughout this book that implementation is a political process and that administrators need to use it to gain allies for their goals. It is natural that they will often turn to the public or to beneficiaries and try to mobilize them as allies. Such mobilization can easily become co-optation. It can also be a part of the natural exchange relationships within which the political process takes place.

Ralf Dahrendorf, the conflict theorist, argues that in fact co-optation is not an aberration; rather it is implicit in any process where people with influence interact with those without influence. He describes how those in authority will frequently try to include representatives of lower-level personnel in decision making. A worker placed on a board of directors or a low-income citizen serving on an advisory board will almost inevitably be co-opted. Each will cease to represent the interests of the workers, or the clients, and will become engulfed by the perspective of management. The only solution according to Dahrendorf and other conflict theorists is for the workers or the public to have their own independent base of authority.[22]

Some participatory strategies are more compatible with an independent base of authority than others are and hence less easily co-opted than others. One listing of strategies is provided by Mary Hollnsteiner on the basis of her work in the Philippines. Reflecting on opportunities for the urban poor, she lists six different means of participation: (1) representation by a "solid citizens" group, (2) appointment of local leaders to official positions, (3) allowing the community to select one of several plans, (4) consultation throughout the planning process, (5) representing the public on decision-making boards, (6) control by the community over funds and expenditures. Only the last three modes Hollnsteiner observes actually constitute participation; the others are forms of co-optation in that they allow elites or bureaucrats to dominate the process.[23]

Those concerned with the ease with which co-optation occurs often turn their attention to protest. From their perspective, protest is not a natural or preferred strategy; rather it occurs when formal channels do not work.[24] Consider the example of "nuisance tactics," which groups often use. "Squatter women in Cebu, tired of appealing to the local community development authorities to facilitate a piped water connection to their site, simply marched into the agency offices' premises and calmly proceeded to do their laundry under the faucets there. The agency quickly got the new connection installed."[25] On a more massive scale the same tactics have been used by squatters to take over vacant lands on the outskirts of cities. Such actions become possible when other channels fail to serve the interests of various groups of the public.

Participation as a Value in Its Own Right

Part of what empowerment means as it was discussed in Chapter 1 is an enhanced sense of efficacy. Efficacy is especially important for peoples who have been colonized — it is the antidote for the psychological pain of colonization. As Goulet writes, "I include optimum participation among development's strategic principles because unless efforts are made to widen participation, development will interfere with men's quest for esteem and freedom from manipulation."[26] This emphasis is in some contrast to most of the other perspectives that emphasize the instrumental nature of participation and its contributions to projects.

Dilemmas in Development Administration

It is apparent from these descriptions that although there are different ways to define participation, the dominant perspective in the literature is to treat it pragmatically, to view it as a strategy to improve the development process. In the rest of the chapter we continue on this basis but also try to incorporate a concern for issues of power and self-development.

Even when participation occurs within the administration arena, it is a profoundly political process. The public can affect organizational dynamics; they can either be allies or offer vetoes. They can facilitate decisions by offering useful information, or they can slow down the process. One study of four participatory projects concludes that the major contribution of participation is political rather than technical; that is, participation does not necessarily enhance a project's effectiveness as much as it enables the participants to influence what is meant by effectiveness. Participation is one way for the poor to "contribute to establishing a definition of project effectiveness that serves their interests."[27]

Some of the specific dilemmas that confront administrators as they work with participatory projects are the following:

Access. Which groups or members of the public should be included?

Responsiveness. To whom should administrators be responsive, to the organized public or the unorganized and less visible public?

Professionalism. What is the best way to evaluate citizen preferences when they contradict professional training and judgment?

Effectiveness. What can an administrator do if organized publics either veto or dilute a project so that little is done?

The implication of these questions is that the value of participation is not in its presence alone. The value of participation varies depending on who is participating at what stage of the administrative process and what kind of activity they are doing. Rather than valuing participation per se, the important issue is what kinds of participation are appropriate to a given task and given environment. "Having 'more' participation is not always 'better', as the value depends on what kind of participation, under what circumstances, by and for whom?"[28]

But although the above questions tend to assume administrators want to be responsive to the public, the dilemma for the public is that this assumption is not always accurate. They may be easily manipulated by administrators who feel primarily accountable to their agencies or supervisors. The public's problem is to hold administrators accountable and to find some ways to influence them. Accountability is particularly important precisely where political institutions are weakest. Citizens within a developing country would therefore view the same problems differently.

Access. Assuming that bureaucrats are trying to build coalitions with supporters, what voice or access can nonsupporters have?

Responsiveness. Administrators often benefit from participatory processes. But what about those instances when this is not the case and opposition threatens them? How can the concept of loyal opposition be instilled? What recourse do the poor—the peasants—have to be taken seriously?

Professionalism. Based on their professionalism, administrators may readily assume they know what is best for project beneficiaries and others in the community; this presumption is particularly popular in the third world, where there is often a great social distance between bureaucrats and the public. At the same time it is easy for the public to be intimidated by the expertise and training of administrators. The problem for citizens is therefore to develop an independent source of authority.

Effectiveness. The public may define effectiveness very differently than administrators; peasants, for example, may have other goals they are seeking quite separate from those of the experts.

Administrators and citizenry therefore have different perspectives on the participatory process. One way to incorporate both is to view participation as a learning process, as mutual interaction. Administrators need to share their judgments with citizens, at the same time that they need to temper their professional judgment with an awareness of citizen preferences. The mutuality of the process will work best if the public has its own organizational base and is not totally dependent on administrators to listen to them.[29] Many of the details of this learning process have been discussed in former chapters where project design, implementation, and evaluation were considered. The point here is that process should not only be useful to the administrators, but facilitate and protect the interests of the public as well.

The Calculus of Participation

Benefits and Costs

Thus far we have considered the place of participation in the administrative process, assuming that if participatory processes exist, people will want to get involved. But it is also true that sometimes people are not interested in participation or at least do not choose to make that investment. Therefore it is important to consider under what circumstances groups and individuals will participate in the political process.

As suggested in Chapter 5 behavior can be viewed from a sociological or an economic perspective. The former examines the socioeconomic influences on people, the latter focuses on the choices that people make to accomplish their goals. For many years, development studies emphasized sociological factors such as the poverty and isolation of small farmers and peasants; they used them primarily to explain why peasants were often reluctant to participate in development. If change depended on peasant initiative, it was unlikely to occur. More recently economic models have been used; they emphasize the choices that people do in fact make, rather than the influences on those choices. They therefore provide a new perspective on the reasons why people may be reluctant to participate. Their utility for this study is that they suggest strategies for development administrators to use in designing projects to include participation.

Several studies have used economic models to explain why peasant farmers respond to new agricultural technology, but they can be generalized to explain participation more broadly conceived. Economic models predict that individuals will pursue their goals in such a way as to balance the benefits they hope to achieve against the costs they expect to pay. Some models define the benefits and costs solely in terms of economic gain;[30] others find that goals can be more varied. One study found, for example, that in Mysore villages, farmers optimized economic benefit with some goods and not with others. And in Papua, farmer behavior was better explained by familial patterns than by strictly economic behavior. The point is that cultural and social characteristics contribute to the ways in which people define their goals.[31] These variations can be included in choice models by referring to the concept of utility rather than simply economic gain. In both cases the models predict that people determine how likely these utilities are and then choose accordingly.

Research on the validity of this model in rural development has added two important qualifiers, risk and opportunity costs. Peasants do not in fact always participate in programs that would optimize their utility or income. Given their meager resources, often the risks of gambling on optimizing their income are too great. Farmers may therefore accept less than the minimum mean income in order to reduce risk; their decisions, however, are still rational because given their income they are still minimizing the accompanying risk.[32] The point of the analysis is that when farmers fail to adopt innovations or to contribute to a project, the problem does not necessarily derive from apathy or traditionalism. Rather the lower their income, the less risk they can afford and the less incentive they have for enlisting in a project or trying a new method of fertilizer.

A second qualification is that farmers will include "opportunity costs" in their calculus. In estimating their benefits from an activity, they also consider what *alternative* benefits they would have gained if they had spent their time doing something else. If they attend a meeting, they have not only paid the cost of their time, but also the cost of not having enjoyed some leisure time. In deciding whether to participate in a local co-op, they thus compare the benefits they expect to gain, their cost in time and resources, the costs of not being able to have something else, as well as how much risk they feel they can afford. This gives us the following formula: $P = [(B \times Pr) - (DC + OC)]R$. Participation (P) is a function of the benefits (B) to be gained times the probability (Pr) of gaining them, minus two kinds of costs – direct costs (DC) and opportunity costs (OC), all times the amount of risk they can afford to take (R). It is readily apparent that the poor will be much less likely to participate than those with more resources.

Farmers as Managers

This formula tells us that estimates of risk can vary with a farmer's income; they can also vary according to whether or not the farmer plays a part in designing the project. According to Allen Jedlicka, it is important to remember that "the farmer is himself a manager, a man who has control over his productive enterprises (no matter how small), who is responsible for his efforts and his rewards." He continues,

> Before this kind of person is going to risk his survival by attempting to adopt a series of new and untested (by him) technologies and survival mechanisms, he is going to request extensive participation in the planning, discussion, and decision-making phases of the process. Above all, if he is not allowed to participate, express his views, and be considered, by change agents, as a mature adult who understands why he has a rational reason for behaving the way he does, one should not seriously expect an overwhelming positive response toward attempts to change him.[33]

Special Problems of Women

Women also undergo common experiences in the development process, and so we can ask how they would think through the "calculus of participation." There is no consensus as to whether women are more influenced by their sex or by their class. It is an important question because "one position would target programs to reach and assist women primarily, whereas the second would treat women in the context of their social class opportunities."[34] Although the weight of each factor varies by locale, it is also true that the effects are cumulative and that women are particularly adversely affected by poverty. Among those who are powerless, poor women in rural areas are at the bottom of the pyramid. One of the cruel ironies of rural poverty is that these women also play a major role in producing food. In some instances, women work nearly twice as many hours in the fields as men because of the sexual division of labor.[35] (Weeding and stoop labor is usually women's work.) Yet malnourished themselves, often pregnant or lactating, these women have little or no access to influence and as a result receive few of the benefits that flow from their labors. They often eat last; they surely eat least.[36]

In many instances, it is not only that poor rural women have not fared as well as men, but that they are sometimes positively worse off than they were prior to the onset of modernization. As Uma Lele points out, Western project planners often tend to see African women, for example, in Western terms—their work is in the home, not in the field.[37] As a result agricultural extension services have not been designed to assist women in their work outside the home. Further, if household incomes are kept separately, as is often the case in Africa, increases in a family's income from exports may not be used for domestic expenses. In other cases, work is mechanized and jobs are no longer available to women, again reducing their income. To make up for the lost income, women simply work harder, eventually lowering their life expectancy.[38]

Given these several characteristics, it is predictable that the cost side of the equation would be higher for women. Because they often work at home and in the field, their opportunity costs are greater; and because they have less experience and fewer resources, the direct costs of participation are higher. At the same time, there are few offsetting benefits, either from their families or from project designs. They are thus an illustration of the equation that powerlessness equals little participation in benefits as well as in influence. Unfortunately the reverse does not always hold; projects that provide them benefits do not necessarily enhance their influence.

Collective Action

The above discussion concerns the way in which people calculate whether or not to get involved as individuals. An economic calculus is also useful to understand people's decisions to participate or not to participate in collective or "horizontal" activities. In economic terms, *collective action* is essential in order to bring about a public good. A public good is generally available to people in the community, whether or not they have actually contributed to its existence. Once it is provided, no one can be excluded from its use. If several neighbors decide to join together and build a road, it is there for others to use as well. From an economic perspective, the problem is that people will decide not to work on the road since they could use it anyway, and hence they would choose to "free ride" on the work of others.

The problem can be illustrated by examining a decision whether to build an irrigation system. Consider the choices available to two communities (see Table 10.1). Let us say that community A would receive four units of benefits from the irrigation system, but that cost would be six units. Obviously they would not build it. Then suppose they find that

TABLE 10.1

Calculus of Cooperative Action

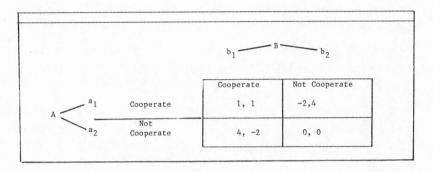

if community B shared the cost, they would each receive four units of benefits, but only pay half the cost, or three units. It seems clear that they would both agree to cooperate on the project since each would have a net gain of one unit of benefit. However, because the irrigation system is a public good, each community might reason that if it held out until the other did all the work, it could free ride and get the benefits without paying any costs. By this reasoning, *neither would participate* in developing the irrigation system, even though it would provide a net benefit for both of them. The point is that people will often choose not to participate in collective action, even if they are in favor of it, because their enjoyment of its benefits does not depend on their contributions.

The utility of these economic models is that they have implications for administrative strategies in designing participatory projects.[39] First, they suggest that it is imperative to understand how members of the community perceive benefits and costs and how they assess risks. Second, administrators need to find ways to lower the costs of participation. They might work through traditional groups in the community, or they might be sure they keep the project simple and manageable. Third, administrators need to find ways to lower the risk of participation in new efforts. Leadership and small groups have both been used to handle problems of risk, either by sharing the risk or by increasing the likelihood that projects will pay off. Finally, it is useful to find ways to ensure that only those who contribute will share in the benefits. Perhaps special benefits can accrue to those who shared in building a health clinic or in constructing an irrigation system. Next we explore several of these strategies more fully.

Strategies to Mobilize Participation and Increase Its Effectiveness

Designing Projects to Be Simple and Manageable

One cluster of strategies focuses on the kind of project being designed. *Providing Direct Benefits.* As the model described above suggests, people are more apt to participate when the benefits accrue directly to them. For example, in the Upper Volta, residents were willing to contribute to an irrigation project, but not to developing a storage capacity for sorghum.[40]

Small Size. When a project involves a small community, everyone's contribution is more apt to be noticed and make a difference, and thus the free-rider problem is less important.[41] Saunders found that in Malawi where credit groups were kept at a size of twenty-five, repayment of loans was over 90 percent, in contrast to a much lower return in Thailand where groups were required to have at least fifty members.[42] Other studies indicate that when smaller projects are expanded regionally their initial success is often diluted.[43] One reason is that as projects expand in size their organizations expand and tend to become more top-down and institutional (See Chapter 3).[44]

Simple Tasks. In her study of farmer organizations in Ecuador and Honduras, Judy Tendler repeatedly stresses the value of simple organizations that have a single task and do not require elaborate skills.[45] A project in Malaysia was successful for similar reasons. Machinery to process rubber was jointly owned by the community; it was decided to have members use it strictly on a cash-and-carry basis in order to eliminate the need for bookkeeping.[46] As discussed in Chapter 6, projects are best kept small and simple. Robert Chambers lists the following characteristics for projects designed to help the poorest: they should be small, administration-intensive rather than capital-intensive, and highly dispersed. Chambers continues that because of these characteristics, they will obviously be difficult to monitor, slow to implement, and not suitable for complex techniques of project appraisal.[47]

Self-Help. Often individual action may not be rational, but if a community were given the opportunity and resources to create or build or maintain a project activity, they might find it rational. Self-help projects are one way to multiply the resources in any community and also to ensure that people have an investment in their work. A self-help project in a squatter settlement in Lusaka is one example.

Groups of householders can decide to work collectively on trenches for water supply or community facilities such as clinics. When they do, any savings from work which would otherwise have to be contracted accrue to those who worked — sometimes in the form of chits redeemable from supply depots for materials, windows, door frames, cement etc., which the squatter can than use in improving his own house. . . . The process is a skillful use of motivation and incentives coordinated in such a manner as to enhance collective action. And the results are far-reaching, for there is a sense of mutual ownership of the project which could not otherwise be generated.[48]

Self-help approaches can be used for very pragmatic reasons — they increase available resources, and they usually mean that people get the good or service they prefer. One argument adds that they are also important to people's sense of self. Consider housing for instance. Housing is so central to a family's life that it is important for the family to have a central role in choosing and constructing it.[49]

Voucher Systems. One version of self-help projects is to set up a formal voucher system. The central government provides vouchers or coupons to a community, which can then be used to "buy" development projects. The role of the government is to prepare a catalog describing possible projects and their cost. In deciding which to purchase, members of a community may prefer to stretch their resources by contributing some of the labor themselves; they may choose one elaborate project, or several small ones. The point is that they will choose preferred projects, they will have the incentive to stretch their resources and to maintain their investment, and finally their capacity for decision making will be increased.[50]

The point of any and all of these strategies is to include a concern with motivating people's involvement in the life of a project. Their interest, energy, and resources are scarce goods in an economic sense, and projects need to find ways to make community involvement and contribution rational and rewarding.

The Use of Organizations

A second cluster of strategies emphasizes the importance of organizations in mobilizing publics and designing participation.

Indigenous Organizations. In a study of World Bank projects, Robert Saunders found almost no instances where projects were designed to work with traditional groups in a community; they either created new groups or assumed that the potential benefits of a project would offer a sufficient inducement to the community. Indigenous groups, however, are an important resource because of their cohesiveness and their reliance on mutual trust. Frequently these can neutralize the free-rider problem. He found that in Indonesia traditional groups and leaders have been used as a basis for organizing people around irrigation systems, and they have proved very effective in allocating water efficiently and in maintaining the canals. The point has been made that groups organized around social and familial ties break down when they are enlisted to accomplish specific tasks. He concludes, however, that the lesson is not to ignore such groups, but to integrate them gradually and sensitively. Ironically he adds that one reason the value of such groups has been overlooked is due to an emphasis on institution building, which often implies starting afresh and building formal organizations, rather than drawing from informal ones.[51]

Some examples illustrate the potential of such groups. The Barrio Magsaysay Project in the Philippines begun in 1966 was a community development effort. It drew on existing groups in the community that had emerged several years previously when residents united to counter eviction threats. The core of the program was to encourage self-help programs by stimulating imaginative, small-scale, immediate civic improvements. One of the leaders of the project was Aprodicio Laquian, who himself had grown up in a barrio family. He surveyed the existing community and found evidence of many community organizations throughout the squatter communities. The lack of urban services in the barrios was usually overcome by communal efforts among the squatters themselves. "In almost all communities associations and organizations were in existence, although many have been organized and mobilized for very specific purposes (to celebrate the fiesta, provide fire protection, hold a social event)."[52] Respondents valued cooperativeness and appeared to find it in their neighbors. The percentages of affirmatives on a question asking whether neighbors joined together for action ran from 70 percent in Davao to 80 percent in Manila. According to Laquian's analysis these are a natural outgrowth of traditional motives and patterns of behavior.

Very similar organizational capabilities and attitudes conducive to community participation and self-help were documented in a study of squatters in Mathare Valley, Nairobi. "The most striking aspect about (the community) is neither the marginal existence attributable to economic conditions nor the inadequate physical conditions. . . . What is so striking about the community is that it is highly organized and politically integrated." The squatters, through self-help, have organized, built, and maintained several nursery schools, community work projects, and a community social hall in the center of the village. This social hall is the only building in the village with electricity. "Unlike virtually all other neighborhoods in Nairobi, there is a relatively well developed sense of community and a series of effective local political and social institutions in the community which provide for the peaceful resolutions of local problems. Actual data on participation in community affairs bear out this conclusion—some 88 percent turned out to vote in the recent village election.[53]

Building Organizations. Whether based on indigenous groups or not, organizations are critical in facilitating effective participation and indeed in general project success. David Korten reviewed a variety of social organizations that had been part of successful efforts to bring about change and development in their areas. The common element in all of them was that each had developed an organization appropriate to the work it had to do. Other than their attention to the importance of organization, the experiences were very diverse. Some were bottom-up on inspiration and momentum; others were top-down and spurred by government initiative. Some were focused on a specific good, such as distributing milk, whereas others took a more comprehensive approach. "Each was successful because it had worked out a program model responsive to beneficiary needs at a particular time and place and had built a strong organization capable of making the program work. Put another way they had achieved a high degree of *fit* between program design, beneficiary needs and the capacities of the assisting organization."[54] (See Chapter 4.)

Other studies confirm the importance of organizations. According to Norman Uphoff and his colleagues, organizations can broaden the base of participation, increase the access to resources, and promote change.[55] A study of thirty-six rural development projects made the following points:

> 1. Local organizations can assist in the development of an effective two-way communications system for the project design, monitoring and evaluation. . . . 2. Local organizations are vehicles for encouraging and reinforcing behavioral changes such as the adoption of new agricultural practices. . . . 3. In areas where there are poor delivery and market systems, local organizations can facilitate the provision, integration and administration of these services. . . . 4. Farmer resource commitment can be increased by means of risk-sharing arrangements, with local organizations facilitating and enforcing these arrangements.

In addition, the use of existing organizations can increase problem-solving capabilities at the local level and can allow projects to become self-sustaining.[56]

Use of Small Groups. Several analysts have stressed the value of using small groups as a way to mobilize farmers and peasants. David Leonard and Allen Jedlicka draw on their respective experiences in Kenya and Mexico to illustrate the value of small groups for stimulating effective participation.[57] In Chapter 9 we discussed how small groups can enhance the effectiveness of field agents. They can also be an efficient mechanism from the public's perspective. In one case, mothers in a maternity hospital were given instructions on the value of cod-liver oil. Those who were taught in a group were much more likely to give oil to their children than those who were taught as individuals.[58]

In addition to being more efficient, groups can also encourage participation and innovative behavior. According to Jedlicka they can contribute to satisfying the needs that people have for being part of a group, for status, and even for self-actualization. Small groups can stimulate participation and involvement, which he describes as a "freedom-to-participate" phenomenon. The group atmosphere makes them feel more secure and "freer to speak out."[59] But such freedom will only occur when the group emphasizes openness and trust, flexibility, clarity of expectations, and a participatory process.

The positive role that groups can play in satisifying workers' needs and in encouraging participation is illustrated by an account of the introduction of automated looms into an Indian textile plant. Surprisingly, the new looms did not increase production. A study focused on the fact that the new looms relied on performance by individual workers, whereas the old ones had been based on interactive processes. Managers deduced that the latter type of loom satisfied people's needs for being part of a group and instituted changes to allow for group effort. The result was a dramatic increase in output.[60]

Based on his own experience in working with small groups as part of the Puebla Project in Mexico, Jedlicka argues that in addition to stimulating participation, groups enable people to take risks that they would not take as individuals. As noted above, many development changes constitute risks for members of the public which they are hesitant to take. These same people, however, when they are part of a group that discusses the risk and arrives at a consensus, are more willing to try it. Jedlicka feels that the key factor is whether an agent is present to explain all of the factors involved in making the change. Part of the explanation is that members probably feel they will be sharing the risk with other members. Again experiences in the Puebla Project confirm the role of groups in encouraging risks and change.[61]

Changing the Capacities of People

A third cluster of strategies deals with the various ways to equip members of the public to take an informed and useful role in development activities. Instead of taking people as they are, this approach raises the possibilities of educating or training people to new insights and new capacities.

Conscienzacione. One of the most penetrating arguments is put forth by the Brazilian Paulo Freire. His initial concern has been with the narrow outlooks and horizons of those people who are locked into poverty and often live out their lives in isolation and squalor. What is needed, he writes, is to alter the consciousness of these people — the way they look at themselves and the way they view the world. The major point is to give them a sense that things could be different, that there are alternatives. But instead of communicating these insights directly, Freire has developed some imaginative educational techniques to elicit awareness from people in small group settings. For example he has developed a method of teaching illiterate farmers to read called *conscienzacione*. One lesson might focus around a figure of a farmer standing by a well. Questions are raised, "Who made the well?" "Why did he do it?" "When?" The purpose of the discussion is to get the farmers to reflect on the difference between things we choose to do and things we have to do. By stimulating them to think about their work, they begin to see how their labor has transformed their surroundings and to ask why they do it and what else they would prefer to do.[62] According to Freire these kinds of discussions are essential to stimulate forms of participation that are not so easily co-opted and that express the preferences of the peasants themselves.

Training. In Chapter 6 reference was made to a series of exercises collected by the United Nations that are designed to equip people to respond to and take part in development activities. Many of these extend the theories of Freire. For example, in Turkey a package of training materials has been developed to educate people about family planning.

> The specific curricula that have been developed are based on the actual conditions of Turkish villiages. . . . The approach uses story-telling; this takes advantage of the fact that Turkish villagers gather in groups to listen to the radio or to readers. It assumes that the problems and the impetus towards modernization that are created by dramatic open-ended stories will not only bring the villager to the point of demanding information on how to improve his life but also encourage him to learn to read the pictures, captions and materials that are made available in the program.[63]

Many of the exercises included in the UN manual involve participants in exercises designed to develop their interpersonal skills and their abilities to work with others. The project design methods described in

Chapter 6 are also appropriate ways to include groups among the public. Finally, there are more traditional training programs, often to equip local leaders to carry out some specific tasks. The point in all of these is that training is important for members of the public as well as for staff.

Conclusions

Participation can easily turn into a cliché for those administering development; it is all too easy to affirm its value, while doing little to make it a reality. Traditionally those concerned with participation have emphasized the political process. Now there is an increasing tendency to look to administrative processes as the arena within which people can be more effective and more easily involved. If the implementation process becomes a major point at which participation occurs, a great responsibility is placed on administrators. No matter how committed they are to participation, it will always be tempting to co-opt the participants to meet the needs of the administrators. The temptation is all the greater considering the scarcity of resources that almost all administrators confront. And yet it remains true that the very process of development requires involvement by the people in shaping their future, and thus it is worth continuing to wrestle with the dilemmas that participation presents.

Notes

1. Carroll Behrhorst, "The Chimaltenango Development Project in Guatemala," in *Health by the People,* ed. Kenneth W. Newell (Geneva: World Health Organization, 1975), pp. 36–37.

2. Robert S. Saunders, "Traditional Cooperation, Indigenous Peasant Groups and Rural Development: A Look at Possibilities and Experiences," August 29, 1977, unpublished.

3. Coralie Bryant, "Squatters, Collective Action, and Participation: Learning from Lusaka," *World Development* 8 (1980):80.

4. Joan Nelson, *Access to Power: Politics and the Urban Poor in Developing Nations* (Princeton, N.J.: Princeton University Press, 1979), pp. 163–167, 202–213.

5. On India see Shriram Maheshwari, "New Perspectives on Rural Local Government in India: The Asoka Mehta Committee Report," *Asian Survey* 19 (1979):1110–1125.

6. An excellent version of this traditional view is Karl Deutsch, "Social Mobilization and Political Development," *American Political Science Review* 55 (1961):493–514.

7. See, for example, Samuel Huntington, *Political Order in Changing Societies*

(New Haven, Conn.: Yale University Press, 1968). In a subsequent book with Joan Nelson, Huntington continued to be concerned about the possible negative effects of participation, *No Easy Choice* (Cambridge, Mass.: Harvard University Press, 1976).

8. John Cohen and Norman Uphoff, *Rural Development Participation* (Washington, D.C.: AID, 1978), p. 11. Participation, as this point reminds us, is a classical issue in political theory. Although Marx said that class consciousness is an essential precondition, much of the Western tradition within which nationalist leaders were schooled evolved from Locke and Mill and their emphasis on participation by individuals. They argued that an elected representative government makes it more difficult for counterinsurgents to win popular support.

9. Merilee Grindle, "Introduction," *Politics and Policy Implementation in the Third World* (Princeton, N.J.: Princeton University Press, 1980).

10. Kenneth Arrow, *Social Choice and Individual Values* (New York: John Wiley, 1951). Robert Bates has examined the utility of the public choice perspective to the problems of development. See "Revenue and Taxation," mimeographed.

11. Uma Lele, *The Design of Rural Development: Lessons from Africa* (Baltimore: Johns Hopkins, 1975), p. 150. Other studies of participation in development include Yusuf Ahmad, "Administration of Integrated Rural Development Programmes," *International Labour Review* 3 (1975):119–143; Patrick Ollawa, "On a Dynamic Model for Rural Development in Africa," *Journal of Modern African Studies* 15 (1977):401–425. A comprehensive review of the literature and the issues that surround development participation is found in Norman Uphoff, John Cohen, and Arthur Goldsmith, *Feasibility and Application of Rural Development Participation: A State-of-the-Art Paper* (Ithaca, N.Y.: Cornell University, Rural Development Committee, 1979).

12. Elliot R. Morss, John K. Hatch, Donald R. Mickelwait, and Charles F. Sweet, *Strategies for Small Farmer Development: An Empirical Study of Rural Development Projects* (Washington, D.C., Development Alternatives, May 1975), 1:29–44. They used these measures to get a single index for success and for the extent of participation; the local action measure accounted for 49 percent of the variance in the success of the projects.

13. Uphoff et al., *Feasibility and Application*, pp. 13–31. Also see Stanley Heginbotham, *Cultures in Conflict* (New York: Columbia University Press, 1975) pp. 44–47.

14. Norman B. Schwartz, "Community Development and Cultural Change in Latin America," *Annual Review of Anthropology* 7 (1978):237. A case of community development was the Vicos project in Peru; for an analysis see Paul L. Doughty and Harold D. Lasswell, eds., *Peasants, Power, and Applied Social Change: Vicos as a Model* (Beverly Hills, Calif.: Sage Publications, 1971).

15. Maheshwari, "New Perspectives."

16. Uphoff et al., *Feasibility and Application*, p. 22.

17. Schwartz, "Community Development"; and Theodore Owens and Robert Shaw, *Development Reconsidered* (Lexington, Mass.: D.C. Heath, 1974), pp. 17–30.

18. David Korten, "Community Organization and Rural Development," *Public Administration Review,* forthcoming. Korten bases his analysis on research conducted by Lane C. Holdcroft in 1978.

19. Uphoff et al., *Feasibility and Application,* pp. 28–30.

20. John Mellor, *The New Economics of Growth: A Strategy for India and the Developing World* (Ithaca, N.Y.: Cornell University Press, 1976); Owens and Shaw, *Development Reconsidered.*

21. David Schumann, *Bureaucracies, Organizations, and Administration* (New York: Macmillan, 1976).

22. Ralf Dahrendorf, *Class and Class Conflict in Industrial Society* (Stanford, Calif.: Stanford University Press, 1959). Bengt Abrahamsson develops a similar conflict model in the context of a critique of organizational theory in *Bureaucracy of Participation: The Logic of Organizations* (Beverly Hills, Calif.: Sage, 1977).

23. Mary R. Hollnsteiner, "People Power: Community Participation in the Planning of Human Settlements," *UNICEF, Les Carnets de L'Enfance/Assignment Children* 40 (October-December 1977):11–49.

24. Janice Perlman, *The Myth of Marginality* (Berkeley: University of California Press, 1976).

25. Hollnsteiner, "People Power," p. 15. Within the United States, Saul Alinsky has written extensively about this approach, *Rules for Radicals* (New York: Vintage, 1971).

26. Denis Goulet, *The Cruel Choice* (New York: Atheneum, 1971), p. 148.

27. Derick Brinkerhoff, "Participation and Rural Development Project Effectiveness: An Organizational Analysis of Four Cases" (Ph.D. diss., Harvard University, 1980), p. 263.

28. Ibid., p. 19. These distinctions were originally used in Uphoff et al., *Feasibility and Application,* pp. 5–8.

29. Korten, "Community Organization"; Mary Parker Follett, *Creative Experience* (New York: Longmans, Green, 1924); John Friedmann, *Retracking America* (New York: Anchor, 1973).

30. Maxwell Owusu, *Uses and Abuses of Political Power: A Case Study of Continuity and Change in the Politics of Ghana* (Chicago: University of Chicago Press, 1970), p. 171. For a general treatment of the issue of the calculus of participation, see Coralie Bryant and Louise G. White, *Managing Rural Development: Peasant Participation in Rural Development* (West Hartford, Conn.: Kumarian Press, 1980).

31. T. Scarlett Epstein, "The Ideal Marriage Between the Economist's Macroapproach and the Social Anthropologist's Microapproach to Development Studies," *Economic Development and Cultural Change,* p. 20.

32. Robert Bates provides a useful review of recent literature in this area, "People in Villages: Micro-Level Studies in Political Economy," *World Politics* 31 (1978):129–149. Three case studies that make this point are R. D. Sanwal, "Agricultural Extension in a Kumaonese Village," *Journal of Development Studies* 1 (1964–1965):384–398; Michael G. Schluter and Timothy Mount, "Some Management Objectives of the Peasant Farmer: An Analysis of Risk Aversion in

the Choice of Cropping Pattern, Surat District, India," *Journal of Development Studies* 12 (1975–1976):246–257; James Scott, *The Moral Economy of the Peasant* (New Haven, Conn.: Yale University Press, 1976). For a somewhat contrasting perspective see Kusum Nair, *In Defense of the Irrational Peasant* (Chicago: University of Chicago, 1979).

33. Allen Jedlicka, *Organization for Rural Development: Risk Taking and Appropriate Technology* (New York: Praeger, 1977), pp. 42–43.

34. Uphoff et al., *Feasibility and Application*, p. 123.

35. Ford Foundation Task Force on Women, *Women and National Development in Africa: Some Profound Contradictions* (New York: Ford Foundation, 1973).

36. Lisa Leghorn and Mary Roodkowsky, *Who Really Starves?* (New York: Friendship Press, 1977); and Irene Tinker and Michele Bramsen, eds., *Women and World Development* (Washington, D.C.: Overseas Development Council, 1976).

37. Lele, *Design of Rural Development*, p. 77.

38. Margaret Haswell, *The Nature of Poverty* (New York: St. Martin's Press, 1975).

39. The basic theory behind this claim is found in Mancur Olson, *The Logic of Collective Action* (Cambridge, Mass.: Harvard University Press, 1971).

40. Saunders, "Traditional Cooperation," p. 20.

41. Louise G. White, "Rational Theories of Participation: An Exercise in Definitions," *Journal of Conflict Resolution* 20 (1976):255–278.

42. Saunders, "Traditional Cooperation," p. 22.

43. Vernon Ruttan, "Integrated Rural Development," *International Development Review* 17 (1975).

44. William Niskanen, *Bureaucracy and Representative Government* (Chicago: Aldine-Atherton, 1971).

45. Judith Tendler, *Inter-Country Evaluation of Small Farmer Organizations: Ecuador, Honduras* (Washington, D.C.: AID, 1976).

46. Saunders, "Traditional Cooperation," p. 30.

47. Robert Chambers, "Project Selection for Poverty-Focused Rural Development: Simple Is Optimal," *World Development* 6 (1978):209–219.

48. Bryant, "Squatters," pp. 79, 80.

49. John C. Turner, "Housing in Three Dimensions," *World Development* 6 (1978):1135–1145.

50. Gene Ellis, "On Development from Below," mimeographed, n.d.

51. Saunders, "Traditional Cooperation"; Milton Esman, "Development Administration and Constituency Organization," *Public Administration Review* 38 (March-April 1978):166–172; Uphoff et al., *Feasibility and Application*, pp. 36–51.

52. Aprodicio Laquian, "Slums and Squatters in Six Philippine Cities" (New York: The Asia Society, 1972), p. 65.

53. M. H. Ross, "Community Formation in an Urban Squatter Settlement," *Comparative Political Studies* 6 (1973):299.

54. Korten, "Community Organization."

55. Uphoff et al., *Feasibility and Application,* pp. 33–36.

56. Donald Mickelwait, Charles Sweet, Elliot R. Morss, *New Directions in Development: A Study of U.S. Aid* (Boulder: Westview Press, 1980), pp. 145–146.

57. David Leonard, *Reaching the Peasant Farmer* (Chicago: University of Chicago Press, 1977), pp. 224–226; Jedlicka, *Organization for Rural Development,* pp. 60–116.

58. Jedlicka, *Organization for Rural Development,* p. 73.

59. Ibid., p. 69.

60. Ibid., pp. 80–81.

61. Ibid., pp. 117–141.

62. Paulo Freire, *Education for Critical Consciousness* (New York: Seabury Press, 1973), especially pp. 63–84.

63. United Nations, *A Manual and Resource Book for Popular Participation Training* (New York: United Nations, 1978), 2:11. It is also worth noting that the Food and Agriculture Organization (FAO) of the United Nations has undertaken a major sixteen-country survey of participation of the poor in rural organizations. See Bernard van Heck, *Participation of the Poor in Rural Organizations* (ROAP) (Rome: FAO, 1979).

11
Development Planning and Its Management

Introduction

Planning is a paradox: the more you need it, the less able you are to do it. On the one hand, planning is more essential the greater the scarcity of resources and the need for their strategic use. On the other hand, that same scarcity makes formal planning more difficult. Urgent needs cannot be predicted, top-level decision-making time is consumed by responding to immediate crises. Poor people, poor organizations, and poor countries are all trapped in this dilemma. Control over their future is desired, but it is virtually unattainable as short-term emergencies consume resources, time, and energy. Any realistic discussion of planning must begin with this problem and realize how deeply embedded it is in the life of organizations. Tony Killick's comments about development planning reflect Herbert Simon's concerns about organizations in general. "The existing stock of knowledge, the current flow of information, the capacity to absorb and interpret information—all these are gravely deficient in developing countries. . . . Economists are well aware of this [shortage] but have failed to recognize its uncomfortable implications for development planning."[1] If, as he says, economists have failed to recognize the reality of these constraints, development administrators cannot refuse to do so.

The advent and spread of planning in the third world paralleled that of development theory; in the beginning there were high hopes and ambitious expectations. Models of development were put forth, and planners incorporated them into five-year plans. As Albert Waterston remarks, "The national plan appears to have joined the national anthem and the national flag as a symbol of sovereignity and modernity."[2] Yet just as development theory has been through a period of serious critique and revision, so has its progeny, development planning. "By and large," writes Robert Seidman, "planning in Africa worked poorly. . . . Not only in Africa but world wide, planning was notable mainly for its lack of implementation."[3] Yet the story is more complex than is reflected in the numerous catalogs of shortcomings. The core of the problem is that the management of planning never received the attention that the economics of planning attracted. "Most planners assumed that planning meant allocating resources, not planning institutional change."[4] Reflecting Western economic models, planners treated institutions as if they comprised a mystical "black box" and ignored any attention to institutional change. If and when those resource allocations were resented by ministries, they were either ignored or undermined. Since development usually requires institutional change, planning processes that ignore that component undercut their own possibilities.

The History of Planning

Historical antecedents to the national development planning that spread around the globe following World War II are few in number. Albert Waterston, a noted authority on development planning, recalls planning efforts in Mesopotamia and pre-Columbian Indian civilizations in Mexico; but with the notable exception of the Soviet Union, there was very little national development planning in other countries before World War II.[5] Following the war, several events conspired to make national planning a necessity for Western Europe and most of Africa, Asia, and, later, Latin America. In the first place, Marshall Plan reconstruction finance was contingent upon national planning. And with the advent of independence of India, the idea of national planning captured the imaginations of nationalists in Asia and quickly became linked in their thinking with the possibility of development.[6] Later, major lending countries, especially the United States, insisted upon comprehensive national plans prior to granting assistance, and this practice spread throughout the major international organizations—the United Nations, the World Bank, the regional development banks (Interamerican Bank, Asian Development Bank, and the African Development Bank.) As Waterston notes, U.S. insistence on a form of national planning that it has never accepted for itself is at best an anomaly.[7] International institutions continue to look closly at the technical proficiency and content of national plans as part of their assessment of a country's capacity to absorb assistance and capital.[8] Although some academics, such as Aaron Wildavsky, are increasingly critical of the utility of planning in poor countries, this emphasis on planning by the major lending institutions and donors leaves developing countries little alternative to planning, short of withdrawal from the international monetary system.[9]

The attention and resources given to planning vary with the country. In India, national planning is done by the prestigious Indian Planning Commission at the center, and state planning by state planning authorities within each state. The idea of national development planning was born inside the Congress party and given a central ideological place by Jawaharlal Nehru. Although never given statutory authority (and contrary to all those experts who claim that such authority is necessary), the idea was presented to the prime minister, gained his approval and won singular status within Congress party leadership.[10] The Indian Planning Commission was, and remains, one of the largest planning institutions of its kind with over 1000 staff members in an elaborate organization. Most countries have smaller planning staffs than those of India, although at one point Iran's plan organization had about 1000 staff members. Most Eastern European (Bulgaria, Romania, and Poland) planning staffs have from 350 to 500 members. More typical, especially of the small to middle-sized developing countries, are staffs between 35 and 100 members.

In federal systems, one of the more difficult issues is negotiating the subnational and national planning agreements; experimentation and constant revisions are endemic. Again India is in the forefront, both in terms of its experience in this area and of the complexity of its plans. Each Indian state has a planning and development authority that has a liaison system downward with district and block planning units, as well as upward with the National Planning Commission. Each state also has a series of sectoral working groups that parallel those of the central government.[11] Nigeria, also a federal system, initiated regional planning in 1955 and reorganized it following independence (1960), again following the civil war (1966–1969), and again with successive governments as the federal structure evolved.[12] The Nigerians experimented with a Central Planning Office that services a Joint Planning Board, which in turn draws its memberships from the Statistics Office, the Central Bank, the Ministry of Finance, and the Nigerian Institute of Social and Economic Research.

In the case of Latin America, it is worth noting that the big push toward planning came from the Alliance for Progress. Following its establishment, no less than nine countries instituted central planning agencies where previously none had existed. The locations of the agencies, their authority, and the scope of their mandates vary. In a review of planning in Central America, Gary Wynia stresses the extent to which planning efforts were circumscribed by political realities. Planners exacted political costs by threatening both dominant interest groups and leaders within the bureaucracy. As a result most of the efforts of the planners led only to disappointments.[13]

What Is Planning?

Planning is an elusive concept, more preached than practiced, more discussed than defined.[14] John Friedmann, the noted planner, tells the story of teaching a seminar on planning in the Brazilian city of Belém to young professionals from the Amazon Development Authority. As part of the course, the group held a series of seminars while steaming up the Amazon. The query, What is planning? was hotly debated for all 2000 miles of the journey.[15] The question remains with us today. It is easy enough to begin by distinguishing among town and country planning, anticyclical planning, and national development planning. These kinds of planning categories describe the different kinds of planning that go on. But what is involved within the exercise of planning?

Much of the impetus for planning has traditionally come from economic models; they tend to vary according to how much they allocate to various sectors of the economy. After a country selects one of the models, planning then involves aggregating relevant data, predicting what is likely to happen, deciding what might be a preferred alternative, and which of the variables need adjusting.[16] Waterston, as he prepared to study the accumulated experience of over 100 third world nations, came up with two guideposts for national development planning. First, it involves the economizing of scarce resources on the part of the publicly constituted authority. Second, it has to involve organized, conscious, and continual attempts to select the best available alternatives to achieve specific goals.[17]

Whereas those are operational ways to decide what experiences will be included in a comparative study of national development planning, there are more broadly conceived definitions that also bear remembering. Russell Ackoff argues that "the attempt to deal holistically with a system of problems is what planning, in contrast to problem solving, should be all about."[18] Frequently planning means setting goals and priorities and establishing a sequence of activities to accomplish them. Friedmann provides a more provocative definition when he writes that "planning is not merely concerned with the efficient instrumentation of objectives, it is also a process by which society may discover its future." He continues saying that we need to make a distinction between the allocative and innovative forms of planning. "The former is concerned with the distribution of limited resources among competing users; the latter with producing a structural change in a system of societal relations."[19] Yet a third point about planning is offered by Raymond Apthorpe. Planning must be interdisciplinary and include social as well as economic planning. Although both elements are necessary, because of the present emphasis on economic models, the immediate task is to find ways to incorporate social information into the planning process.[20]

To the extent that the planner is charged with guiding social changes as well as mobilizing resources and indicating their future use, some serious political and management questions must also be addressed. What about the responsibility of the planner? To whom is he accountable? Guiding social change is not a technical issue, but rather a normative issue about what is the good society. To date, we have little indication that planners have significantly better answers to that question than anyone else, and hence accountability becomes the compelling question.[21]

There have always been serious tensions between the technician planner and the political decision maker. Often these tensions grow out of the different mandates that each has and the different information with which each deals. Sometimes they grow out of differences between short-term and long-term consequences. Political leaders have to be elected or stay in power in the short run; planners by definition are considering long-run questions and draw up recommendations in light of longer-term consequences. Political leaders, in marshaling support, may share concern for the long run, but must respond to public opinion about the short run.

Tony Killick, after considerable experience with planning in India, adds that frequently planners are politically naive, if not presumptuous. Temperamentally they are more at home quantifying problems than negotiating about them. Their training leads them to make unrealistic assumptions about political behavior, which in turn increase the gap between planning in theory and actual performance.[22] Planners tend to assume they are addressing the long-run general good and that political leaders also vaguely endorse this same course of action. But, Killick says, this is unlikely; ministers are "at least as often concerned to evade issues as to confront them and will often prefer to react to problems rather than to anticipate them." Carrying the point one step further, he writes, "Government will, moreover, often be right in deferring action in the real world of imperfect knowledge and large uncertainties, especially in open economies highly susceptible to movements in trade and capital flows beyond their control."[23] Therefore the holistic perspective of planners needs to be tempered by the pragmatism of the politicians.

A variety of recent case studies of planning reveals the same perspective. Gary Wynia on Central America, Tony Killick on India, Robert

Chambers on East Africa, and Wolfgang Stolper on Nigeria write of the shortfall between plans and their performance.[24] But they go on to argue that planning requires a continuous learning process and that it is intrinsically a political process. Politics is after all conflict over the allocation of resources, the very substance of planning. Planning cannot therefore give scientific and politically neutral answers to what are essentially political questions.

The tension between planners and politicians goes to the heart of a dilemma about the nature of the political process and how to make decisions that are in the best interests of citizens. Traditionally, the political process has been used to aggregate citizen preferences; but we also know that the political marketplace is a very inadequate reflection of real public opinion. And because politicians respond to short-term issues of necessity, public policy is further skewed away from dealing with broad public interests. This is the void into which planners have willingly stepped, on the claim that their insulation from political whims and their professional expertise enable them to better interpret public mandates. The problem, however, is obvious. It is precisely their insulation and professionalism that cause them to pursue plans that fit their own and frequently narrow views of public life. Thus neither the politician nor the planner can lay claim to an ideal perspective. The wisest course is therefore to somehow include both of them in the process, however many tensions that produces. Planning is a political process, it involves particular rather than comprehensive interests, and both the planner and the politician need to have a part in it.

Thus the planner faces a dilemma. Although some argue that a further development of his or her political skills is necessary, there are good reasons for responding to political leadership rather than usurping it — and even better reasons for considering every conceivable way to increase decentralized and participatory approaches to the planning process. It may be that such participation does not have to come through traditional political channels, that planning offices and project organizations can establish their own channels of including the public. And as was discussed in Chapter 10, it often makes most sense to involve citizens around implementation issues that are immediate for them, rather than around broader political issues. Thus the challenge for planning is to take seriously its political nature and the need for participation, but to find innovative ways to involve a variety of interests in the process.

This emphasis does not mean that national development planning should not be undertaken at all. The realities of resource scarcity and international trade mean that national governments need to have the capacity to make choices. They need to reconcile the competing demands and needs with current resources, provide a sense of the future for the polity, and maintain coherence in the priorities that are politically determined.

Planning and Administrative Capacity

Every observer of planning has commented on the failure of development planning. Many claim it is rooted in the lack of administrative capacity. As Waterston expresses it, "Few countries can cope with the administrative problems which development planning brings. These problems are so complex that in most less developed countries the limitation in implementing plans is not financial resources, but administrative capacity."[25] Plans are routinely criticized because of poor implementation or because they could not be implemented. Most critics point out that five-year plans are stylized, formalistic, even ritualistic, and have little or no effect on day-to-day decisions. The plans are idealized statements of goals based on predictions and forecasts, and there is little hope that these goals can be remotely approximated. Thus they are shelved, and the daily decisions continue, rendering increasingly less possible the very goals that were eulogized in the comprehensive plans.[26] S. A. Bessanov makes a typical case: "By and large, planning in Africa worked poorly. Plans remained on paper. Governments abandoned one-third of the national plans before their term; practically all of them underwent major revisions during their course."[27]

Some of the more extreme critics argue for the abolition of national planning, if not its serious curtailment. Wildavsky and Caiden, after reviewing national planning and budgeting in a dozen poor countries, conclude that the effort at comprehensive planning has done more damage than good. Planning itself is the problem, they argue, and the better approach would be to use the budgeting process to accomplish control and direction. Since budgeting continues throughout the course of governing and since budgets are revised at close intervals and are hence more controlling, there is more opportunity to marshal those programs worthy of the effort by budgeting than by comprehensive planning.[28]

Whatever the merits of this perspective, it is not one with much credibility or acceptance within the third world. For any country to eschew national development planning would be tantamount to eschewing the struggle for control over the nation's future. The five-year plan has symbolic roots; and, as mentioned earlier, it is also required by the whole plethora of international and bilateral development assistance organizations. How then can the national development planning process be effectively managed? How can that process be made congruent with a more participatory, bottom-up, learning process that facilitates self-correcting mechanisms as it progresses? Chambers talks about planning as a learning process that works through "incremental grafting and modification of procedures" rather than through formal plans.[29] The latter may sometimes be wasteful. More useful, he says, is the "sharpening of objectives and implementation of existing projects, the gathering of experience with implementation which can feed back into future proposals, improvements in the budget process and allocations, and the organization of search procedures and rural research and development."[30] Planning in his model is part of an ongoing dynamic, rather than a formal single stage in the policy process. But most of the time, Chambers is talking about subnational planning. Planning at that level is more appropriate to his learning-adapting model. National planning, precisely because of its larger, more comprehensive mandate and authority, represents a problem of a different magnitude. Documents of considerable technical proficiency are required and will be scrutinized by the IMF, IBRD, and the UN system. The amounts of aggregation necessary pull the process away from that which can be done at subnational levels. And there is another problem. The very raison d'être for national planning is that it takes a *national* perspective over the longer time horizon; too ready a "grafting and modifying of procedures" can make it too vulnerable to short-term special interests. In short, national development planning needs to walk a fine line between being removed from day-to-day skirmishes, and yet responsive enough to be accountable to political leadership.

Recent events have also added another reason for, and yet complication to, national planning. Increased regional cooperation calls forth regional planning of multinational groupings. And political leaders are quick and rightfully sensitive to the fact that they need to be sure of their national priorities when negotiating with neighbors over international agreements. Just as the Common Market in Europe increased the planning efforts of its respective member states, so has the Economic Community of West African States had much the same effect.

In giving us some important historical perspective, Waterston also reminds his readers that when it comes to the management problems inherent within national planning, the public administration field has been strangely mute.[31] Planners and public administrators have rarely talked about these problems, and when they have, they have talked past one another rather than in dialogue, without sharing insights from their respective disciplines. On the one hand, planners have not been interested in administrative improvement, at least not in the way in which public administration has proposed it. But not all the fault lies with the planners, for, on the other hand, few experts in public administration seem deeply interested in development or concerned with the special dimension of the management problem surrounding national development planning. In the early 1960s, the public administrators who were working in developing countries were not conceptualizing *development* or thinking through its broader implications. They did talk about the needs for large-scale sweeping civil service reform, but that did not address the needs of the planners, especially those trained as economists who could not conceive of any feasible way to wait for wholesale administrative reform before they could move ahead with their five-year plan. As Waterston points out, "Those in public administration have not been development minded. They sometimes think of public administration as a separate matter from development . . . something in and of itself."[32] This depiction of the field is not completely accurate. Yet if we recall the limited approaches of the public administration field in the 1960s, we can see that Waterston is not far from the truth. Planners have also worn disciplinary blinders. The serious need for institutional reform they have treated as unimportant, if not irrelevant. Planners as economists have not seen why institutional change could not simply follow as part of the general trickle-down effect of growth. Interestingly enough, only in the Eastern block socialist states has there been ready acceptance that institutional change must precede effective development planning if redistribution (equity) is to be realized.[33]

There have thus been many lapses and inadequacies within the planning profession. Robert Chambers places these failings in a useful perspective. "To blame only the planners for these problems would be unfair. Like field staff and peasant farmers their behavior can be understood in relation to their experience and work environments and there is no reason to suppose that their responses are any less rational. The explanation for these problems lies much less in plan formulation than in the development of management procedures."[34]

We are therefore directed back to management issues and such questions as, How can the planning function be organized so that learning can occur among planners and among other agencies in the government? And how can the holistic perspective of the planning function be institutionalized within the government and integrated into the political process? As stressed throughout the book, no single or optimal organization can be defined. Rather one needs to emerge from and fit with the tasks of planners. Therefore we next consider what planners do, the range of their tasks, and the strategies they employ.

Tasks of National Development Planning

National development planning, as the term is most often used, means a conscious effort to undertake some, if not all, of the following tasks:

1. Collecting and assessing aggregate indicators of the nation's economic and social conditions.
2. Collecting and assessing data on major sectors within the nation's economy.
3. Identifying the relationships between sectors in order to specify areas of essential activity for key problems.
4. Specifying alternative approaches for the amelioration of problems affecting the whole economy and those affecting particular sectors.
5. Identifying the allocative implications of alternative approaches.
6. Identifying and specifying alternatives to top decision makers, usually at the cabinet level. Laying out their implications in light of sectoral linkages.
7. Following up on decisions taken in earlier planning discussions.
8. Continual monitoring of the indicators of national economic and social well-being and of the sectoral linkages.
9. Carrying out evaluations and insuring that results are included in successive plans and policy discussions.

Not all these tasks are done by all planning agencies, but they are the major ingredients of the planning process. Each of the tasks must be managed; some of them amount to coordination of the work of other agencies, such as the central statistics office, with the planning process.

But in considering the optimal organizational fit for the planning agency, the extent to which these tasks are part of the assignment affects the way in which the authority should be staffed, located, authorized, and related to other line agencies in the government.

Strategies for Public Action

Development planning affects, and is affected by, the amount and nature of intervention in an economy that are considered necessary to ensure the provision of goods and services. The choice is not only whether the good or service is to be provided, but *how* that provision is to take place. Broadly, there are five alternatives. A government can (1) decide *not to provision* or supply the good or service, but rather to leave it to individual action, a private sector, or simply undone; (2) decide to *directly provide* residents with goods or services—for example, to build public schools and clinics or do extension work with public monies; (3) *coproduce* goods and services with the active involvement of citizen groups—self-help housing for example; (4) *induce* the private sector to provide the goods or services—tax incentives or vouchers for example; and (5) use sanctions or penalties to discourage certain behavior. In short, a government has the choice of using either carrots or sticks, much as the boy trying to drive the proverbial donkey. Sticks are controls, regulations, or some form of coercion to prod the production of goods or services; carrots are inducements or incentives to reward someone or a group for providing the service.

Consider the advantages and disadvantages of each alternative. The direct supply choice, for example, is the oldest and most straightforward. And the very laxity of colonial governments in this regard meant that new governments were very anxious for the direct supply of as many goods and services as possible. But the obvious expensiveness of this approach is its own constraint. Public provision of schools, housing, transport, and so forth quickly reaches its limits. And this approach is more costly administratively; the full weight of implementation falls on the government, and neither the manpower nor the money is readily available. The third strategy saves some financial cost and some implementation for the government, but it requires both the active cooperation of the citizen and a flexibility on the part of the government to grant a significant role to the public. The fourth, the inducement strategy, may be less administratively costly, but it requires a more active private sector than is present in many third world nations, and it can be difficult to encourage broad and equitable distribution through the private sector. (Indeed, many countries nationalized industries in the hope that such nationalization would ease the work of planning. Often the hope was not realized.) The strategy of using sanctions can involve taxes to penalize those who do not follow government priorities and plans. The third strategy, the use of coproduction and incentives, deserves more attention than it often receives, particularly its implications for development planners.

Coproduction means that services and goods depend on the mutual production of citizens and governments.[35] The point for planners is that if governments can stimulate the public to increase its share, then the government's resources will go further. Self-help and self-reliance approaches, which are well established in many third world countries, are a variant of this approach.[36] One example is housing. Housing results from what the public and private sectors produce and also from what people build on their own. If planners can devise mechanisms to encourage and reward citizens to do more, perhaps by providing them with lower cost supplies, by providing them with access to location, then the total amount of housing can be increased without exhausting public accounts. One major advantage of this approach is that government is encouraging or facilitating what groups are already doing on a modest scale. Examples include improvements on irrigation projects, communal forestry projects, or the development of village fish ponds.

A related strategy is the use of vouchers. Governments issue "money" in the form of coupons, which can be used to "buy" specific goods or services. These vouchers are then a form of carrot or inducement for either individuals or groups in the private sector to produce certain goods. This approach is one way to increase opportunities for the public to select the amount and kind of service or good that it wants.

The utility of this approach, and the trade-offs between carrots and sticks, can be illustrated by ways in which the government might choose to deal with food shortages. As many small farmers change from food crops to export crops, domestic food supply declines. When this occurs, prices tend to rise, urban interests complain vigorously, and governments put on price controls to keep the price of food arbitrarily low. The result is that the producer gets less in return for his/her efforts, cuts back even further on production, and may turn to other ways of earning income.

An alternative approach is for the government to use food vouchers to reverse the trend and stimulate a demand for specific food crops. Small farmers and women hawkers complain that they cannot market ordinary food crops in their villages, that there are too few who can afford to buy them.[37] A system of food vouchers, distributed locally and good for specific foods, would increase *effective* demand and thereby the production of more food, meet some nutritional needs, and save on food lost in storage and transport.

Few policies have had so many harmful effects as poorly conceived price controls. Yet many countries persist in this anomalous practice. Controlling the price of food to keep it cheap in urban areas has exactly the opposite effect than the vouchers discussed above. It keeps people out of the food-producing business for local markets and abets the urban bias so prevalent in much current planning practice.[38] If a country has had price controls for a long time, however, they can only be removed gradually in order to allow for the necesary structural readjustment. Since food shortages and food riots are politically destabilizing, it is no surprise that political leaders are unresponsive to advice to remove price controls.

Fiscal policy can be used either to offer incentives or to impose penalties. Taxation and tax policies, licensing, and regulatory policies all affect the provision of goods and services. Taxation is all too often sadly neglected within the third world because of its political opposition and its administrative requirements. If no one is punished for tax evasion, then no government should be surprised at serious problems in implementing tax policies.[39] Monitoring tax collection requires administrators who have some insulation from the political battles of the day; that insulation is unfortunately often missing in many developing countries. And, finally, planners need to think through strategies of working with public enterprises, or parastatals, as part of the planning strategy. Nationalization did not often bring the kind of access to information or control that its proponents had hoped. Public enterprises vary in their degrees of de facto, if not de jure, autonomy from the planners' needs. In some instances, the public enterprises know more ways to evade and avoid requests for information and data than the planning agency has ways to get that information. The management of public enterprises is the least well-developed part of the development management field.[40]

Location of the Planning Office: Establishing Fit

A recurring theme in this book is that there needs to be a fit between the *task* of administration, in this case national development planning, and *the way in which administration is organized*. Observers note a variety of locations that countries have tried for their planning organizations.[41] Although they agree that location matters, unfortunately there has been too little empirical examination of the ways in which it matters. Yet drawing on that which is known, location affects (1) access to decision making, (2) access to information, and (3) possibilities for subnational and sectoral planning and programming.

The most commonly chosen locations for a national planning office are (1) in the office of the chief executive, (2) as a separate ministry, (3) within another ministry—usually finance, and (4) as an independent board or commission.

The weight of opinion appears to be that the planning organization is likely to be most effective when it is located in the office of the chief executive. (And some would add that it ought to have its foundations in legal authority, statute, or legislation.) The argument for being in the office of the chief executive is that of optimizing leverage, being at the apex of the government where it can serve as final arbitrator. George Gant argues for this location, adding that a small staff in this location is suited to provide general guidance rather than being involved in programs. He writes, "The planning agency should keep itself as small as possible to reserve its energy and talents to the central planning and coordinating function and to avoid as far as possible the assumption of operating functions that, although closely related, can be undertaken by others as well or better, at least in time."[42]

In spite of the cogency of this argument, the reality is much more varied. The following comparison of the experiences of planning departments illustrates some of the tensions they experience, as well as the politics involved in deciding where to locate. Some countries have tried all four of the locations. Zambia, for example, has a development planning unit of twenty-five to thirty people in what is now called the National Commission for Development Planning. This organization has variously been in a division within a Ministry for Planning, within the Ministry of Finance, and a separate Ministry of Development Planning. It is now an independent commission in the prime minister's office.[43] The constant changes in location are symptomatic both of the serious problems afflicting planning in Zambia and the lack of clarity in the thinking of leaders about how planning should be undertaken. In addition to the pressures brought about by the drop of copper prices, the problems in international trade, and conflagration on every border, Zambia's major planning problem has been to gain control over the huge parastatal enterprises. Among these enterprises, the Zambia Industrial and Mining Corporation, Ltd. (ZIMCO), is among the five largest corporations in the world. Needless to say, a country that serves as the location for a corporation whose annual revenues and expenditures are many times that of the entire nation has a planning problem.

Planning in Zambia is at best an effort to coordinate the various sectors. But coordination requires access to information, and skilled staff members who could interpret available information were in desperately short supply. The problem is that planning was not given the same political commitment that it had in neighboring Malawi. In Malawi, the planning organization, the Economic Planning Division (EPD), is in the Office of the President. Interestingly enough, the Malawians do not have a plan as such, but rather a *Statement of Development Policies* listing projects of each sector, along with their goals and objectives.[44] The Economic Planning Division pulls together information from each ministry and has the full backing of the president in ministry requests for this information. The EPD analyzes project functions, does evaluation and appraisal, and analyzes the recurrent cost implications of projects. It also monitors the overall performance of the economy, trade relations, and productivity within sectors. The Malawian planners have used their location to gain leverage within the government, building skillfully on the initial commitment from the chief executive. The Zambians, in contrast, had weaker commitment initially and have tried successive locations with differing numbers of expatriate assistants to achieve a footing for planning. Not only were their constraints more serious (large parastatal organizations with their own expertise), but their constant shifting and reorganizing eroded their fragile institution.[45]

The Indian Planning Commission operates in parallel with other ministries and is more comparable to a separate ministry. In this instance, the leverage of the commission is derived from its standing with the chief executive. Malaysia's Economic Planning Unit is in the Office of the Chief Executive, whereas Kenya's planning authority is inside of the Ministry of Development and Finance. In each instance the location affects what access to data and information is available to the planners, as well as their power and influence vis-à-vis other ministries. Their influence is also determined by their standing with the chief executive and the dominant political party. For example, in the case of Malawi, the planners have acquired hegemony in large part because the president has decided on the primacy of technical considerations. On the other hand, under some Indian governments, political considerations weigh heavily on the Indian Planning Commission, which sits on top of a far more intricate system of localized planning organizations and issues than is true elsewhere. Some would also say that the failures of planning in Zambia had far more to do with external political and military pressues than any location could have solved.

Interestingly enough, even controlled one-party systems committed to planning have experienced a shifting balance between technical and political considerations. This is apparent in Alexander Eckstein's account of planning in China as well as in the much earlier studies by Dudley Seers of planning in Cuba.[46] Seers points out that which was often forgotten or overlooked by subsequent studies of planners. "What has been thrown into sharp focus by the experience of Cuba, and this is of wider significance for all development policy, is that organization, rather than capital, is the clue to really rapid structural change."[47] One location issue deserves separate and more detailed attention, going as it does to the heart of the planning process, and that is the location of the planners in relationship to the budget.

Planning and Budgeting

Part of the location issue concerns the relation of the planning office to the budgeting function. Since planning is an effort to understand and control future commitments, it has to be undertaken in conjunction with the budgetary process.[48] Years ago it was assumed that there could be two separate budgets — a capital budget and an operating budget. It is increasingly evident that capital expenditures affect recurrent expenditures; in other words today's actions change the scope and range of possibilities in the future. Making capital expenditures on schools, clinics, irrigation projects, conference centers, or agricultural research has long-range implications for recurrent operating costs for maintenance, staff, supplies, and follow-up programs. Because of the close relationship between current and future expenditures, planners need to consider the recurrent budget implications of every capital budget project. Although this sounds straightforward, the institutional arrangements are usually not conducive to doing business in this manner; the planning agency or commission may be located where it cannot have much effect on the budget. If it is a separate ministry, it must bargain as any other ministry for its share of the pie. If it is within the ministry of finance, it is able to look at the recurrent costs of projects, but this puts it in an adversary relationship with the ministries within which those projects originate. If it is independent but within the office of the chief executive, it may be able to recommend disapproval of projects in light of their recurrent costs, but how much authority the commission holds with the budget decision makers depends upon the political leadership. The final authority in that instance is usually the cabinet.

Budgeting within developing countries is afflicted with the same management and organizational problems that trouble all other line agencies. In most instances these problems are worse with budgeting because it is here that resource scarcity is so painfully apparent. Tax collection is weak throughout the third world. Fiscal policy is not always used as frequently as it might be because it is so deeply resented by those who are most powerful. To the extent that the country depends upon external support for part of the budget, as the planners do for the development budget, it is virtually impossible to make accurate estimates. Legislatures (or Congress) halfway around the world can decide to turn off the flow of resources that a five-year plan may estimate is available. For all these reasons, budget officials and planners are often in an adversary relationship. Although observers of planning speak of the need for close communication between budgeting and planning, few appear to appreciate fully why such communication runs counter to the reality of organizational politics.

In spite of these political difficulties, it is the case that planners need to estimate and evaluate the budgetary implications of the development proposals that come to them from ministries and local governments. The budget officials, working for the ministry of finance, may ask that the cabinet rule on disputes between the finance ministry and the planning organization. At least in this manner, the choices open to the cabinet would be clarified, rather than subsequently buried within, or excluded from, the budget. Planners must have a role in examining recurrent cost implications and recommending against projects with cost implications that the future budget cannot support. Added impetus to induce planners to play this role will probably come from international agencies and multilateral banks as they become concerned about financing the increasing levels of third world indebtedness.

Planning and Decentralization

Planning in the 1950s and 1960s was centralized: the development models of the day encouraged, if not abetted, centralization. Enmeshed in their models, and committed to industrialization, planners lived and worked almost wholly in capital cities. Not only did early models neglect rural development, but early planners had little experience or exposure to rural areas and their potential place in national development. This unfortunate situation began changing in the 1970s, but not as far or fast as it could have.

There are two methods used for decentralizing or at least of deconcentrating national planning. First, sectoral planning can be one way of reaching down to subnational areas through functional arenas. (A sector is a functional arena of productive activity within an economy such as mining, livestock, industrial production, housing, education, or communications.) Second, subnational planning can be initiated within state or district units.

Sectoral planning grew out of the earlier concerns with the appropriate balances between sectors.[49] In planning practice it has come to mean that a section within a ministry will have responsibility for planning for that sector, for gathering the necessary data, and for communicating the plan to the central planning office. The difficulty is that this organizational arrangement means that officials within the sectoral planning unit get caught between two different offices. Wildavsky provides an example from Peru citing a central planning official who lamented, "If they were responsible totally to us, we wouldn't receive any information from the ministries. If they were responsible totally to the ministries, we couldn't get them to help make the national plan."[50] Sectoral planning requires that the planner be a skilled negotiator, in order to negotiate between two authorities. Good central planning is built upon sectoral planning and upon devising management strategies to improve the quality of coordination.

Subnational planning is an older approach to decentralization and one that has had an uneven history. The interest in subnational planning seems to swing like a pendulum. Subnational planning was encouraged in

Nigeria with the creation of new states in the 1970s. It was encouraged in Tanzania as a cornerstone in the Arusha Declaration and the *ujamaa* villagization process. Although there was always some interest in India, the 1970-1983 Five-Year Plan calls for local panchayati raj elections and a renewed emphasis on block-level planning.

The effective management of subnational planning calls for some rare but essential attitudes and skills among planners. First, planners need to be posted to regional or local governments to assist and facilitate local-level planning. Second, both the planners away from the center and those within the central office have to be open and flexible about the diversity, some would say chaos, that local-level planning generates.[51] Third, the final documents will be less technically elaborate, but also more honest reflections of the empirical realities within a country. Just how to reconcile this situation with external donors' insistence upon technical sophistication requires diplomacy and artful reconciliation. Local subnational or area planning should have to emphasize the practicality of the plans; that is, they should not be "wish lists" that lead to frustration. Rather they should include a short inventory of major resources, an assessment of current growth patterns, identification and selection of projects, and suggestions for an implementation strategy.[52] Subnational units should do this exercise in conjunction with their budget process. Every effort should be made to involve people within the area in the social assessment, identification of projects, and discussion of their feasibility. Forums, *barazas,* public meetings are but a few of the ways in which local input into the local planning process can take place. But the clear warning to all should be to keep the discussions on the possible and feasible; otherwise well-founded cynicism sets in and generates conflict.

Conclusion

Planning has frequently served as a whipping boy for the failure to accomplish the goals of development formalized in such documents as five-year plans. But planning encompasses far more activities than designing these plans, and it includes a greater variety of skills than simply deciding on long-range goals. Essentially planning is an effort by the government to enlarge its capacity to make choices to consider and select among its alternatives. According to Kalman Silvert this task is actually the heart of the development process. "The essential measure of political development is the relation between the range of choice open to a polity and the range it actually explores."[53] Many developing countries hunger for the opportunity to widen the range that they are currently exploring, and planning is one of the ways in which this might be done. It includes both an ability to use information well and to operate in the political process. A large part of its success will depend on how well it is managed and how much credence it is given by those in the political arena.

Notes

1. Tony Killick, "The Possibilities of Development Planning," *Oxford Economic Papers* (July 1976):173.
2. Albert Waterston, *Development Planning* (Baltimore: Johns Hopkins Press, 1965), p. 28.
3. Robert B. Seidman, "Development Planning and Legal Order in Black Anglophonic Africa," *Studies in Comparative International Development* 14 (Summer 1979):5.
4. Ibid., p. 21.
5. Waterston, *Development Planning,* Chapter 2.
6. Rajni Kothari, *India* (Boston: Little, Brown, 1970), pp. 111–112.
7. Waterston, *Development Planning,* p. 36.
8. World Bank country reports usually have lengthy discussions of the five-year plans, their efficiency as well as the effectiveness of the planning process in the country under consideration.
9. Naomi Caiden and Aaron Wildavsky, *Planning and Budgeting in Poor Countries* (New York: John Wiley & Sons, 1974).
10. See Richard L. Park and Irene Tinker, eds., *Leadership and Political Institutions in India* (Princeton: Princeton University Press, 1959); and A. H. Hanson, *The Process of Planning* (London: Routledge & Kegan Paul, 1966).
11. Waterston, *Development Planning,* p. 543.
12. The introductions to Nigeria's five-year plans usually detail the changed organizational arrangements. See, for example, *The Second National Development Plan 1970–1974* (Lagos, Nigeria: Federal Ministry of Information, 1970).
13. Waterston, *Development Planning,* p. 525.
14. Ibid.
15. John Friedmann, *Retracking America, A Theory of Transactive Planning* (New York: Doubleday, 1973), p. 49.
16. A good summary of the economics involved in planning is available in Michael P. Todaro, *Economic Development in the Third World* (London: Longman, 1977), Chapter 15.
17. Waterston, *Development Planning,* p. 21.
18. Russell Ackoff, *Redesigning the Future* (New York: John Wiley & Sons, 1974), p. 21.
19. Friedmann, *Retracking,* p. 4.
20. Raymond Apthorpe, *People, Planning, and Development Studies* (London: Frank Cass, 1970), p. 8.
21. Merilee Grindle, "Power, Expertise and the 'Technico': Suggestions from a Mexican Case Study," *Journal of Politics* 39 (1977):399–426.

22. Killick, "Possibilities of Development Planning," p. 168.

23. Ibid., p. 173.

24. Wolfgang Stolper, *Planning Without Facts* (Cambridge, Mass.: Harvard University Press, 1966).

25. Waterston, *Development Planning,* p. 289.

26. Mike Faber and Dudley Seers, eds., *The Crisis in Planning* (London: Chatto and Windus, 1972).

27. Robert Seidman cites S.A. Bessanov in "Development Planning and Legal Order," *Economic Planning for the Developing Countries of Africa* (Budapest: Hungarian Academy of Science, 1974).

28. Caiden and Wildavsky's *Planning and Budgeting* is the single most complete discussion of this relationship.

29. Robert Chambers, *Managing Rural Development* (Uppsala: Scandinavia Institute of African Studies, 1974), p. 146.

30. Ibid.

31. Waterston in *Development Planning* discusses this issue throughout, but see especially pp. 278-285.

32. Ibid., p. 283.

33. Seidman refers to this point in "Development Planning and Legal Order," especially pp. 15-21. See also Irving Louis Horowitz, *Three Worlds of Development* (New York: Oxford University Press, 1972), for a discussion of the Russian model.

34. Chambers, *Managing Rural Development,* p. 146; see also Chapters 5 and 6.

35. Richard Rich, "Voluntary Action and Public Services," *Journal of Voluntary Action Research* 7 (January-April 1978):4-14.

36. John Turner, "Housing in Three Dimensions: Terms of Reference for the Housing Question Redefined," *World Development* 6 (September-October 1978):1135-1145. See also Coralie Bryant, "Squatters, Collective Action, and Participation: Learning from Lusaka," *World Development* 8 (January 1980): 73-85.

37. In in-depth interviews with women migrants in Botswana, Coralie Bryant heard this point constantly discussed. For a report on that survey, see Coralie Bryant, Betsy Stephens, and Sherry MacLiver, "Rural to Urban Migration: Some Data from Botswana," *African Studies Review* 30 (September 1978):85-99.

38. Michael Lipton, "Urban Bias and Food Policy in Poor Countries," *Food Policy,* November 1975, pp. 41-52.

39. Gunnar Myrdal discusses the tax evasion and tax avoidance problems in *Asian Drama* (New York: Random, 1968). See especially vol. 3, pp. 1039, 2096, 2098-2103. Albert Waterston discusses this issue in *Development Planning,* pp. 18-20.

40. P. N. Agarwala, *Public Administration and Public Enterprises in the Indian Sub-continent* (Bangalore: Indian Institute of Management, n.d.).

41. George F. Gant, *Development Administration* (Madison: University of Wisconsin Press, 1979), pp. 131-161, for one of the best discussions of the relevance of location.

42. Ibid., p. 140.

43. Coralie Bryant, Richard Blue, and Tom DeGregori, *Planning, Budgeting, and Management Issues in Zambia, Malawi, and Swaziland,* Case Studies in Development Assistance No. 4 (Washington, D.C., Development Studies Program, U.S. Agency for International Development, April 1979).

44. Another document put out annually by the Economic Planning Division in Malawi that summarizes the division's work is the *Economic Report.* See, for example, *Economic Report 1978* (Zomba, Malawi: Government Printer, 1978).

45. Bryant, Blue, and DeGregori, *Planning, Budgeting, and Management Issues.*

46. Alexander Eckstein, *China's Economic Revolution* (London: Cambridge University Press, 1977).

47. Dudley Seers, ed., *Cuba* (Chapel Hill: University of North Carolina Press, 1964), p. 49.

48. See Caiden and Wildavsky, *Planning and Budgeting,* for the discussion of this relationship.

49. One of Albert Hirschman's major points has been that "balanced growth" is not necessarily as meaningful in development policy as some had assumed; instead decisions should be analyzed to discover possible linkages with other decisions; *The Strategy of Economic Development* (New Haven, Conn.: Yale University Press, 1958). For a good discussion of the similarities and differences between Hirschman and Charles Lindblom, see "Economic Development, Research and Development Policy Making: Some Converging Views," *Behavioral Science,* 8 (1962):211–222.

50. Caiden and Wildavsky, *Planning and Budgeting,* p. 225.

51. Robert H. Jackson, "Planning, Politics, and Administration," in *Development Administration: The Kenyan Experience,* ed. Goran Hyden, Robert Jackson, and John Okumu (Nairobi: Oxford University Press, 1970), pp. 171–200.

52. Chambers, *Managing Rural Development.* See his list on p. 145. Also note his concern about self-help projects that have gone astray on pp. 100–106.

53. Kalman Silvert, *Man's Power* (New York: Viking, 1970), p. xxiv.

PART THREE

Implementing Development: Urban and Rural Arenas

Part 1 has addressed questions of administrative behavior and organization theory, and Part 2 has dealt with program and project implementation. Part 3 applies these concerns to the changing urban and rural environments in the third world. Chapter 12 considers the impact of rural to urban migration and the effect of this migration on urban management. The problem is that the formal powers and political resources of local governments are insufficient to cope with immediate crises. Chapter 13 turns to the crucial issue of rural development. Rural development has become a major concern as the term *development* has come to mean social change. The problems of widespread poverty and isolation present special challenges for administrators trying to bring about this change. This chapter concludes the book by relating rural development to the process of national development and the management problems therein.

12
Managing Urban Development

Introduction

The daily migration from rural to urban areas throughout the third world is one of the historic changes of our times. This single change—the movement of people from villages to town—has far-reaching repercussions. Discussions of urban growth in developing countries commonly begin with litanies of figures—figures that are overwhelming in their magnitude. Whether the focus is on population, disease, unemployment, illegal squatting, the numbers are so large they appear to foreclose the possibility of effective administration. As long as development was equated with growth, it seemed to depend on both industrialization and urbanization. Only later, with criticisms of early growth models, was consideration given to the impact of urban policies on other sectors of the economy. As development was defined in broader terms, however, questions began to be raised about the impact of urban policies on other sectors of the economy, especially on rural areas. The concern now is whether urban and rural development can be conceived and planned so that they interact positively rather than countermand one another.[1]

In the meantime, people continue to come to the cities, and housing, sewage, water supply all become more needed and less available. Broad debates about development recede before the immediate issues confronting urban administrators. How can services be delivered most effectively? How can local administrators work within their limited powers and meager resources? What can be done for migrants to stem their crowding and squalor? How can this be done without inducing yet more migration from the rural areas?

Dimensions of the Urban Problem

With continued migration and natural increases, it is projected that the urban population of the developing countries will expand by more than 1 billion between 1960 and 2000.[2] One problem is that the increase is not evenly spread out but targeted to a few already large cities. Although all cities are growing, and most of them at very rapid rates, central cities generally outpace the smaller urban places. In 1970, the population of Buenos Aires was approximately 9,410,000; Cairo, 5,600,000; Calcutta, 5,153,000, with a metropolitan area of another 2,000,000.[3] It is estimated that by the year 2000, developing countries will have 200 cities with populations over 1 million. Even in Africa, the least urbanized continent, more than one-third of the people will be living in cities by 2000.[4] Rural to urban migration continues even in countries with extensive controls. China, for example, has experienced persistent migration pressures, and now has over 31 cities with more than 1 million population.[5] Part of this growth, of course, is due to natural increase and rising birthrates in general, but it is estimated that more than half of each year's increase is due to migration.

Given the likelihood of such growth, one would expect that serious preparations are under way for the management of these urban areas; yet that is far from the case. In part there are few preparations being made precisely because policymakers feel ambivalent about urban growth and its long-run implications for the nation generally. The problem they face is to find ways to manage growth without adding to the lure of urban life and hence inadvertently increasing the absolute level of migration. Improved housing and better jobs and health care will only draw more away from their villages.

Migration has another implication for administrators. As people move into urban areas their needs for government services increase. Part of this increased demand is the inevitable nature of urban life. Many services cannot be provided by individual efforts as may have been done in the rural area. Waste disposal, for example, becomes a wholly different concern; whereas rural authorities do not deal with waste disposal, most urban areas have to design policies for sewage and waste treatment. Villages often can ignore problems of water supply, but once people move to the cities their need for water becomes an issue to be settled by public authority, rather than left to the whims of nature.

The impact of urbanization is complicated by the generally weak condition of most local governments in developing countries. Understaffed, underfinanced, and lacking in authority, there are few resources that third world cities can marshal to meet the challenges they confront. Historical patterns and colonial experiences often precluded the development of local authority, and frequently nationalist impulses countered efforts to develop them following independence. The central government, its ministries, and the parastatal organizations continue to circumscribe severely the role and authority of local units. Hence, as discussed in Chapter 8, urban problems are legal and constitutional as well as economic and sociological. This fact means that we need to consider how urban governments relate to other levels and what possibilities exist for some further decentralization of resources and authority, as well as for coordination.

Migration and Migrant Behavior

Since migration is such a central fact of urban life, it is useful to examine it more closely and explore the varieties of responses that governments can make. The literature on migration suggests that the calculus that rural residents make in deciding whether or not to migrate is very similar to the calculus that they make about participation in general. It is essentially a rational effort to determine the various costs and benefits of moving to the city. And because it is rational, policymakers and administrators can try to discover what goals people have and offer new incentives for them.

It appears that economic incentives play a large role in the decision to migrate, that people "tend to move from places of lower economic opportunities to areas of higher potential opportunities."[6] The crucial point is how villagers estimate this potential. Generally, they perceive that urban areas have the greater potential for increasing their income, a perception that often persists throughout long periods of job searching.[7] Periods of unemployment after all are no more risky than the uncertainties of weather for subsistence crops. And many have had no access to land in the first place and thus have relied on the vagaries of farm labor for a livelihood. It is therefore not surprising that respondents who are surviving as pavement dwellers or squatters tell surveyors that they are better off in their new urban environments than they were back home.

In many instances their assumptions are well founded. Figures indicate that unemployment tends to run higher among the more educated, longer-term urban residents than among those who arrived during the past year.[8] It is also not uncommon for urban incomes to be five to ten times greater than in rural areas. It is therefore easy to see how urban areas are equated with opportunity and greater potential.

Surveys also indicate that two other factors explaining migration decisions are the presence of relatives in the city and the distance from the village to the city.[9] Either of these can lower the risk of a decision to migrate and hence increase the perceived opportunities from doing so. These various factors are illustrated in Figure 12.1.

Often there are special historical or political problems that encourage migration, such as political instability, drought, or famine. In some parts of Africa, the cities were the special province of the white colonialists,

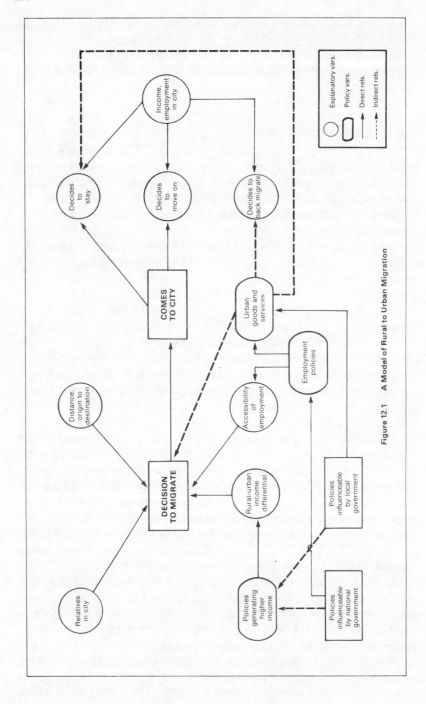

Figure 12.1   A Model of Rural to Urban Migration

whereas Africans were made to settle for homesteads on the fringes of urban life. A great psychological hunger for town life and its attendant status reinforces the obvious economic benefits in these cases. Everywhere urbanism is associated with modernity, with a faster pace of life, with the media and their attractions. It evokes symbols and status all the more valued, indeed coveted, when they had been long denied.

Since the differential between rural and urban incomes is the single most important factor, migration can be stemmed either by keeping urban incomes low or by improving rural incomes. Urban administrators therefore have a reason to favor income generating rural enterprises, off-farm employment, and improvements in farm-earned income. Since improvements in urban services or incomes will only increase migration, they need to be coupled with policies directed at rural incomes.[10] It is also useful to know what proportion of the migrants are sojourners, who have every intention of returning to their rural homesteads after they acquire some capital.[11] Efforts can then be made to facilitate their return rather than encouraging them to remain. In the final analysis, however, urban areas will probably continue to grow even if rural incomes are improved and two-way movement is encouraged. The differential in incomes is already so significant in many countries that closing the gap actually becomes less possible with each five-year plan.[12]

In addition to these urban-pull factors, there also are rural-push considerations, characteristics of rural areas that act as disincentives. Serious land shortages add a migratory push as the landless move to urban areas. Limited access to factors of production—water, animals, tools, credit—also encourage migration.[13] Another factor is the reality of social or ethnic discrimination; for ethnic minorities the urban area can be a haven from their rural isolation and vulnerability to persecution. For women, migration can be an escape from the privations of desertion or widowhood coupled with limited access to land, credit, and animals.[14] For the young, it can be an escape from the tenure and authoritarian control of the elders.

This emphasis on the rationality of migration challenges some of the traditional views of migrants. Frequently observers describe them as unstable malcontents and conclude that the swelling tide will prove to be politically destabilizing. At one point, for example, the Nairobi City Council became concerned about the growing squatter settlement in Mathare Valley and periodically tried to burn it down to encourage residents to return to their villages. However, a large body of recent research indicates that, in fact, the migrant is not an especially likely candidate for disruptive political behavior. To the extent that the migration is undertaken voluntarily, migrants have every incentive to get on with the business of carving out a more viable life for themselves and their families. Their primary interest is to secure such immediate benefits as security of tenure for their dwelling, shelter, education, and work.[15] Wayne Cornelius, for example, found that once a migrant achieved security in what he considered "primary benefits" his demands dropped off significantly.[16] Working in Brazil, Janice Perlman has also documented that migrants generally are not marginal or disruptive; rather they are marginalized by the local-level decision makers. The latter find that the myth of disruptive migrants is a useful rationalization for policies to relocate migrants and deny them access to urban services.[17]

Role of the Central Government

The reality of institutional and political life in many third world countries is that local city councils and executives have little authority even as they have overwhelming responsibilities. The management of urban development requires a high degree of coordination between central government ministries and local councils and authorities. Even when they are not directed at cities, the decisions of central governments have far-reaching impacts on urban growth. The range of central government decisions such as those dealing with labor, land use, investments, taxation, and employment have a direct impact on migration and urban development. Often these are considered in relative isolation from each other and with little attention to their impact on rural to urban migration. Even decisions that appear quite separate from urban growth, such as rates of pay for the civil service, affect migratory flows quite directly.[18] The reason is that increases in civil service salaries affect the demand for goods in the urban area, and migrants perceive that those increased needs will in turn generate employment opportunities.

Virtually all ministries have some impact on future urban development. The ministry of commerce, which negotiates locations for future industrial sites, affects income differentials within a wide radius of each location. The ministry of education affects urban development and migration indirectly through the nature of the curriculum used in the school system and through the location of the schools. The mismatch between school graduates and the labor force needs directly affects migration. The ministry of health affects urban development with its location and staffing of clinics and facilities. The ministry of finance affects organization through its fiscal and monetary policies and its input into the ministry of agriculture's pricing policies.

The central government also gets involved in local problems for political reasons. Even countries that espouse a rural development model find that urban areas need constant attention. Part of the problem is that urban densities generate needs for governmental action, or at least call for government action, more than do rural areas; this pressure occurs even though rural areas may have more critical and pressing needs. Urban needs capture attention, especially those of key decision makers, in ways in which rural needs frequently do not. Often urban problems are placed on the political agenda because they are new and therefore more dramatic. Consider the case of health problems. High infant mortality rates and disease in rural areas tend to be seen as inevitable and thus not amenable to policy initiatives. But in the urban areas health problems are often generated by density, and in these cases the sheer numbers involved tend to attract immediate attention.

Although part of the reason for the urban bias in policy decisions is the greater political activity of urban residents, the more serious problem is that the urban middle class is more active and more politically relevant. This same middle class frequently opposes efforts to address the needs of migrants. They know that every tax dollar that goes into a project to upgrade a squatter settlement is not available for renovating middle-income housing. The political reality is that local authorities rely on elections and it is difficult for them to embark on long-term policies that do not benefit the middle class.

It is important not to overdraw the dichotomy between rural and urban life, for in reality there is a rich and complex fabric of linkages between cities and villages. These are an important part of a country's culture, as well as its political economy, and frequently they serve to diffuse benefits from one sector to another. Townspeople in much of the third world are socially and economically interdependent with their rural kinfolk. In one survey taken in Botswana, for example, migrants reported a steady flow of return visits to their rural homesteads. One purpose was trade, and they indicated that such items as medicines were traded for foodstuffs to be brought back to the squatter settlement.[19] Another study of Nairobi confirmed that rural connections continued to provide urban residents with what amounted to a social security system.[20]

Local Government's Role

A major characteristic of the colonial heritage is a feeble and emaciated local government. It is not that the structure is weak, although it often is; the devastating weakness is the lack of awareness that local governments have a potential contribution to make to national vitality. Lackluster and unimaginative, local authorities often are the very backwater of government service. There are variations depending on the nature of the colonial experience, the kind of fight that national independence required, and the length of time since that independence was gained. The weakest tradition of local governance was that of the Spanish and Portuguese in Latin America, Mozambique, and Angola. In most of these areas, the violence that accompanied the struggle for independence had a centralizing impact and diminished the possibilities for local self-help and initiative. Even though Latin American governments have had over a hundred years to rebuild, they have grown more centralized over time, with a cacique tradition at the local levels, rather than one of local government.[21] French rule was patterned after the metropole with a strong center and administrative powers reaching well into the countryside. Even today, military governments in post-French-speaking countries tend to take a Gaullist approach to local governance and to treat self-help as a method of enlisting free labor for public works.[22]

The English colonialists, with a tradition of local government at home, made several efforts to transplant local government institutions to their colonies. The nature of the transplant varied slightly from Tory to Whig in the colonial office, but its residue is still to be found in local governments in many countries in Africa and somewhat in India, Bangladesh, and Pakistan. For example, in many cities from this tradition, planning will often be modeled on an old English Town and Country Planning Act, with its emphasis on closely regulated land use and a failure to provide for informal sector work.

A major task assigned to local governments is to administer the delivery of local services. Even in developing nations, however, local governments play a very weak role. In her study of government and administration in Lagos, Anne Marie Hauk Walsh found that regional and federal levels of government dominated urban services and development.[23] Major works and public services "are provided by these governments or their statutory corporations, and local authorities not only derive their existence and powers from them, but also are subject to close control by them."[24] As a result, local governments are seen primarily as caretakers rather than effective decision makers. Citizens in turn do not perceive that local governments could or should make a difference; they do not consider the elected local government as primarily responsive to their needs.

Because of these institutional weaknesses it is probably fair to conclude that the major administrative task for urban areas is to improve their capacity. And as always capacity depends on financing. Local governments are seriously underfinanced partly because of their limited taxing authority.[25] A recent IMF study underscored the reluctance of other levels of government to share their taxing powers. It pointed out that "higher levels of government may not relinquish for local use those revenue sources which they themselves value, or consider potentially valuable, until forced to do so by crises at lower government levels."[26]

Ironically, some efforts to ameliorate financial problems only increase the incapacity of local governments. Some donors, for example, in giving aid to cities, have responded to the evident weakness at the local level by creating separate authorities to administer special projects. Although the project may be very successful in meeting its goals, and the needs of the beneficiaries, little is learned by the local government that leads to its improved performance in the future.

Whether spurred by donors or by central governments fearing to expand local governmental powers, many of the larger cities—Nairobi, Manila, Calcutta—have recently established citywide agencies outside of the existing governmental structures to carry out planning and development activities. Predictably they draw resources, supports, and energy away from the traditional structures, thus making it more difficult for these structures to carry out their ongoing service delivery functions. Although they may make it easier for donors, for central authorities, or for private interests to maintain an influence over development, separate institutions weaken local political capacity.[27]

Interestingly, a very similar debate has been going on within the United States. During the 1960s the national government funded a variety of projects and structures at the local level that were not accountable to local leadership. Although the poor often benefited in the short run, the local governments were weakened in the process. The core of New Federalist policies in the 1970s has been to pass all federal funding through locally elected leadership, and the result has been to strengthen the role of mayors and councils and thus to enhance their capacity.[28] With evidence that the international community is beginning to renew its interest in urban development, it is important to consider the implications of financial management for institutional capacity.[29]

Thus far we have argued that local governments need to have their powers and financial capacities strengthened if they are to cope with the enormous problems confronting them. Those who realize that it is important to expand local government capacity, however, frequently have a very top-down, professionalized, and nonparticipatory model in mind. Consider the example of community development. Most commonly professional land use planners are put in charge of community development efforts, and the plans focus solely on physical land use. Colin Rosser has given us a description of an urban planning effort in Calcutta during the 1960s that grew out of this perspective. In this case, however, a multidisciplinary team was convened to oversee the development plans, and they gradually came to the view that a more radical approach was necessary given the crushing problems of Calcutta. They insisted that urban planning had to be more than the creation of a physical plan. In fact, it was better described as a *process*, rather than a specific end product—not a "'one-shot exercise' conducted by experts in a special 'back-room' agency, but a permanent, continuous process fully integrated with the normal structure of government." Only in this way would urban planning be integrated with those who would implement it.[30]

The staff went one step further. They decided that the enormity of the problems meant that any planning process had to mobilize the contributions, resources, and supports of the public and integrate these into the planning process. The program that they developed to involve the public included many of the steps described in Chapter 10. They tried to work through local voluntary organizations and existing leadership. They also focused on immediate neighborhood improvements in order to elicit local contributions. Rosser's major point, however, is that in order to fully integrate and draw on these voluntary groups, the participation must be carefully organized. "Skillful organization is the main requirement based on full consultation with local leaders and with government departments."[31] The implication for this discussion is that local governments need financial support from the national level, and they also need to give careful attention to organizational structures for involving the public and to procedures for linking planning into the ongoing policy and implementation process.

Policy Responses

The major task of local governments continues to be the efficient and effective delivery of local services—waste disposal, water supply, transportation, health care, education. As described in Chapter 11, there are generally four different approaches available to governments in providing these services: supply, demand, negative sanctions, and coproduction. For most services, it is possible for the government to supply them directly, to stimulate demand indirectly through the marketplace, to penalize people for not producing them, or to coproduce them with residents and consumers. Some services may require large investments and public provision. Generally, it is true, however, that governments do not give adequate consideration to efforts to use the private sector, to work with citizens, or to develop a diversified system. Consider waste disposal for example. Most central cities require a large public sewage system in the core of the city. In less dense residential areas, where middle-income people own homes, it may be more efficient to induce the private sector to put in septic tanks. In outlying low-income areas, however, the most useful role for the government may be to provide residents with plans and supplies to build their own pit latrines.

Housing is another arena where governments are exploring a variety of strategies. Traditionally, governments have dealt with the inability of the private sector to provide housing for the poor by building public housing. Such housing, however, is usually expensive, difficult to maintain, and frequently very unpopular with those who end up living in it. One alternative is to explore possibilities for self-help housing. Governments then provide some materials and other inducements to encourage citizens to participate in building their own housing. Sometimes they do so as individuals, but more often they do so as a community of neighbors. Charles Abrams, who wrote eloquently about "man's struggle for shelter," called attention to the viability of roof loan schemes. Putting the roofing on a shelter is the most difficult and expensive part of the home. Abrams reasoned that if the government provided loans for roofs and people were organized into small groups among whose members loans could rotate, people would be able to construct safe and decent housing for themselves. A community would join together to build a roof for one person. As this person paid back the loan for the materials, it would be used to buy material for a second roof that the community would then build. This process would continue until all of the participants had a roof on their homes. Expanding upon this idea, self-help housing has become a strategy widely used in developing countries.[32]

A major challenge for urban governments is to devise ways to have major needs met through self-help approaches. Shrewd squatters have already devised a wide variety of self-help techniques, often in open disregard for the legal aspects of their situation. Governments may want to explore these efforts and determine if they are aberrations or undesirable. Picture the usual scene in a barriada in Latin America where the squatters have jerry-rigged their electrical hookup to the existing electricity lines along the highway. Their efforts are essentially self-help approaches, and it is worth asking what can be learned from their activities. It may be tempting for public officials either to overlook the illegal hookup or endeavor to tear it down. In the first response they assume that the electricity is a free public good, in the second that it is a stolen good. It is important to see that there are alternatives that avoid both of these extremes. For exmple, the government could assess user fees based on group rates. Such an alternative would establish the authority of the government, would collect some revenue, and would encourage conservation among the users. Table 12.1 lays out some of the alternative approaches that governments can take, some more costly than others, to improve local services, especially for the urban poor.

In brief, there are a variety of options available to local governments not requiring large capital expenditures that they could adopt as part of their strategy for responding to urban growth. Table 12.1 points to some of these options, designating those involving low and medium expenditures. Most local governments have sufficient authority to undertake these approaches and are doing so, although many hesitate when they consider their political costs.[33]

Notice that many of the low-expenditure strategies are controversial and that they pose difficult dilemmas for urban managers. Their controversial nature means that low-expenditure items are most often rejected for political or organizational reasons and that narrow cost-benefit analyses are of limited utility. These political realities place a premium on organizations that reward officials for taking initiatives, being willing to encounter risk, and coping with uncertainty. Unfortunately that is not the common organizational environment for most local-level managers.

If the focus is shifted from the kinds of *services* that can be undertaken in urban areas to strategies to improve urban *incomes,* especially those of the poor, another set of options can be delineated. Table 12.2 suggests several, again distinguishing between those that involve low and medium costs. (The lists are intended to be suggestive rather than comprehensive; there are other possible options such as manipulating taxation or fiscal policy.)

In many respects urban managers confront the same management problems as those extension agents face. Urban administrators are field agents too; however, because there is less public consensus over their goals than there is for agricultural agents, they are less likely to take initiatives. It is useful to consider the political costs and benefits that local administrators have to take into account. Norman Uphoff, for example, stresses the utility of cost-benefit analysis to understand the importance of political resources to the decisions of administrators. His conclusion is that political leaders have to calculate their political resources with as much care as economists use when they offer advice on investments. "Political will" is not a given that can be relied on.

On the contrary, [political will] is something conditioned by the structure of political situations: On which sectors does the government depend for

TABLE 12.1

Strategies for Improving Urban Services

Low Expenditure	Medium Expenditure
1. Organize local self-help to build and staff local facilities.	1. Provide essential services at minimal levels (water, sewer hook-ups); charge user fees for any provision above the minimum.
2. Support and train local Community Development staff.	2. Secure tenancy rights in self-help housing areas. Use Community Development assistance to encourage self-help efforts.
3. Organize non-formal education projects around, e.g., nutrition, health, job skills.	3. Generate revolving credit schemes to improve local facilities and services.
4. Monitor industrial location decisions affecting jobs and services.	4. Establish facilities to cooperatives to expand their services.
5. Add local projects to existing centrally funded projects.	5. Support local associations in exchange for services they take on for the community.
6. Involve voluntary associations in local programs.	
7. Review local codes and regulations which inhibit local service delivery.	
8. Train para-professionals in essential area (e.g., mid-wifery).	

TABLE 12.2

Strategies for Increasing Income and Productivity of Urban Poor

Low Expenditure	Medium Expenditure
1. Revise licenses which restrict employment.	1. Set up credit facilities for small-scale enterprises.
2. Review land use regulations which discourage local employment.	2. Establish small-scale training programs in management for enterpreneurs.
3. Review local regulations restricting hawkers and vendors.	3. Require job training in businesses moving into area.
4. Support self-help building of facilities: market stalls child care centers, clinics.	4. Offer loans for small equipment essential for local businesses -- sewing machines, adding machines, bicycles, tools.
5. Provide tax exemptions for small businesses.	5. Give transportation vouchers for marketing goods.
	6. Negotiate contracts with small enterprises wherever possible.

what resources to sustain its authority and pursue overt and tacit policies? What demands and expectations do these sectors have? What are their respective capabilities for making the political equivalent of "effective demands"? What are the capabilities of political and administrative infrastructures on which the government can draw?[34]

Given this political logic, consider the options facing governments in cities experiencing steady and significant rates of rural to urban migration. Figure 12.2 details some of these options and their probable economic, political, and administrative costs. The figure helps to explain why some of the choices that appear "irrational" or unresponsive to the poor are in practice very rational for local decision makers. They are rational because they are responses to existing organizational and resource incentives. A restructuring of incentives is therefore important in order to accomplish any significant change. One example of such a change is the role that some major international donors have played in encouraging innovative policies. For example, the support of institutions such as the World Bank for self-help housing programs has encouraged, sometimes induced, local governments to consider what had earlier been disregarded. For example, the Lusaka self-help housing project financed by the World Bank's Urban Projects Division is a successful project responding to the shelter needs of the urban poor. Organizational incentives also were used to encourage a well-trained community development team to work closely and consistently with squatter groups over the life of the project.[35]

The Urban Informal Sector

Many of these low-cost policy strategies assume that the informal sector in these communities offers potential opportunities for development. They suggest that the informal sector is not necessarily a threat to urban development, but that it can be a source of impetus and creativity. The informal sector refers to the unprotected sector, to the fringe areas of work outside of the regular system of wage employment. The point is that informal sector workers have no legal protection, no contracts, no employee rights. Poor people, not always newly arrived migrants, move constantly in and out of the informal sector as they contrive to earn enough to stay alive on a day-to-day basis. Brewing beer, making sandals from scraps, hawking food, carting and peddling water, making clothing or rudimentary furniture are all examples of informal sector activities.

Most empirical studies indicate that there are frequently more women than men in the informal sector.[36] Tied closer to home to care for dependents between earning periods, a woman will brew, hawk, peddle,

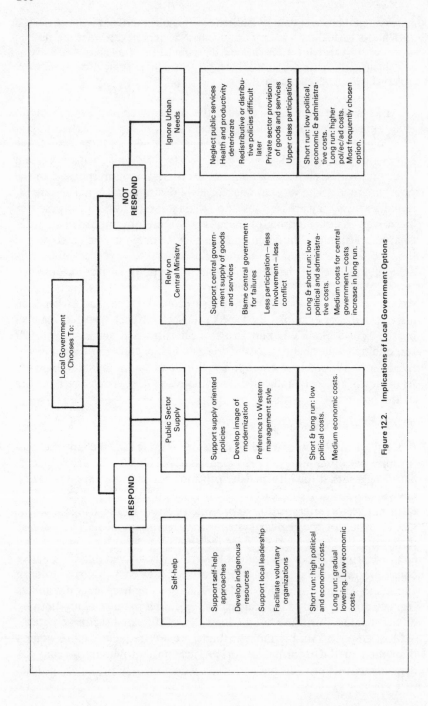

Figure 12.2. Implications of Local Government Options

Local Government Chooses To:

RESPOND

Self-help
- Support self-help approaches
- Develop indigenous resources
- Support local leadership
- Facilitate voluntary organizations

- Short run: high political and economic costs.
- Long run: gradual lowering. Low economic costs.

Public Sector Supply
- Support supply oriented policies
- Develop image of modernization
- Preference to Western management style

- Short & long run: low political costs.
- Medium economic costs.

NOT RESPOND

Rely on Central Ministry
- Support central government supply of goods and services
- Blame central government for failures
- Less participation — less involvement — less conflict

- Long & short run: low political and administrative costs.
- Medium costs for central government — costs increase in long run.

Ignore Urban Needs
- Neglect public services
- Health and productivity deteriorate
- Redistributive or distributive policies difficult later
- Private sector provision of goods and services
- Upper class participation

- Short run: low political, economic & administrative costs.
- Long run: higher pol/ec/ad costs.
- Most frequently chosen option.

and work without any assurance of earnings on a regular basis. Hemmed in by local restrictions on land use that constrain her to growing "European" vegetables, or hawking in particular neighborhoods, most of what she experiences from local government are curtailments, if not harrassment, as she tries to earn a living.

There are two interpretations of the role and nature of the informal sector.[37] One argues that it is a migrant's major point of entry into urban employment and further that the migrant tends to move up from this point to more secure and lucrative employment. The other view is that the informal sector represents the dead end for those who fail to get or keep regular wage work. People fall back into these jobs after some catastrophe—an illness, a forced relocation—has spoiled whatever chances they may have had for more regular employment. Some surveys indicate that the informal sector is primarily populated by the not-so-recent migrants, hence lending some credence to the latter view. But the evidence is mixed, and it is a difficult area to research. The very nature of this kind of work means that it will often be illegal, brewing beer for example. In the meantime there is enough evidence that these various activities have the potential for employing and servicing sufficient numbers that governments should reconsider the many ways in which they discourage such activities. To take only one example, the English Town and Country Planning Act sets forth standards of performance and land use regulations in order to create homogenous practices. And local interests have grown up around these local codes, making them difficult to change. It is very possible that many of the codes need to be rethought in order to allow a greater variety of economic activity. Revising such regulations may be one very effective and low-cost way to respond to urban needs.

Conclusions

Urban areas in developing nations, with their vast concentrations of people, are simultaneously a storehouse of energy and resources and a center of poverty and misery. As real as the poverty is, the migration to cities continues, intensifying the problems. The administrative issue is to deal with these problems without luring more peoples to the cities or diverting resources from the primary task of rural development. The dilemma is that few local governments have the capacity or resources to be either creative or effective. The central government therefore needs to assume a large part of the burden of the urban areas, but to do so in a way that will strengthen the capacity of their fragile and resource-starved institutions. Both levels of government—central and local—need to be more imaginative in thinking of a variety of strategies to build on the strengths within the community and optimize their resources. One noteworthy strategy is to find more ways to tap the resources of the informal sector and to provide it with the protection it needs to grow and flourish. In the administratively heavy governments of developing nations, it is all too easy to ignore anything that does not occur under government sanction. But the informal sector provides a rich resource for urban development activities.[38]

Notes

1. One of the most important articles to call attention to the deleterious effects on rural development of an urban bias in development models is that of Michael Lipton, "Urban Bias and Food Policy in Poor Countries," *Food Policy*, November 1975, pp. 41-52. For a thoughtful balancing of urban and rural policies, see also Bertrand Renaud, *National Urbanization Policies in Developing Countries*, World Bank Staff Working Paper no. 347 (Washington, D.C.: World Bank, July 1979).

2. There are many sources for demographic data on urban growth. The standard one is Kingsley Davis, *World Urbanization I; Basic Data* (Berkeley: University of California, 1969). See also *The Task Ahead for the Cities of the Developing Countries*, World Bank Staff Working paper no. 209 (Washington, D.C.: World Bank, 1975). These figures are also in John D. Herbert *Guidelines for Formulating Projects to Benefit the Urban Poor in the Developing Countries*, vols. 1-2 (Washington, D.C.: Agency for Interior Development, 1976).

3. Joan Nelson, *Access to Power* (Princeton, N.J.: Princeton University Press, 1979).

4. One well-known model of rural to urban migration is the Harris-Todaro model; although it illuminates many of the relationships that explain migration, it neglects the importance of the informal sector. Michael Todaro, "A Model of Labor Migration and Urban Unemployment in Less Developed Countries," *American Economic Review* 1 (1969). This discussion is also available in his textbook *Economic Development in the Third World* (England: Longmans, 1978).

5. Thomas P. Bernstein, *Up to the Mountains and Down to the Villages* (New Haven, Conn.: Yale University Press, 1977).

6. Lorene Yap, *Internal Migration in Less Developed Countries: A Survey of the Literature*, World Bank Staff Working Paper no. 215 (Washington, D.C., World Bank, 1975).

7. Todaro, *Economic Development*.

8. Survey data tends to reconfirm this finding. See Coralie Bryant, Betsy Stephens, and Sherry MacLiver, "Rural to Urban Migration: Some Data from Botswana," *African Studies Review* 1 (September 1978):85-99.

9. Ibid. We would like to thank Shaik Ismail for his assistance in developing the model in Figure 12.1.

10. Yap, *Internal Migration*; Todaro, "Model of Labor Migration."

11. See Joan Nelson, "Sojourners Versus New Urbanites: Causes and Consequences of Temporary Versus Permanent Cityward Migration in Developing Countries," *Economic Development and Cultural Change* 24 (July 1976).

12. There are several studies of this issue dealing with single countries. For example, see Patrick Eze Ollawa, "Rural Development Strategy and Performance in Zambia: An Evaluation of Past Efforts," *African Studies Review* 21 (September 1978):101–124. Also see Donald Rothchild and Robert L. Curry, *Scarcity, Choice and Public Policy in Middle Africa* (Berkeley: University of California Press, 1978).

13. Historically access to land or security of tenure affected rural to urban migration. The enclosure movement in England increased the rate of such migration and the growth of cities throughout northern England. Indeed the problems of enumerating the landless in any country are complicated by the fact that those who migrate to urban areas are often not counted; yet historically landless people have always migrated. For more discussion of the problem of landlessness, see Chapter 13.

14. See Irene Tinker, "The Adverse Impact of Development on Women," in I. Tinker and M. Bramsen, *Women and World Development* (Washington, D.C.: Overseas Development Council, 1976). See also Nancy Hofkin and Edna Bay, *Women in Africa* (Berkeley, Calif.: Stanford University Press, 1976); Kenneth Little, *African Women in Towns* (London: Cambridge University Press, 1973); Nwanganga Shields, *Women in the Urban Labor Markets of Africa: The Case of Tanzania,* World Bank Staff Working Paper no. 380 (Washington, D.C.: World Bank, 1980).

15. Nelson, *Access,* and also her earlier *Migrants, Urban Poverty and Instability in Developing Nations,* Occasional Paper no. 22 (Cambridge, Mass.: Harvard University Press, 1969).

16. Wayne Cornelius, "Urbanization and Political Demand Making: Political Participation Among Migrant Poor in Latin American Cities," *American Political Science Review* 68 (1974):1125–1146.

17. Janice Perlman, *The Myth of Marginality* (Berkeley: University of California Press, 1976). A useful discussion of this same problem in India can be seen in P. Ramachandran, *Pavement Dwellers in Bombay City* (Bombay: TaTa Institute of Social Sciences, 1972). Ramachandran interviewed the heads of 828 households who were pavement dwellers. One of his interesting findings, revealing something of the nature of marginalization, is that nearly 12 percent of those interviewed indicated they were paying something to the police as "rent" for their street sleeping location.

18. Bryant, Stephens, and MacLiver, "Rural to Urban Migration." The rate of rural to urban migration in Botswana increased significantly the year following the increase in civil service salary rates.

19. Ibid.

20. Marc Howard Ross, *Grass Roots in an African City* (Cambridge: Cambridge University Press, 1975).

21. Perlman, *Myth of Marginality;* see also John Collier, *Squatters and Oli-*

garchs (Baltimore: Johns Hopkins University Press, 1976). Wayne Cornelius has written about this phenomena in several articles. See, for example, "Contemporary Mexico: A Structural Analysis of Urban Caciquismo," in *The Caciques: Oligarchical Politics and the System of Caciquismo in the Luso-Hispanic World,* ed. Robert Kern (Albuquerque: University of New Mexico Press, 1973).

22. Sometimes these approaches draw upon the *loi indigénat* as practiced under early French colonial rule. For a straightforward account of French colonial policy toward local government, see Lord Hailey, *An African Survey, Revised 1956* (London: Oxford University Press, 1957).

23. Ann Marie Hauk Walsh, *The Urban Challenge to Government* (New York: Praeger, 1969). This volume followed a whole series of studies of cities and their governance, such as Lagos, Paris, Zagreb, Stockholm, and so forth, that the Institute of Public Administration had undertaken. See, for example, Ann Marie Hauk Walsh and Babatunde Williams, *Urban Government for Metropolitan Lagos* (New York: Praeger, 1968).

24. Walsh, *Urban Challenge,* p. 54.

25. Roger Smith, "Financing Cities in Developing Countries" (Washington, D.C.: International Monetary Fund, July 1974).

26. Smith, "Financing," p. 330.

27. Dr. Sivaramakrishnan of the Educational Development Institute, World Bank, made the point speaking at the annual conference of the Washington chapter of the Society for International Development, May 28, 1980. Sometimes this lack of diffusion is because the project is quite autonomous from the local city council and its staff, and sometimes because many of the urban services are turned over to a development corporation. On the former, see Coralie Bryant, "Squatters, Collective Action and Participation: Learning from Lusaka," *World Development,* 1980, pp. 73-85.

28. Paul R. Dommel et al., *Targeting Community Development* (Washington, D.C.: U.S. Department of Housing and Urban Development, 1980), Chapter 3.

29. By the early 1970s, urban development was taken more seriously by international agencies, and urban project offices were established in bilateral agencies and within the World Bank. Additional international pressure was brought to bear with an international conference by the United Nations in 1976, "Habitat, The Conference on Human Settlements." Among its other contributions it established the United Nations Environment Program with its headquarters in Nairobi.

30. Colin Rosser, "Action Planning in Calcutta," in Raymond Apthorpe, ed., *People, Planning, and Development Studies* (London: Frank Cass, 1970), p. 126.

31. Ibid., pp. 121-139.

32. Charles Abrams, *Man's Struggle for Shelter in an Urbanizing World* (Cambridge, Mass.: MIT Press, 1965). See also John F. C. Turner, "Barriers and Channels for Housing Development in Modernizing Countries," in *Peasants in Cities,* ed. William Mangin (Boston: Houghton Mifflin, 1970). Turner more recently has written part of a dialogue concerning self-help housing. See John F. C. Turner, "Housing in Three Dimensions: Terms of Reference for the Housing

Question Redefined," in *World Development* 6 (September-October 1978):1135-1145.

33. *Urban Edge,* a monthly newsletter of the Council for International Urban Liaison, Washington, D.C., regularly carries accounts of the wide variety of new approaches to the delivery of basic services being tried in cities around the world.

34. Norman Uphoff "Political Considerations in Human Development" in *Implementing Programs of Human Development,* edited by Peter T. Knight, World Bank Staff Working Paper no. 403 (Washington, D.C.: World Bank, 1980).

35. Bryant, "Squatters, Collective Action and Participation."

36. Shields, *Women in the Urban Labor Markets.*

37. Keith Hart, "Informal Income Opportunities and Urban Employment in Ghana," *Journal of Modern African Studies* 11 (January 1973):61-89. See also Dipak Mazumdar, *The Urban Informal Sector,* World Bank Staff Working Paper no. 211 (Washington, D.C.: World Bank, 1975).

38. Raymond Apthorpe, *People, Planning and Development Studies* (London: Frank Cass, 1970), p. 10.

13
Managing Rural Development

Introduction

The daily migration from rural to urban areas is a graphic indicator of the depth of rural poverty for most of the third world's population. For millions, rural poverty is so deep and degrading that the only escape appears to be to walk to town and take up subsistence on urban streets. Those who are most able leave; those who cannot frequently starve—either slowly from severe malnutrition, or quickly in the recurrent famines. The nature of this poverty was vividly described by the economist John Kenneth Galbraith after he had lived in India.

> It is rural poverty that is intractable. Here people have lived at or near the minimum necessary for survival for a long time; for practical purposes, always. And here the condition persists because they live in an equilibrium of poverty. Few things allow of escape from life at a minimum level of subsistence; when something does, there are forces which operate to return the people to something approaching their former level of deprivation. Improving income here is not normal. It is and always has been unknown.[1]

In spite of the sheer number who are involved, many officials do not hear or absorb the message. There are several reasons for this failing. In a multitude of ways, as Robert Chambers reminds us, rural poverty is not seen and, not being perceived, is not addressed. Partly out of ignorance and partly out of bureaucratic inertia, administrators find that daily organizational routines insulate them from this pervasive reality.[2] Dealing with rural poverty is also very demanding on administrators. It challenges their organizations, their skills, their roles, and their assumptions. Since they are confronted with repeated failure in improving rural areas, it also challenges their self-confidence and their political support systems. Sometimes administrators consider that the best recourse is to

275

focus on urban areas where problems are at least more visible and political pressures more immediate. In this manner an "urban bias" may provide an escape from confronting the awesome gap between rhetoric and performance in rural development.

Much of what has already been said in this study addresses the problems that administrators face as they deal with the training of field agents or with the most effective means of organizing participation. In this chapter we apply these models to the task of designing an effective approach to rural development. First, we consider the environment within which administrators of rural programs must operate—in particular the world food system, the motivations of the peasant, and the national political arena. After discussing this environment, and the constraints and opportunities it affords, we consider different approaches to rural development. Finally, we discuss various strategies that administrators can consider.

One of the recurring themes of the book has been a consideration of the relative merits of top-down and bottom-up strategies. The former focuses on the decision-making and analytic approaches of managers; the latter examines appropriate processes out of which an effective development strategy can emerge. We will be considering the implications of this latter approach to rural development problems, underscoring what Richard Nelson refers to as "the saliency of organizational structure" and the "open-ended evolutionary way in which policies and programs do and should unfold."[3]

The Environment of the Rural Development Administrator

Rural Development and the World Food System

Growing interdependence, discussed in Chapter 1, is dramatically evident in the operations of international trade and agricultural marketing. Within any single country, food policy involves farm policy, domestic economic policy, foreign policy, welfare and development policy. Each of these arenas has its own constituency and set of interests. Each "is represented by individuals and institutions inside and outside government who give it priority. They are different communities with different questions of the policy arena."[4] Decisions that appear to be domestic and internal to one nation also have immediate impact upon farmers halfway around the globe. For example, a decision to control the price of food in one nation means that there is less incentive to local producers elsewhere to plant for the next harvest. Similarly, if a country meets its shortages by importing subsidized food, it is apt to further depress local production, while encouraging the farmers elsewhere to plant more. (Critics of the U.S. Food for Peace program (Public Law 480) argue that it is apt to help the farmers in Iowa and to create new problems in third world nations.)

Many developing countries that were once able to feed their own populations are no longer able to do so; most in fact have become net food importers. In the early stages of development, a country tends to concentrate on the growth of export crops. This concentration often induces greater malnutrition and even hunger within the country as people turn their energies from food crops toward export crops. Aggregated data available from international organizations indicate absolute levels of malnutrition using indicators such as calorie counts per capita.[5] But those figures need to be disaggregated by region and sector in order to understand the real hunger in rural areas, for poverty is not distributed evenly. Even in instances where food crops do receive attention, those food crops are marketed in urban areas, and the farm families whose labor produced them may consume little of them and may even suffer from varying degrees of malnutrition.

Not only is food production frequently diverted elsewhere, it has often not increased. For example, during the past fifteen years, in fifty-three developing countries, staple food production fell behind population growth. In 1979, although developing countries had 70 percent of the world's population, they only produced 40 percent of the world's food supply.[6] At the same time, their incomes are insufficient to import the balance of what they need. Writing from the political economy perspective, Richard Barnet points out that "malnutrition is the hidden holocaust of our day. . . . The technological revolution needed to feed the anticipated global population in the year 2000 is within our grasp but political, social, and institutional conditions stand in the way."[7] The problem goes beyond per capita agricultural productivity, however; it involves problems of access to land, water, animals, technology, and capital. And often it is this lack of access, or landlessness, that continues to account for hunger. In some countries land reform has been a major development strategy, but it has not always been effective.[8]

The Moral Economy of the Peasant

Throughout this text, the point has been emphasized that both policy choices and administrative strategies are deeply affected by the assumptions that decision makers hold about peasant behavior and motivation. These assumptions are a significant aspect of the working environment of the rural administrator. In Chapter 10 we discussed the way in which peasants balance benefits, costs, and risks in deciding whether to adopt new technologies. These trade-offs constitute what James Scott describes as the "moral economy" of the peasant and demonstrate that what might appear to be irrational behavior is actually very rational when the peasant's perspective is taken into account.[9] The logic of this rationality is described as follows by Michael Todaro:

> Subsistence agriculture is a highly risky and uncertain venture. It is made even more so by the fact that human lives are at stake. In regions where farms are extremely small and cultivation is dependent upon the uncertainties of a highly variable rainfall, average output will be low and in poor years the peasant and his family will be exposed to the very real danger of starvation. In such circumstances, the main motivating force in the peasant's life may be maximization not of income, but rather of his family's chance of survival.[10]

As Todaro goes on to explain, this logic underpins the reasoning of the peasant farmer contemplating the possibility of changing technology or crop pattern from those that are well known to those that are purported to be profitable. If current crop patterns mean a low yield per hectare, if their variance or fluctuations are also low, that will be preferred to even higher yields that have higher variance. Todaro's diagram, reproduced below as Figure 13.1, illustrates the point.[11]

This figure describes how attitudes toward risk among small cultivators may countermand narrow economic incentives. The lower horizontal line illustrates the peasant's view of the minimum necessary for the family's physical survival. The upper sloped line illustrates the minimum level of food consumption he desires, a level that may increase with rising expectations. The more well-to-do farmer whose past performance and crop experience has been that of farmer B, is more likely to experiment, to take on risk, than farmer A, whose experience over the past few years has been very close to the family's minimum consumption requirement. (Actually this approach rediscovered empirically points that Mao and Gandhi had made earlier, albeit in different ways and for different reasons. Both of these leaders held that the peasant has a wisdom and a rationality that can be called his own moral economy. When peasants reject opportunities for expanding production, it is not due to "an immutable Oriental personality" that is different from an "economically rational Western personality." Rather they are responding to the realities of their situation.[12])

This model helps to explain several aspects of peasant choice and behavior. For example, it explains why price incentives will tend to work better for farmers who are not operating close to a subsistence level. Since farmers closer to subsistence are more preoccupied with risk than

Figure 13.1.

Small Farmer Attitudes toward Risk

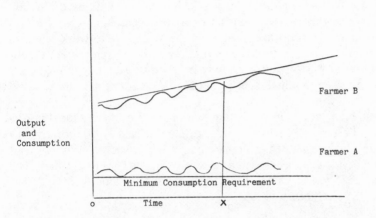

Output
and
Consumption

Farmer B

Farmer A

Minimum Consumption Requirement

o   Time   X

Source: Based on Michael Todaro, Economic Development in the Third World (London: Longmans Press, 1972), p. 221. Permission granted by publisher.

with profit, they are actually behaving rationally when they reject price incentives to expand production. Among the policy implications that this approach suggests is that full consideration be given to the supports necessary to buffer the risks involved for a subsistence farmer confronting change. If there is little in the way of such support (credit, or guaranteed prices, for example), then it is more likely that only farmers with a good margin (the better-off farmers) will adopt the new technique.

Not everyone agrees that this model accurately reflects the way the peasant approaches reality. Some repudiate the idea altogether, arguing that peasants are often stubborn, sometimes stupid, and frequently suspicious; others amend the concept to take into account a different interpretation of peasant motivation and behavior.[13] Often these differing interpretations either expand upon the concept of rationality or revise the concept to incorporate logical explanations for apparently irrational behavior. Two of these latter revisionists are Goren Hyden and Kusum Nair, who write on Tanzania and India respectively.

Goren Hyden's argument is that peasant modes of production differ in different regions both within and without Africa.[14] Latin America, he says, has been far more penetrated by Western capitalism, whereas much of Asia has a severe problem of landlessness. One of the most important differences is therefore the amount of independence the peasant can, and does, exercise due to his particular position. In Tanzania, the peasant can be very independent of government action. Further, he argues, the peasant's motivation is deeply affected by what Hyden terms "the economy of affection," the network of interpersonal norms and needs of the extended family whose survival and status are often paramount. In the third world peasants work to live, not, as in the West, live to work. He also notes the difference that rain-fed agriculture makes, reinforcing the independence of the peasant producer; irrigation systems typical of Asia require more communal sharing and negotiation than do rain-fed systems.

Kusum Nair, however, holds that peasants are neither rational nor irrational. Therefore, she is reluctant to rely too heavily on incentives to motivate the peasant to produce that which society needs. Instead peasants need sanctions as well as incentives if they are to produce. The state needs to use coercion in the form of taxes or land reform, rather than positive inducements. She argues:

> Change strategies based on education, demonstration, and incentives have not been successful in bringing about the requisite transformation. But it can be done, if farmers are also regarded as normal human beings – neither more nor less stupid, rational or irrational. It means that, as in every other field of economic activity, farmers too must be required to fulfill their obligations to society and maintain certain standards of land use and production. And if they fail to do so, instead of being subsidized, as now, they too must be penalized – for non-use, neglect, or wastage of scarce resources.[15]

Tax policy should therefore penalize wasteful behavior and inaction, by being based on the potential productivity of the land rather than on a farmer's income.

National Commitment to Rural Development

Given the pressures from both the international and domestic environment, it should come as no surprise that few countries are deeply committed to rural development. Those interests committed to increasing equity and enhancing the access of small farmers to the means of production are often a small group with little political muscle. Rural development options are constrained by the interests and goals of large landowners, agricultural businesses, and weak small farmer organizations. Thus although the rhetoric of national plans is that of rural developmnt, the reality of national budgets is more frequently that of urban development.[16] Official reports are replete with accounts such as that of Zambia where more money was spent in the first national development plan in the two urbanized regions than in the remaining six rural provinces combined.[17] And all too often the approach to rural development is a simplistic one of "how can we keep them down on the farm." Policies framed within that perspective are ill-conceived. There is not an urban rural dichotomy, but rather an interdependence among rural areas, villages, and towns. Awareness of this interdependence must underpin policy strategies.

Development assistance agency officials often lament the lack of national commitment to rural development without appreciating its origin. Third world officials perceive they have little control over the crucial variables and feel there is too much uncertainty over the key factors of production. Their environment is full of uncertainties, the magnitude and likelihood of which the administrator can only estimate, but rarely control. But in any case, the very use of the term *national commitment* is suspect for it encompasses national decision makers, as well as provincial and local political interests. Any national commitment to rural development lies beneath a welter of decisions on agricultural policy, land use and regulations, tax policy, credit and financial institutions, and export-import strategy.[18]

Most every third world nation has experienced a vigorous debate over the importance of rural development. The debate has been heavily influenced by Western theories of development that argued for a strategy based on industrialization and meant that investment in rural production was not seen as important as it would later become. In the meantime, many third world leaders disagreed with the Western prescriptions. Gandhi was outspokenly critical and emphasized the possibility of small-scale projects that might have the potential for rural people to recombine change with traditional values.[19] Within his own political following there were many who considered Gandhi arcane in his preoccupation with rural development; even his protégé Jawaharlal Nehru disagreed with the "village-industry-first" strategy. Nevertheless, Gandhi's influence was profound and led to the panchayati raj movement, one of the world's largest experiments with rural and community development.[20] Other third world countries have had their own versions of this complex debate; Mao's greatest difference with the Russian Communists was his insistence upon the role of the peasants in the revolution.[21] The commitment of China looms as the largest single experiment in rural development and food self-sufficiency.

While socialist leaders in the third world often place rural development first, some capitalist systems have also taken this approach. The startling growth of the Japanese agricultural sector illustrates that when rural people have political power, the rural sector can flourish and provide a stable base for industrial growth. Taiwan has also followed this path, and with similar positive benefits. Sri Lanka invested in both rural development and basic needs to devise a mixed approach that has been quite successful.

A major complication in achieving support for rural development in many countries since 1973 has been the rapid rise in oil prices. Not only is oil a major import for industrial production, but it is essential for agricultural production. Recent fluctuations in prices—both of the key imports and of the key primary crop exports—have greatly constrained rural development. For example, the Philippines imports fertilizer for rice paddy production. In 1974–1975 imported fertilizer prices increased 400 percent, and there was an immediate decline in the uses of fertilizer and a consequent drop in rice yields. To the vagaries of climate, weather, and credit must always be added this price instability of prime imports and exports.

The Environment of Rural Development

Prior chapters stressed the importance of the environment or context of administration and the constraints and possibilities it offers. This section has selected only three of the many environmental factors affecting rural administrators. To use the terms introduced in Chapter 4, they are factors that at least need to be *appreciated* and to some extent can be *influenced* (See Figure 4.1, p. 73). Insofar as peasants respond to positive incentives and development practices can cushion the risks they experience, administrators can often *influence* the extent to which peasants invest themselves in change and expanded production. Therefore it is important for managers to reconsider and periodically reevaluate the impact of their strategies on peasant behavior. Since field agents, working far from the capital, and remote from the point where decisions are made, are often the only ones who are aware of the motives of peasants, it is important to establish organizational means to elicit this kind of information and feed it into the policymaking process.

The global agricultural system is certainly less subject to an administrator's control, but its implications need to be appreciated. Without an awareness of the extent to which subsistence farming is part of a broader agricultural system, changes could be counterproductive. For example, the introduction of cash crops, without attention to their impact on the consumption and income of the peasants, could result in the substitution of one form of subsistence for another. Structural changes in the distribution scheme may be necessary. These choices relate to the national policies toward rural areas. And here the local administrator needs to appreciate the pressures that national policymakers confront, while trying to communicate to them the realities of the subsistence agricultural system. Again the issue becomes how to establish organizational procedures that incorporate ways to learn from new information or, in David Korten's words, how to insure that programs and policies are based on and institutionalize the results of local projects.[22] (See Chapter 4.)

Approaches to Rural Development

Three Definitions of the Problem

Given these environmental factors — global interdependence, peasant behavior, and national policy commitments — three different ways of diagnosing the problem of rural underdevelopment can be distinguished. And just as the diagnoses differ, their policy implications also differ.[23] The approaches are important because they have different adherents both within third world countries and inside the organizations that administer development assistance.[24] The first group argues that rural development can best be approached as a technological problem.[25] Low-yield seed, little or no use of fertilizers, minimum water, and little or no mechanization relegate the producer to back-breaking labor with too few returns for that labor. For this group, the problem requires research into technologies, their improvement, and their delivery to those most likely to take advantage of them. This group has been identified with the Green Revolution and its emphasis on new seed and growing techniques.

A second group argues that this first explanation is incomplete in some instances and wrong in others.[26] They claim that small farmers are frequently neglected and that there is a mistaken assumption that economies of scale and larger holdings are more efficient.[27] They argue that an emphasis on small producers and a recognition of their efficiency would result in more food being grown. Thus they emphasize reaching the small farmer and improving his or her access to the means of production. But they emphasize only those inputs that are directly and immediately related to production and not issues they see as ancillary to small farmers, such as nonformal education, political access, and problems of landlessness. Landlessness, according to this group, is not a farming issue, since, by definition, the landless are not farmers.

A third group disagrees with both of the earlier approaches and claims that the rural poor farmers are poor because they are powerless.[28] This group also argues that rural development needs to deal with the problem of landlessness. For this group, rural development requires far more than a focus on agriculture and its technologies; it requires an expanded focus on rural incomes and rural needs. Policies prescribed by this group are for small farmer cooperatives and organizations, attention to agrarian reform, and attention to rural works programs to provide employment for the growing numbers of landless.

These three competing perspectives have different administrative implications. Generally speaking, those of the first group are most interested in agricultural innovation and dissemination. They would support agricultural research and strengthen extension services. The second group is concerned with opening up market mechanisms so that prices reflect the contributions of small farmers. Prices might then serve as incentives to increase productivity. Focus is also on factors directly contributing to that productivity, such as access to land, credit, water, and markets. The third group, however, argues for a more comprehensive approach to rural development and for less preoccupation with agriculture and its techniques per se, claiming that improving rural *incomes* is at least as important. With an eye toward improving the political leverage of the rural small producer, this group also argues for encouraging cooperatives, for farmer organizations, and for mobilizing farmers in bottom-up planning.

The Special Problem of Land Reform

Each of the above policy responses is influenced by the problem of land tenure and reform; and land reform in turn is influenced by the environment of rural development described above. If the politics are such that even a discussion of land reform is politically impossible, then commitment to rural development will be greatly affected. Some countries in fact have opted for a heavy emphasis on industrialization precisely because of the intractable problems with legislating, let alone implementing, land reform. Similarly, if most national administrators tend to believe that peasants are irrational, stubborn, and hopelessly opposed to improving productivity, they tend also to have diminished interest in, or commitment to, rural development.

Rural peoples have only two resources—their land and labor. Yet access to land is increasingly limited, and gross inequalities in the distribution and rights to land remain a most serious problem impeding rural development. This lack of access can be traced to several different factors each requiring different policy considerations. For example, technological change can alter the speculative value of land. The World Conference on Agrarian Reform and Rural Development concluded, "Where shifts to entrepreneurship were more rewarding than usury and rentier ownership, the large owner bought out the small one, pushed out the sharecropper and leased in from the marginal owner who had lacked the inputs, credit, and extension services needed to benefit from the new production methods."[29]

Land reform is particularly significant in studies of administration since its manner of implementation is as important as the original policy decision. Frequently implementation involves the building of organizations and new administrative units. According to the World Bank,

> A major factor in making reform effective is the creation of institutions to implement the reforms once legislated, and to press for continuing development. This has usually involved organizing the beneficiaries. [For example, in] Venezuela suitable institutions were established to ensure that land was indeed transferred. In other countries a community of interests between landowners and officials, combined with an absence of organized pressure from the beneficiaries, largely nullified positive reform efforts. . . . Some form of rural organization, especially involving local representation may be a critical condition for successful land reform.[30]

An attempt at land reform that is not adequately managed can worsen an already difficult land use situation. If large landowners perceive the absence of a complete implementation and follow-up system, they will move to forestall land reform by evicting sharecroppers and tenants. In some cases there are moves to capital-intensive mechanization precisely because this reduces the number of tenants who can claim access through a "land to the tiller" movement.

The role of administration in rural development depends upon the kind and type of land use and land ownership system that prevails. The World Bank categorized the different kinds of land relationships according to the confluence of political, social, legal, demographic, economic, and agricultural characteristics.[31] This provides six different types of land use: feudal Asian, feudal Latin American, traditional communal, market economy, socialist, and plantation ranch. These categories are useful in order to understand the broad differences that land use patterns can and do make for rural development strategies. The most striking difference, for example, is between the feudal Latin American landlord-tenant relationships and the communal land ownership patterns in parts of some African countries. The communal system has relatively egalitarian land access, and differentiation is less marked. But both situations confront difficulties as the man-land ratio changes and technology is introduced. In the former, the landed elite may be responsive to innovation, from which great profits can be extracted, but tenants will be displaced by mechanization and serious deprivation will result. In the latter, or communal system, there is little incentive to consider introducing technology. At the same time, overuse of land often happens creating soil degradation and erosion.

The optimal size of landholdings has long been an issue in reform movements. Holdings that are too small require some kind of consolidation in order to realize economies of scale. For example, one of the reasons for Tanzania's villagization program has been to overcome the limitations imposed when the rural population is scattered over a very wide area. Simply reaching the peasant farmers became an issue; and supplying them with technology, credit, and water was not feasible. But when grouped into villages, with continuous blocks of land, it is easier to improve the factors of production. Improvement in productivity, as was done in Tanzania, depends in such situations upon how that regrouping process is organized, institutionalized, and supplied. It cannot be assumed that changing the pattern alone will be sufficient, as some nominal efforts at land reform in Latin America indicate. Although not all land reform necessarily encourages rural productivity, small-to-medium-sized holdings are generally more productive than extremely large holdings. Since they are usually labor-intensive, there often is less waste than with mechanization. Since it is also true that mechanization can do serious damage to the soil, policymakers and managers need to take into account both the long-run and short-run implications of alternative land use and tenure patterns.

Role of Administration and Organizational Strategies

Top-Down and Bottom-Up Strategies

The fundamental task for rural development administrators is to select the most approriate processes and organizations for accomplishing needed change.[32] An administrator can opt for an efficient, direct delivery and top-down approach to policy implementation. Alternatively one can choose an approach aimed at mobilizing increased productivity with more attention given to bottom-up participatory strategies. In his analysis of the organizational problems of agricultural extension work in Kenya, David Leonard makes the case for the former approach. He first distinguishes between "mechanistic" and "organic" organizations and then continues, "Many scholars have concluded that the best structure for change agencies is the organic type. So firm is this conclusion that it has become common to use the term bureaucracy for mechanistic structures and development administration for organic ones."[33] He goes on to argue that perhaps in the third world accountability in a predictable structure may be more useful than organic kinds of structures. In many respects the debate is similar to the point made by Weberians, discussed in Chapter 3. Weber argued that predictable structures with firm rules would at least not be arbitrary, while theorists such as Herbert Simon add that they provide coherence and structure in the face of complexity. Leonard is making the point that the limited institutional capacity in these nations makes some structure useful.

At several points we have argued that under certain environmental conditions, such a structured approach may be very appropriate. The problem, however, is to avoid what David Lehmann calls "bureaucratic or technocratic omnipotence" and to create learning organizations. For, as Lehmann continues, "measures may be distorted, cancelled out, or defeated by their administration and the political effects will depend greatly on the relationship between the peasantry and a bureaucracy on which they depend increasingly for inputs, public works, etc."[34] Russell Stout provides a useful approach to the question of organizational strategies with his concept of management. Management, he stresses, is not the same as control. The issue is how much certainty there is, how much information, and how much ability to predict results. (Recall Table 4.2 and the discussion on management in Chapter 4.) "Good management requires an acknowledgement that there are situations in which control is appropriate; refusing to control in known domains can lead to organizational collapse. But a more powerful danger lies in trying to control in inappropriate circumstances."[35] Thus there are occasions where some top-down control may be relevant, but only in the context of a learning organization that is aware of its environment and the problems and possibilities it presents.

It is tempting to think that the choice is similar to one between efficiency and equity. That reasoning would claim that top-down strategies are more efficient. Or, to return to the issues raised in Chapter 1, insofar as rural development involves doing or accomplishing productivity, top-down strategies are crucial to create momentum, to protect the assets from co-optation, and to manage the implementation process. In the long run, however, the nature of development and the fact that it involves capacity and equity and empowerment mean that *both* equity and efficiency are enhanced by at least some attention to bottom-up strategies. For example, insofar as including field agents and members of the public in implementation increases accountability, efficiency will also be served. Such efforts also mobilize additional support and make the best use of existing resources.[36]

Some of the dimensions of the choice of strategies is illustrated by a comparison of the Kenyan and Tanzanian models of rural development.

Kenya has made a serious effort to apply the top-down efficiency model of delivery of services, while Tanzania has been openly committed to a bottom-up mobilization approach to improving rural productivity. According to Uma Lele, each approach has encountered management problems and each has had shortcomings. Kenya still has far to go to improve program planning and implementation, and Tanzania needs to work more to "ensure genuine grass roots support." She adds, "Tanzania's tendency towards self criticism suggests that the strategic difficulties with ujamaa may eventually be ironed out internally, provided the political roadblocks do not prove insurmountable."[37]

The Tanzanian model has had to deal with several very basic problems. Its approach requires a certain level of saturation; it must be tried on many fronts with consistent applications in order to begin to work. It is rather like the effect of penicillin when fighting an infection—a small limited dose without a follow-up can mean that antibodies develop to the dosage and then the infection becomes more virulent. A little effort at mobilization meets with similar reactions and will make future efforts more difficult. Yet the moral dilemma for the policy's architect, Julius Nyerere, is also very real. He expresses a reluctance to use coercive activity for many good reasons—his information may be incomplete, and hence he might be forcing peasants to undertake changes that might be wrong. And there is a bigger cause for hesitation. If one is fighting dependency on many political and psychological levels, it is inconsistent to replace the newly won self-determination with an overt coercion. Recent evidence that Nyerere has used more coercion than originally intended is all the more disquieting precisely because he has been sensitive to these dilemmas.[38] The evidence is not in on the ultimate effects of the Tanzania experiment; nor is it clear whether and how the external international environment will be responsive or supportive of its efforts.

The Kenyan and Tanzanian approaches illustrate another aspect of the debate between Weberians and Marxists. According to Weber, an orderly administration with established rules is justified in terms of its freedom from ascriptive or ethnic politics. The Tanzanian planners have used this model and have built their approach on the assumption that class rather than ethnicity is the more important variable in organizing efforts. In the process, it has become somewhat self-fulfilling, and mobilization has tended to occur around class lines. By contrast, Kenyan planners assumed the greater saliency of ethnicity and these ascriptive ties have become increasingly salient.

The extensive communalization of Chinese agriculture is one effort to use both approaches—top-down mobilization of peasants around bottom-up inputs into planning. The commune was designed to be an administrative unit as well as a political and agricultural one. It used behavioral psychology on as wide a scale as any endeavor seen to date in the third world.[39] The instance of China illustrates that the two approaches are clearly not mutually exclusive, and yet efforts to combine them can be both very costly and politically difficult for any government. Elsewhere in the text it is suggested that the appropriate choice, or combination of choices, needs to vary with the nature of the policy and the political context. Yet choosing the best model for the problem at hand is by no means an easy task. In the third world, its severe constraints in trained manpower and the limits of the administrative corps may set the parameters within which the two approaches can be mixed. For example, as discussed in Chapter 9, field agents may often require a more structured setting within which to function. However, it is easy to rely too much on this administrative network. Recently the Overseas Development Institute in England held an intensive seminar with leading authorities on managing rural development. One of their conclusions was the need for a radical policy revision to correct some "existing and dangerous illusions." As they said, "One such illusion is that almost wholly stereotyped bureaucratic management is adequate to maintain the morale of a very large field of staff, mostly working on their own and often in difficult conditions of weather and travel. [Let us] strike at the illusion. There will never be enough officials for personal services to a mass of holdings of only one to four hectares. *The job is one of stimulating farmer organization* as well as giving technical help and this can only be done through groups"[40] (emphasis added).

A most interesting and successful effort to change rural social institutions to achieve both greater productivity and greater local control over decision making was that of the folk school movement in Scandinavia. Folk schools were initiated by the political interests and political parties that had also brought about the sweeping Scandinavian land reform movements of the 1850s. Confronted with a largely illiterate rural population and a need for greater food and export crops, the folk school movement was a large-scale and successful effort to work with rural peoples. The rural folk came to schools and played a role in designing the curriculum and in the teaching. The system was developed to reinforce self-awareness, skill, and pride. The result was a profound change in the quality of rural life as well as a dramatic increase in agricultural output in Scandinavia.

Tinbergen refers to the folk school movement as a possible model for third world countries, and in fact both Nyerere and Nehru were impressed enough with the experiment to try folk schools in their own countries. The folk schools were remodeled in Tanzania into regional training centers and have made an important contribution to Tanzanian rural development.[41]

Problems and Possibilities in Integrated Projects

Another choice that governments need to make is whether to focus on a single task or whether to take a multiple approach to rural problems.[42] The projects of the 1960s tended, on the whole, to concentrate on a single crop and to be done on a regional basis. The Gezira Scheme in the Sudan, for example, concentrated on cotton within a province. The Kenyan Tea Development Authority, as its name implies, concentrated on the production of quality tea for export. From this model several alternatives began to be apparent to planners. The government could expand the coverage of the project, in terms of the population it served, or in terms of the crops it covered, or in terms of the related ancillary services provided. From among these possibilities, the concept of the integrated rural development project took root and began to spread in the 1970s. The integrated rural development project is usually a multisectoral, multifunctional project located in one or several different locations. The Comilla project in Bangladesh, for example, involved many different sectors in its effort to improve the income of the poorest. Yet even this relatively examplary project faced the familiar problem of having its benefits siphoned off by the more well-to-do farmers. This concern, addressed elsewhere in this book, seems to afflict all distributive projects the world over. There is a "leaky bucket" syndrome as benefits leak to middle income groups before reaching their intended beneficiaries.[43]

But beyond the leaky bucket, integrated rural development projects have management difficulties. Integration is rooted in the fundamentally correct observation that the poverty of the rural small farmer stems from a host of problems from health to literacy to access to credit and technology. Hence the idea was to try to address the many problems simultaneously. The management problem comes in at this point. The more integrated the project, the more coordination there must be, and all the weight of coordination is thrown upon the project-level administration. For example, in any given project, health clinics may be under authority of the ministry of health, the extension services under the authority of another ministry, the nonformal education under yet a third ministry. The project staff not only have responsibility for the substantive project, but are forced into a constant series of negotiations with central ministries over staff, supplies, budgets, and lines of command. If staff are seconded to the project, they work knowing that future promotions depend upon decisions of others within the ministry, not on project performance. In most cases integrated projects also mean that there is little diffuson of learning throughout the provincial administration; if and when the project funding is gone, the administrative capacity is not there to carry on.

Improving Agricultural Extension Services

Perhaps the most straightforward attack governments can take on rural poverty is to improve the quality and availability of their agricultural extension services. The problem according to Uma Lele is that "extension agents are few and far between, ill paid, ill trained, ill equipped with a technical package, and consequently very poor in quality. That the farmer often knows more, at least about what is wrong with the new innovations, and that extension agents often do not follow their own advice, have become part of a folklore of extension in developing countries."[44]

Some of the more often cited shortcomings of agricultural extension services is that they are (1) not available to many farmers, (2) not technically equipped, (3) not unbiased in their outreach, (4) not supported by their outreach, and (5) not able to travel widely or frequently in the area. There are, however, wide variations in the extent and nature of these shortcomings. Third world countries inherited very different agricultural extension services depending upon the nature of the colonial system, the presence or absence of settlers, and the nature of the primary export crop. Yet even after a long period of independence there are wide variations in the size and nature of the extension services. The Kenyan agricultural service was traditionally one of the largest in East Africa. By 1968, Kenya, with a rural population of 10 million people, had 5,277 extension workers; Tanzania with 11 million had less than half as many agents with 2,455. Yet Ethiopia, which was never a colony, had a rural population of 22 million and 124 extension agents.[45] When Malawi introduced the Lilongwe Rural Development Project the original design called for a ratio of 1 agent to 200 farm families. The project, however, never reached that goal as there were not sufficient trained extension agents to meet that ratio, and draining the regular supply of agents only heightened problems in the nonproject agents.

In addition to the variety of needs it is also true that some efforts to address these problems may only intensify them. Consider the example of training. Training may only make the situation worse. If the training was largely done in an urban setting and was not experimental, then the agent is unfamiliar with the field and the farmer perceives this lack of experience and surmises that the information source is risky at best, or wrong at worst. Leonard also finds that the more secondary schooling the agent has had, the more restless he becomes with the job.[46]

Sometimes agents cannot recognize crop distinctions in the field or discriminate between different kinds of diseases. Errors of this kind cost the agent essential credibility in the eyes of farmers. One answer generally proposed is to require the agent to farm an experimental holding or to work with a small group of experimental farmers under his general supervision. Since soil conditions vary greatly in many third world countries, several small experimental farms are more likely to reflect the diversity of conditions than a few very large ones. In any case, the agents' training has to go beyond that of technological innovation; the agents need training in communication skills and in understanding the farmers within the area. It is also true that nonformal education projects established for the farmers themselves may be more efficacious than training that is only for agents.

Perhaps the most thoroughgoing reform proposed for extension workers is that of the Benor Method, originally designed in India. The Benor Method is based on establishing clean lines of authority from the top of the ministry down to the lowest echelon — the village extension worker.[47] The innovation in the reform is its insistence that the village extension worker live in the very village she or he is to reach. The worker is supplied with a bicycle and required to report at regular intervals on farm visits and their results. Many think that the success of the method derives from this regular reporting and the feedback of information up the line on the results of innovations or problems encountered. Where the Benor Method has been tried there have been dramatic results in agricultural productivity. The major problems are that it is not effective when it is modified; the need to follow the method makes it expensive and it does not allow for much participation. The authors recommend that economy can best be achieved by reducing the size of the area served rather than the intensity of the visitation. Then the problem is that, at some point, the process of concentrating resources in a smaller area carries negative externalities for adjoining areas.

Finally recall how easily ethnic and sexual discrimination are woven into agricultural extension services. Colonial officials assumed that the European patterns of male plowing and farming were ubiquitous and hence trained the local men. Their efforts were largely wasted when, as often is the case, women managed the fields.[48] The role and importance of women in rural development continue to be underestimated; they are often of central importance. Many countries have experienced significantly improved extension services as more women are recruited into agricultural extension work. The female farmer must be provided increased access to the means of production. She must also be encouraged to participate in small-farmer organizations, credit unions, and cooperatives.

Conclusion

Rural development is an appropriate issue with which to conclude this text. It both draws upon and illustrates the issues and possibilities raised throughout each of the prior chapters. It is also appropriate as a concluding theme because its importance illustrates the scale and saliency of the issues in managing development. People killed by war and people killed by famines are morally equivalent, and the prevention of famines becomes as important as the prevention of war. Famines are not inevitable; they are avoidable. Their avoidance will require that we harness our institutional imaginations to the social sciences and to managerial skills. The task is as important as it is challenging.

Rural development illustrates the dimensions of development as it was conceptualized in Chapter 1. It illustrates the linkages between administrative incapacity and underdevelopment discussed in Chapter 2. It requires thinking through the organizational dilemmas and behavioral issues of Chapters 3, 4, and 5. It will not happen without skillful program and project design and implementation. The needs for simplicity and empirical approaches covered in Chapter 6 and 7 are important ingredients. And thus, it is the case that each topic that has been considered has something important to contribute to the arena of rural development. Among the recurring themes, there are three that are particularly crucial: the importance of participatory learning organizations, the danger in relying solely on technocratic competence, and the importance of listening to the specific needs of farmers and peasants within their own diverse and culturally specific situations.

Participatory learning organizations represent one of the main ways to cope with errors and uncertainty in the highly uncertain environment of development. Learning from errors should be the hallmark for all organizations that work on rural development. An openness to examine error in order to better understand what happened needs to be the sine qua non of these organizations—from the small-farmer organizations and cooperatives to the large international donor-assistance organizations, however remote from the scene.

Similarly the test has emphasized the trap of assuming that technocratic competence can cope with the painful choices involved in development. There are no technocratic "quick fixes" for the problems discussed. Instead the key is to focus on organizations and processes. Indeed, one of the major reasons for a preference for market mechanisms wherever and whenever possible is precisely in order to change organizational rigidities and encourage learning and responsiveness. Peremptory decision making is the hallmark of a top-down bureaucracy, and it tends to be part of the problem rather than part of the solution.

Small farmers and peasant producers living on the land have innate understanding of the dimensions of their environment. The cultural complexity of that environment is an important part of their story; anyone working on rural development must be constantly listening for the variations within that diversity. And this diversity occurs from area to area within single regions of any one country. Managing rural development, therefore, requires constant attention to these very specific differences and problems that farmers face as they work with their land, water, animals, and seed.

H. L. Mencken once said, "To every human problem there is a solution which is neat, simple, and . . . wrong." Right solutions to rural development do not exist. They especially do not exist when development is defined in terms of capacity, equality, and empowerment in a sustainable and interdependent world. Right responses will most assuredly be messy and complex — and, even then, many will be wrong. Anyone involved in rural development management must avoid the two extremes of pessimistic withdrawal and simplistic solutions. Just as the rocks of Scylla and Charybdis lured the ancient Greeks onto one or the other course, both withdrawal and Band-Aid approaches are tempting. The scale and scope of the rural problems are nearly overwhelming and pessimism abounds. But pessimistic withdrawal will consign millions living in rural poverty to further degradation. The opposite course is to try anything that appears to work in the short run and that appears to have a visible payoff. The creative and important course is to strive for a longer view and to build the kinds of organizations and institutions that deal with specific problems at the same time that they build a self-sustaining capacity for the future. In the last analysis, managing development is an innovative, creative, responsive process where learning and adaption will always be occurring. That, in practice, is what the development process is all about.

Notes

1. John Kenneth Galbraith, *The Nature of Mass Poverty* (Cambridge, Mass.: Harvard University Press, 1979), p. 52.

2. Robert Chambers, "Rural Poverty Unperceived: Problems and Remedies," Institute of Development Studies, University of Sussex, Brighton, England, January, 1980 (Washington, D.C.: World Bank Staff Working Paper no. 400).

3. Richard Nelson, *The Moon and the Ghetto* (New York: W. W. Norton, 1977), p. 79.

4. I. M. Destler, *Making Foreign Economic Policy* (Washington, D.C.: Brookings Institution, 1980).

5. See, for example, *World Bank Tables* (Washington, D.C.: World Bank, 1976). For another description of the problem, see "Report to the President from the World Hunger Working Group," *World Hunger and Malnutrition: Improving the U.S. Response* (Washington, D.C.: White House, 1978).

6. Kenneth L. Bachman and Leonardo A. Paulino, *Rapid Food Production Growth in Selected Developing Countries: A Comparative Analysis of Underlying Trends, 1961-76*, Research Report no. 11 (Washington, D.C.: International Food Policy Research Institute, October 1979).

7. Richard Barnet, "The World's Resources II: Minerals, Food and Water," *New Yorker*, March 31, 1980, pp. 40-91.

8. The ineffectiveness of land reform is indicated by the growing problem of landlessness detailed by Milton J. Esman, *Landlessness and Near Landlessness* (Ithaca, N.Y.: Center for International Studies, Cornell University, 1978). See also the reports of the United Nations. The General Assembly of the United Nations and the Economic and Social Council call for the secretary general to submit periodically comprehensive reports on the trends and problems in implementing land reform programs. The most recent of these is *Progress in Land Reform* (New York: United Nations, 1976). This sixth report was the joint effort of the United Nations, FAO, and ILO and covers the period 1968-1974. See also David Lehmann, ed., *Peasants, Landlords, and Governments* (New York: Holmes and Meier, 1974).

9. James Scott, *The Moral Economy of the Peasant* (New Haven, Conn.: Yale University Press, 1976).

10. Michael Todaro, *Economic Development in the Third World* (England: Longmans, 1978), p. 221.

11. Ibid.

12. The Dutch economist Boeke as quoted in Everett Hagen, *The Economics of Development* (Homewood, Ill.: Richard Irwin, 1975), p. 202.

13. See Robert Bates, "People in Villages: Micro-Level Studies in Political Economy," *World Politics* 31 (1978):129-149.

14. Goren Hyden, *Beyond Ujamaa in Tanzania: Underdevelopment and an Uncaptured Peasantry* (Berkeley: University of California Press, 1980).

15. Kusum Nair, *In Defense of the Irrational Peasant* (Chicago: University of Chicago, 1979).

16. Michael Lipton, *Why the Poor Stay Poor: Urban Bias in World Development* (Cambridge, Mass.: Harvard University Press, 1977).

17. Donald Rothchild and Robert L. Curry, *Scarcity, Choice, and Public Policy in Middle Africa* (Berkeley: University of California Press, 1978).

18. For an excellent analysis of the issues surrounding the much used and abused concept of "political commitment," see Norman Uphoff, "Political Consideration in Human Development" in the excellent collection of papers edited by Peter T. Knight, *Implementing Programs of Human Development*, World Bank Staff Working Paper no. 403 (Washington, D.C.: World Bank, 1980).

19. Mohandas K. Gandhi, *An Autobiography: The Story of My Experiments with Truth* (Boston: Beacon Press, 1957, 8th printing, 1968).

20. For one recent analysis of this movement, see Stanley Heginbotham,

Cultures in Conflict: The Four Faces of Indian Bureaucracy (New York: Columbia University Press, 1975).

21. See Alexander Eckstein, *China's Economic Revolution* (Cambridge: Cambridge University Press, 1977).

22. David Korten, "Community Organization and Rural Development: A Learning Process Approach," *Public Administration Review* 40 (September-October, 1980):480–511.

23. For a useful review of the voluminous literature on rural and agricultural development, see Bruce F. Johnston and Peter Kilby, *Agriculture and Structural Transformation: Economic Strategies in Late Developing Countries* (London: Oxford University Press, 1975). One of the forerunners of the changes that were to sweep agricultural economics in the 1960s was Theodore W. Schultz, *Transforming Traditional Agriculture* (1964; reprinted, 1976). Later Yujiro Hayami and Vernon W. Ruttan criticize, amend, and improve on Schultz's work in their book *Agricultural Development: An International Perspective* (Baltimore: Johns Hopkins Press, 1971). They argue that technical and institutional changes must be treated as endogenous factors in a more accurate model of agricultural development. For an excellent review of the current state of the field, see Todaro, *Economic Development.*

24. U.S. Agency for International Development, Agricultural Development Policy Paper (Washington, D.C.: U.S. Department of State, June 1978). This policy paper represents a carefully constructed compromise between the last two positions. John Mellor was, at that time, in the Bureau for Policy Planning and Coordination, U.S. AID. For a discussion of these competing positions, see Steven H. Arnold, "AID's Response to New Directions" (Paper written for the U.S. Congressional Research Service, January 1981).

25. Much of the work on specific crops that led to the Green Revolution took place within the research institutes located around the world and was primarily funded by the Rockefeller Foundation. For more information see the Annual reports of the Rockefeller Foundation. See also Sterling Wortman and R. W. Cummings, *To Feed This World: The Challenge and the Strategy* (Baltimore: John Hopkins Press, 1978).

26. For a review of this argument, see Coralie Bryant and Louise G. White, *Managing Rural Development: Peasant Participation in Rural Development* (West Hartford, Conn.: Kumarian Press, 1980).

27. The major spokesman for this perspective is John Mellor, *The New Economics of Growth* (Ithaca, N.Y.: Cornell University Press, 1976).

28. Esman, *Landlessness and Near Landlessness in Developing Countries.* We are grateful to Harlan Hobgood, Director of the Office of Rural Development, U.S. Agency for International Development, for his emphasis on this issue in our discussions.

29. See *Report of the World Conference on Agrarian Reform and Rural Development,* Rome, July 12–20, 1979, FAO, United Nations, and the accompanying volume, *Review and Analysis of Agrarian Reform and Rural Development in the Developing Countries Since the Mid 1960s* (New York: FAO, United Nations), p. 106.

30. *Land Reform,* Sector Paper (Washington, D.C.: World Bank, 1975), p. 10.

31. Ibid.

32. Hagen, *Economics of Development,* p. 107.

33. David Leonard, *Reaching the Peasant Farmer* (Chicago: University of Chicago Press, 1977), p. 218.

34. Lehmann, *Peasants, Landlords, and Governments,* p. 18.

35. Russell Stout, Jr., *Management or Control: The Organizational Challenge* (Bloomington: Indiana University Press, 1980), p. 12. For an interesting case study of an alternative approach, see Young-Pyoung Kim, *A Strategy for Rural Development: Saemaeul Undong in Korea* (PASITAM, Indiana University Press, 1980).

36. Nelson, *Moon and the Ghetto.*

37. Uma Lele, *The Design of Rural Development: Lessons from Africa* (Baltimore: Johns Hopkins University Press, 1975), p. 62.

38. Louise Fortmann, *Peasants, Officials, and Participation in Rural Tanzania: Experience with Villagization and Decentralization* (Ithaca, N.Y.: Center for International Studies, Cornell University, 1980).

39. For a fascinating and in-depth account of this phenomenon at work inside a Chinese village, see William Hinton, *Fanshen: A Documentary of Revolution in a Chinese Village* (New York: Vintage, 1966).

40. Guy Hunter, ed., *Agricultural Development and the Rural Poor,* Overseas Development Institute (Cambridgeshire: ODI, 1978), p. 19. An earlier work by Guy Hunter that remains a useful addition to this field is *The Administration of Agricultural Development* (London: Oxford University Press, 1970).

41. Peter Manniche, ed., *Rural Development in Denmark and the Changing Countries of the World,* rev. ed. (Copenhagen: Borgen Publishers, 1978). This collection includes a preface by Jawaharlal Nehru and many papers on the founding and approach of folk schools, the Tanzanian experience, and the Indian experience (Mysore, now Karnataka).

42. There have been a large number of rural development projects about which a substantial body of literature exists. Some of those that were studied as part of the preparation for this chapter were the following: Anand Dairy Cooperatives in India, Chilalo Agricultural Development Unit in Ethopia, Comilla project in Bangladesh, BRAC in Bangladesh, Gezira Scheme in Sudan, Lilongwe project in Malawi, Muda Irrigation project in Malaysia, SRDP in Kenya, Ujamaa program in Tanzania, PIDER project in Mexico, Cooperative Agricola Integral Mineros (CAIM) in Bolivia, Bicol and Masagana in the Philippines.

43. The term *leaky bucket* comes from Arthur Okun's important study, *Equality Versus Efficiency: The Great Trade-Off* (Washington, D.C.: Brookings Institute, 1976). For an excellent discussion of how bureaucratic behavior abets the hijacking of project benefits by middle-income farmers, see Harry Blair, "Rural Development, Class Structure and Bureaucracy in Bangladesh," *World Development* 6 (1978):65–82.

44. Lele, *Design of Rural Development,* p. 62.

45. Ibid., p. 67, n.10.

46. Leonard, *Reaching the Peasant Farmer,* p. 111.

47. Daniel Benor and James Q. Harrison, *Agricultural Extension: The Training and Visit System* (Washington, D.C.: World Bank, 1977).

48. See, for example, Kathleen Staudt, "Agricultural Productivity Gaps: A Case Study of Male Preference in Government Policy Implementation," *Development and Change,* July 1978, pp. 438–457.

Annotated Bibliography

The following short list of books and articles most relevant to development management serves as a guide to those initiating study of this field. Readers should note, however, that the notes at the conclusion of each chapter are better guides to the specialized topics within the field. References below are chosen for their general relevance. In the interests of brevity, works published before 1970 are for the most part excluded.

Adelman, I., and Morris, C.T. *Economic Growth and Social Equity in Developing Countries.* Stanford: Stanford University Press, 1973.
   A path-breaking study of the impact (mostly damaging) on the poor of the conventional development programs of the 1950s and 1960s. This empirical study documents that the participation of the poor diminished and their share of the national income decreased under most conventional development programs.
Apthorpe, R., ed. *People, Planning and Development Studies.* London: Frank Cass and Co., 1970.
   A useful collection of articles difficult to obtain elsewhere. Note particularly the study of urban planning in Calcutta by Colin Rosser.
Argyris, C. *Management and Organizational Development.* New York: McGraw-Hill, 1971.
   One of the major works in the organizational development field that has much to contribute to development management. (See Argyris in Index of Names.)
Bates, R. "People in Villages: Micro-Level Studies in Political Economy." *World Politics* 31 (1978):129–149.
   A review of major recent books that explore concepts of peasant rationality and thereby explain behavior that some earlier development authors had considered to be stubbornly resistant to development.
Blair, H. W. "Rural Development, Class Structure, and Bureaucracy in

Bangladesh." *World Development* 6 (1978):65-82.

A work that documents the importance of organizational incentives in explaining field agents' behavior.

Brookfield, H. *Interdependent Development*. Pittsburgh: University of Pittsburgh Press, 1975.

A careful argument by an economic geographer that moves beyond dependency to an analysis of interdependence from a Marxist perspective. Poverty within industrial nations is shown as linked to poverty within colonized peripheries.

Bryant, C., and White, L. G. *Managing Rural Development: Peasant Participation in Rural Development*. West Hartford: Kumarian Press, 1980.

A short monograph that summarizes different approaches to rural development and argues for the central importance of participatory strategies. Specific management ideas for more responsive administrative behavior are discussed.

Caiden, N., and Wildavsky, A. *Planning and Budgeting in Poor Countries*. New York: John Wiley, 1974.

A pessimistic look at the experience of national planners in several developing countries. The authors argue that it is more productive to use budgeting as a planning tool.

Chambers, R. *Managing Rural Development*. New York: Holmes and Meier, 1974.

The best single book on managing rural development. A firsthand account of the author's own field work, along with his programming and implementation management (PIM) system.

Chenery, H., et al. *Redistribution with Growth*. London: Oxford University Press, 1974.

An important collection of thoughtful papers jointly undertaken by the World Bank's Development Research Center and the Institute of Development Studies. University of Sussex. Institutional and administrative issues are given attention, and of particular note is the paper on the political framework. The appendix contains six country case studies.

Coombs, P., and Ahmed, M. *Attacking Rural Poverty*. Washington, D.C.: Johns Hopkins University Press, 1974.

Prepared originally as a report for the World Bank on nonformal education and its potential in addressing rural development. This work is a good source on organizational and staffing issues in rural projects.

Downs, A. *Inside Bureaucracy*. Boston: Little, Brown, 1967.

Although older than most other entries listed here, a classic that remains important for its insights on administrative behavior. It has been widely translated due to popular demand.

Esman, M. "Development Administration and Constituency Organization." *Public Administration Review* 38 (1978):166-172.

An important article that preceded the author's contribution to the *World Development Report* published by the World Bank in 1980, which elaborates on the argument.

Fortmann, L. *Peasants, Officials, and Participation in Rural Tanzania.* Ithaca: Cornell University Press, 1980.
A study of the dilemmas facing the government of Tanzania as it tries to implement local participation while carrying out its development strategy. The author points out those aspects that are more top down than bottom up.
Gant, G. F. *Development Administration.* Madison: University of Wisconsin Press, 1979.
A summary from a practitioner's perspective of agencies' efforts and management processes in the field. The author was an employee of the TVA for sixteen years and a frequent consultant to national planners in Asia.
Gittinger, J. P. *Economic Analysis of Agricultural Projects.* Boston: Johns Hopkins University Press, 1972.
A very practical book that explains how to conduct economic analysis of agricultural projects. The author teaches at the Economic Development Institute of the World Bank.
Goulet, D. *The Cruel Choice: A New Concept in the Theory of Development.* New York: Atheneum, 1971.
A seminal work that forces the reader to consider the position of the powerless and the choices available to this group given its existence rationality.
Grindle, M. *Politics and Policy Implementation in the Third World.* Princeton: Princeton University Press, 1980.
A series of case studies of problems surrounding efforts to implement development policies, with particular emphasis on the political problems encountered during implementation.
Heady, F. *Public Administration, A Comparative Perspective.* 2d. ed. New York: Marcel Dekker, 1979.
A volume containing much useful information, although more awareness of the organizational and behavioral materials relevant to development would improve the text.
Heginbotham, S. *Cultures in Conflict.* New York: Columbia University Press, 1975.
A sensitive analysis of the role of field agents in carrying out rural development in India, detailing the clash between different cultures with their differing views on appropriate roles for government and community development.
Hirschman, A. *Development Projects Observed.* Washington, D.C.: Brookings, 1967.
A very provocative book drawing on the author's experience and creative analysis. Among its major points is the concept of the "hiding hand," which induces action through error as both project costs and the creativity of people to identify inventive solutions are underestimated.
Hunter, G., ed. *Agricultural Development and the Rural Poor.* Cambridgeshire: Overseas Development Institute, 1978.
A landmark book that, while detailing its lessons from India, argues that agricultural development must be organized and administered to be both efficient and equitable.
Hyden, G., Jackson, R., and Okumu, J. *Development Experience: The Kenyan*

Experience. Nairobi: Oxford University Press, 1970.

A series of readings applying insights from the field to the special circumstances in African administrative systems.

Ingle, M. *Implementation: The State of the Art.* Washington, D.C.: Office of Rural Development and Development Administration, Agency for International Development, 1979.

A complete review and summary of that which has been written on implementation.

Jedlicka, A. *Organization for Rural Development: Risk Taking and Appropriate Technology.* New York: Praeger, 1977.

An analysis of management problems facing the Puebla project in Mexico and its efforts to establish a learning approach to project design.

Johnston, B. F., and Kilby, P. *Agriculture and Structural Transformations: Economic Strategies in Late Developing Countries.* London: Oxford University Press, 1975.

A review of the patterns of change in the structures of production in Taiwan, Mexico, and the Soviet Union (latecomers) in contrast with historical patterns in England, the United States, and Japan.

Killick, T. "The Possibilities of Development Planning." *Oxford Economic Papers.* July 1976.

A critique of national planning efforts in India, how they are influenced by economic models of development with too little attention to the political choices available to leaders.

Korten, D. "Community Organization and Rural Development: A Learning Process Approach." *Public Administration Review* 40 (September-October 1980):480-512.

A path-breaking article on the author's experience with the Philippine National Irrigation Administration and its efforts to work with communal irrigators' associations. Detailed examination of what a "learning style" organization can mean to effective development work.

———. *Population and Social Development Management.* Caracas: Instituto de Estudios Superiores de Administracion, 1979.

An eminently readable book in which the author details current field experience and commitment to participatory development projects, arguing that sometimes structural change is essential.

Lehmann, D., ed. *Peasants, Landlords, and Governments.* New York: Holmes and Meier, 1974.

Seminal studies of agrarian reform movements in Latin America, India, and China with important information about alternative official behaviors that can determine effectiveness of reforms.

Lele, U. *The Design of Rural Development.* Washington, D.C.: Johns Hopkins University Press, 1975.

A book based on careful field examination of twelve rural development projects in Africa. In a comparative study, the author discusses management issues frequently and in much detail.

Leonard, D. *Reaching the Peasant Farmer: Organization Theory and Practice in*

Kenya. Chicago: University of Chicago Press, 1977.
> An empirical study of the agricultural extension service in Kenya and the behavioral reasons for its failures to reach the peasant farmer.

Leys, C. *The Underdevelopment of Kenya*. London: Heinemann Educational Books, 1975.
> An exploration of the capacity of dependency theory to explain the underdevelopment of Kenya, with general applicability to much of Africa.

Lipton, M. *Why the Poor Stay Poor: Urban Bias in World Development*. Cambridge, Mass.: Harvard University Press, 1977.
> The arguments about urban bias in development planning are best propounded in this study.

March, J., and Simon, H. *Organizations*. New York: John Wiley and Sons, 1958.
> The single most important book on organizations, conflict within them, innovation, and motivational constraints. Although dense reading, it is a very useful text.

Mickelwait, D., Sweet, C., and Morss, E. *New Directions in Development: A Study of U.S. AID*. Boulder: Westview Press, 1979.
> A book that evolved from the consultants' introspective look at the projects with which they had been concerned and at the role of the Agency for International Development in the project process.

Montgomery, J., *Technology and Civic Life: Making and Implementing Development Decisions*. Cambridge, Mass.: MIT Press, 1974.
> An excellent book on the conflicts and dilemmas of technology and its transfer and on the impact these conflicts have on the quality of life. (See *Montgomery* in index.)

_____. "The Populist Front in Rural Development." *Public Administration Review* 39 (January-February 1979):58–65.
> An article in which the author, concerned about the amount of attention being given to participatory approaches, cautions the audience about administrators' problems with populists.

Nelson, J. *Access to Power: Politics and the Urban Poor in Developing Nations*. Princeton, N.J.: Princeton University Press, 1979.
> The single best book on experience to date with the urban poor's efforts to develop access in developing countries.

Ollawa, P. " On a Dynamic Model for Rural Development in Africa." *Journal of Modern African Studies* 15 (1977):401–425.
> A work in which the author argues for far more commitment to rural development in Africa, illuminating problems confronted to date.

Riggs, F. *Administration in Developing Countries: The Theory of the Prismatic Society*. Boston: Houghton Mifflin, 1964.
> An interesting, perceptive, and early discussion of the ways in which culture influences administrative behavior.

_____, ed. *Frontiers of Development Administration*. Durham, N.C.: Duke University Press, 1971.
> A collection of the best papers from members of the old Comparative Administration Group.

Rondinelli, D. *Planning Development Projects.* Stroudsburg: Dowden, Hutchinson and Ross, 1977.
A selection of articles on project planning, appraisal, and implementation.
Schumacher, E. *Politics, Bureaucracy and Rural Development in Senegal.* Berkeley: University of California Press, 1975.
Interesting argument that points to the difficulties in transforming public bureaucracies into a system of development administration. The author suggests that leaders of new states will forego structural change essential for development in preference to security.
Seidman, R. "Development Planning and Legal Order in Black Anglophonic Africa." *Studies in Comparative International Development* 14 (Summer 1979):3–27.
Documents the shortcomings of development planning in Africa. The author argues for more attention to the skillful use of legal systems to reinforce or secure development.
Sharma, S., ed. *Dynamics of Development.* 2 vols. Delhi: Concept Publishing Co., 1978.
Two very large volumes of original papers commissioned from all over the world. Although uneven, they contain many interesting and useful selections.
Simon, H. "Applying Information Technology to Organization Design." *Public Administration Review* 33 (May-June 1973):268–277.
Part of a dialogue between Simon and Argyris that is highly relevant to development management. (See *Simon* in Index.)
Stout, R. *Management or Control.* Bloomington: Indiana University Press, 1980.
A very important book of special relevance to this field. The author warns of the dangers of trying to control in inappropriate circumstances. His argument, as well as his discussion of organizations, is at the cutting edge of the field.
Tinker, I., and Bramsen, M. *Women and World Development.* Washington, D.C.: Overseas Development Council, 1976.
One of the first, and still one of the best, books on the importance of women in development and their unfortunate treatment by development planners in the 1960s and 1970s.
Turner, J.F.C. "Housing in Three Dimensions." *World Development* 6 (1978):1135–1145.
An article that is but one aspect of the author's continued efforts to have self-help housing considered because of its many positive externalities.
Uphoff, N., Cohen, J., and Goldsmith, A. *Feasibility and Application of Rural Development Participation: A State of the Art Paper.* Ithaca, N.Y.: Center for International Studies, Cornell University Press, 1979.
An excellent 285-page monograph that summarizes experience with participatory projects in many different areas as well as from different points of view—including the congressional mandate. It is one of the most important monographs in a series that grew out of the work of the Rural Development Committee at Cornell University, sponsored by the Office of Rural Development and Development Administration, U.S. AID.

Uphoff, N., and Ilchman, W. *The Political Economy of Development*. Berkeley: University of California Press, 1972.

A book that asks readers to consider political cost-benefit analysis as well as economic cost-benefit analysis in evaluating development policy choices. The argument is both useful and provocative.

van Heck, B. *Participation of the Poor in Rural Organizations*. Rome: Food and Agriculture Organization, 1979.

An overview of several major country surveys by the FAO of the participation of the poor in rural organizations. The project produced many useful works. Where available, as many as possible should be read.

World Bank Staff Working Papers.

Studies directly related to management issues the Bank has published in addition to its studies with economic focus. Two of partciular interest are R. Chambers, *Rural Poverty Unperceived*, no. 400 (Washington, D.C., July 1980); and W. Smith, F. Lethem, and B. Thoolen, *The Design of Organizations for Rural Development Projects*, no. 375 (Washington, D.C., 1980). (Also see *IBRD* in Index.)

Wynia, G. *Politics and Planners: Economic Policy in Central America*. Madison: University of Wisconsin Press, 1972.

A firsthand account of the frustrations and problems in the relationships between political leaders and planners in Central America. Development management issues are an integral part of the discussion.

Index of Names

Subject Index

About the Book and Authors

Managing Development in the
Third World
Coralie Bryant and Louise G. White

This is the first text to focus on the problems and processes involved in organizing, implementing, and managing programs and projects aimed at relieving poverty and underdevelopment in the Third World. During the 1970s there was a shift in development assistance programs toward a greater concern for equity and the basic needs of the poor. The authors emphasize the task of administering development programs that seek to accomplish these goals.

Professors Bryant and White summarize organization theory and behavior and how these apply to development programs. They also give specific guidelines for project design, for evaluating the impact of services, for organizing self-help projects, for improving cross-cultural communication, and for urban planning. This book approaches development from a practical viewpoint but also provides a new and controversial perspective—the potential of redistributive growth to redress the inequities of underdevelopment.

Coralie Bryant is co-director of the International Development Program in the College of Public and International Affairs at American University, where she also serves as a professor in the Schools of Government and Public Administration and of International Studies. **Louise G. White** is assistant professor in the Department of Public Affairs at George Mason University.

Also of Interest

Women and Technological Change in Developing Countries, edited by Roslyn Dauber and Melinda L. Cain

Scientific-Technological Change and the Role of Women in Development, edited by Pamela M. D'Onofrio-Flores and Sheila M. Pfafflin

† *From Dependency to Development: Strategies to Overcome Underdevelopment and Inequality*, edited by Heraldo Muñoz

Science and Technology in a Changing International Order: The United Nations Conference on Science and Technology for Development, edited by Volker Rittberger

Migration and the Labor Market in Developing Countries, edited by Richard H. Sabot

Agricultural Credit for Small Farm Development: Policies and Practices, David D. Bathrick

Transnational Enterprises: Their Impact on Third World Societies and Cultures, edited by Krishna Kumar

Food Security for Developing Countries, edited by Alberto Valdés

Administering Agricultural Development: A Comparative Analysis of Four National Programs, Richard W. Gable and J. Fred Springer

Appropriate Technology for Development: A Discussion and Case Histories, edited by Donald D. Evans and Laurie Nogg Adler

† *Debt and the Less Developed Countries*, edited by Jonathan David Aronson

Economic Development, Poverty, and Income Distribution, edited by William Loehr and John P. Powelson

Food, Politics, and Agricultural Development: Case Studies in the Public Policy of Rural Modernization, edited by Raymond F. Hopkins, Donald J. Puchala, and Ross B. Talbot

A Select Bibliography on Economic Development: With Annotations, John P. Powelson

New Directions in Development: A Study of U.S. AID, Donald R. Mickelwait, Charles F. Sweet, and Elliott R. Morss

† Available in hardcover and paperback.